SIMPL
TO PREVENT, CONTROL
AND TURN OFF
CANCER

MAN MOHAN SHARMA

(Wellness Consultant & Corporate Speaker)

Director Training MAFS –USA
Plant Based Nutrition – Cornell USA
Weight Management Consultant - AFPA USA
Certified Yoga Trainer - India
PGD Wellness Management – Apollo India
5 Star Coach - Wellness Rx India
4 times Half Marathon Runner

S. CHAND & COMPANY LTD.
(AN ISO 9001 : 2008 COMPANY)
RAM NAGAR, NEW DELHI-110055

S. CHAND & COMPANY LTD.

(An ISO 9001 : 2008 Company)

Head Office : 7361, RAM NAGAR, NEW DELHI - 110 055

Phones : 23672080-81-82, 9899107446, 9911310888; Fax : 91-11-23677446

Shop at: **schandgroup.com;** e-mail: **info@schandgroup.com**

Branches :

- 1st Floor, Heritage, Near Gujarat Vidhyapeeth, Ashram Road, **Ahmedabad** - 380 014, Ph: 27541965, 27542369, ahmedabad@schandgroup.com
- No. 6, Ahuja Chambers, 1st Cross, Kumara Krupa Road, **Bengaluru** - 560 001, Ph: 22268048, 22354008, bangalore@schandgroup.com
- Bajaj Tower, Plot No. 243, Lala Lajpat Rai Colony, Raisen Road, **Bhopal** - 462 011, Ph: 4274723. bhopal@schandgroup.com
- 152, Anna Salai, **Chennai** - 600 002, Ph: 28460026, 28460027, chennai@schandgroup.com
- S.C.O. 2419-20, First Floor, Sector - 22-C (Near Aroma Hotel), **Chandigarh** -160 022, Ph: 2725443, 2725446, chandigarh@schandgroup.com
- No. 5, 30 Feet Road, Krishnasamy Nagar, Ramanathapuram, **Coimbatore** -641045, Ph: 0422-2323620, coimbatore@schandgroup.com **(Marketing Office)**
- 1st Floor, Bhartia Tower, Badambadi, **Cuttack** - 753 009, Ph: 2332580; 2332581, cuttack@schandgroup.com
- 1st Floor, 20, New Road, Near Dwarka Store, **Dehradun** - 248 001, Ph: 2711101, 2710861, dehradun@schandgroup.com
- Pan Bazar, **Guwahati** - 781 001, Ph: 2738811, 2735640 guwahati@schandgroup.com
- Padma Plaza, H.No. 3-4-630, Opp. Ratna College, Narayanaguda, **Hyderabad** - 500 029, Ph: 24651135, 24744815, hyderabad@schandgroup.com
- Mai Hiran Gate, **Jalandhar** - 144008, Ph: 2401630, 5000630, jalandhar@schandgroup.com
- 67/B, B-Block, Gandhi Nagar, **Jammu** - 180 004, (M) 09878651464 **(Marketing Office)**
- 1st Floor, Nand Plaza, Hawa Sadak, Ajmer Road, **Jaipur** - 302 006, Ph: 2219175, 2219176, jaipur@schandgroup.com
- Kachapilly Square, Mullassery Canal Road, Ernakulam, **Kochi** - 682 011, Ph: 2378207, cochin@schandgroup.com
- 285/J, Bipin Bihari Ganguli Street, **Kolkata** - 700 012, Ph: 22367459, 22373914, kolkata@schandgroup.com
- Mahabeer Market, 25 Gwynne Road, Aminabad, **Lucknow** - 226 018, Ph: 2626801, 2284815, lucknow@schandgroup.com
- Blackie House, 103/5, Walchand Hirachand Marg, Opp. G.P.O., **Mumbai** - 400 001, Ph: 22690881, 22610885, mumbai@schandgroup.com
- Karnal Bag, Model Mill Chowk, Umrer Road, **Nagpur** - 440 032, Ph: 2723901, 2777666 nagpur@schandgroup.com
- 104, Citicentre Ashok, Govind Mitra Road, **Patna** - 800 004, Ph: 2300489, 2302100, patna@schandgroup.com
- 291/1, Ganesh Gayatri Complex, 1st Floor, Somwarpeth, Near Jain Mandir, **Pune** - 411 011, Ph: 64017298, pune@schandgroup.com **(Marketing Office)**
- Flat No. 104, Sri Draupadi Smriti Apartments, East of Jaipal Singh Stadium, Neel Ratan Street, Upper Bazar, **Ranchi** - 834 001, Ph: 2208761, ranchi@schandgroup.com **(Marketing Office)**
- Kailash Residency, Plot No. 4B, Bottle House Road, Shankar Nagar, **Raipur** - 492 007, Ph: 09981200834, raipur@schandgroup.com **(Marketing Office)**
- 122, Raja Ram Mohan Roy Road, East Vivekanandapally, P.O., **Siliguri**-734001, Dist., Jalpaiguri, (W.B.) Ph. 0353-2520750 **(Marketing Office)**
- Plot No. 7, 1st Floor, Allipuram Extension, Opp. Radhakrishna Towers, Seethammadhara North Extn., **Visakhapatnam** - 530 013, visakhapatnam@schandgroup.com (M) 09347580841 **(Marketing Office)**

First Edition 2012

ISBN : 81-219-4118-0 **Code :** 22 037

PRINTED IN INDIA

By Rajendra Ravindra Printers (Pvt.) Ltd., Ram Nagar, New Delhi-110 055 and published by S. Chand & Company Ltd., 7361, Ram Nagar, New Delhi-110 055

Dedicated to my Dear Mother

Who was an excellent caregiver to my father and grandfather, who suffered through an agonizing year of lung cancer. She served them with selfless devotion and a relentless smile. In addition to her daily chores, she prayed, cooked and held the family together. I salute her courage and commitment.

Mother we all love you!

When the solution is simple, God is answering - Albert Einstein

AUTHOR'S DESK

The name kills. It spares no one. The message from Apple's Steve Jobs death is very clear –money and modern medicine has no answers. Twice in my life I had a very close encounter with world's most deadly disease. I lost my father and grandfather because of Cancer.

From the diagnosis to death it is a misery for the patient and the family. Modern understanding and methods of cancer control are woefully inadequate.

Large drug companies and the medical fraternity have very little faith and interest in the healing power of nutritious foods, spices and body. Obviously, you cannot make much money by selling apples and oranges.

They are dead wrong!

There is hope, a "BIG HOPE". We can practically STOP over 80% of all cancers. The scientific evidence linking diet and lifestyle to cancer is so compelling that even American Cancer Institute estimates that more than 33% of cancer related deaths are due to these two factors.

Right nutrition can have significant impact on preventing, controlling and turning off various cancers. I have been doing research on **Nutritional Healing of Cancers** for the last two decades.

The book is accumulation of world's latest and most creditable research in the field of Nutrition by the best Doctors, Research Scientists and Health Consultants. I salute them for their exceptional hard work and that too without much funding and media support.

Happy & Healthy reading...

MAN MOHAN SHARMA

Thanks

My sincere thanks to Mrs Santosh Kumar, Executive Director, MAFS, for encouraging me, guiding me, and giving me the opportunity in pursuing my dream of nutritional care, in USA. She not only gave me a platform in her organization, but also promoted me in her professional circle.

I want to thank my colleague Smitesh who always encouraged me and promised to make and promote a Gujarati version of the book. Thanks to Ms Promila, Ms Himali and Ms Fatima, my other colleagues, for encouraging me and having extraordinary confidence in my nutritional competence and presentation skills.

Thanks to my enterprising friend Naveen Sharma for helping me in the initial stages of book writing and suggesting the new e-marketing strategies.

Thanks to my son Ashish who gave me very valuable input of writing only 52 most important points about cancer turn-offs instead of 100, which I was initially pursuing. He also took out time to edit my text and listened patiently on my research.

Special thanks to my younger son Shashank, who made me a member of the Chicago library, from where I had unlimited access to the latest books, videos and research papers. He also helped me in simplifying my work by introducing me to drop box.

Last but not the least, thanks to my dear lovely wife Nisha for putting up with my research, dietary madness and irregular routines. Her constant elbowing has encouraged me in striving higher in life.

We are thankful to the Management Team and the Editorial Department of S. Chand & Company Ltd., New Delhi, for all help and support in the publication of this book.

–AUTHOR

Contents

CHAPTER 1

Know Thy Enemy

"The best way to destroy an enemy is to make him a friend".
— Abraham Lincoln

CANCER THE MASTER KILLER

If you are worried or facing a cancer diagnosis, the first thing you should know is that there is real hope in the world of alternative, non-toxic treatments. The second thing you should know is that you are not alone.

"Half of all men and one-third of all women in the US will develop cancer during their lifetimes"
...American Cancer Society

RISE, RISE, RISE...

Cancer continues to defy the progress made by modern medicine. After 40 years of intensive research, it remains the mysterious killer, responsible for the premature death of millions of people.

Each year, globally 12.7 million people are diagnosed with Cancer and 7.6 million die from the disease as per the latest estimates of World Cancer Research Fund (WCRF).

> *"Cancer is on track to kill 565,650 people in the United States this year—more than 1,500 a day, equivalent to three jumbo jets crashing and killing everyone aboard 365 days".*
> *...Newsweek*

LOST WAR

In 1971, President Richard Nixon announced the War on Cancer. He declared that within a decade, a cure for cancer would be found, and the war would be won.

Since then millions of dollars have gone down the drain. World has been waiting for nearly half a century. False promises of cure being "Just round the corner". With hit - and - miss strategies, the real progress and success remain elusive.

> *We Fought Cancer...*
> *And Cancer Has Won*

Now the time has come to reassess and adopt a new approach to get some relief from the curse of Cancer.

EARLY WARNING SYMPTOMS & SIGNS

Unfortunately cancer gives most people no symptoms or signs that exclusively indicate the disease. Some common symptoms that may occur with cancer are as follows:

1. A sore that does not heal, changed color, ulcerates or bleeds.
2. Unusual bleeding or discharge from any opening in the body, example, blood in the urine, stool, frequent or heavy menstruation.
3. A lump or swelling that has progressively enlarged which may or may not be associated with pain.
4. Indigestion or difficulty in swallowing.
5. Change in bowel or bladder habits consistently for a duration of 2-3 months.
6. Obvious change in size or texture in a wart or mole.
7. Non-smokers' cough or hoarseness of voice that persists for more than 2 weeks. Smokers' cough that becomes intense.
8. Unexplained tiredness and /or weight loss of 10 per cent or more within a period of 3-6 months.
9. Persistent pain or discomfort in the abdomen.
10. Unexplained fever.

WE ALL HAVE CANCER CELLS

The cell is the base unit of all life on earth. Human body is made of more than 60,000 billion of living cells. Normal body cells grow, divide, and die in an orderly fashion.

During the early years of a person's life, normal cells divide faster to allow the person to grow. After the person becomes an adult, most cells divide only to replace worn-out or dying cells or to repair injuries.

Doctors and scientists now know that each cancer starts with changes in one cell or a small group of cells.

Usually it is many years before you can feel a lump, or a doctor can see it on a scan, the cells had started to reproduce uncontrollably.

> *"Cancer is the general name for a group of more than 100 diseases in which cells in a part of the body begin to grow out of control. Although there are many kinds of cancer, they all start because abnormal cells grow out of control"*
>
> *...American Society of Cancer*

People can inherit damaged DNA of a cell, but most DNA damage is caused by mistakes that happen while the normal cell is reproducing or by something toxic in our environment like cigarette smoking, exposure to pesticides, paints, chemicals, sun etc.

SEED & SOIL

The process of tumor growth is much like the growth of weeds. Tumors grow in three phases: 1) initiation, 2) promotion, and 3) progression.

Initiation is the phase when a seed settles in the soil, Promotion is the phase when the seed becomes a plant, and Progression is the phase when the plant becomes a weed (developing beyond control, invading flower beds and growing right up to the sidewalk).

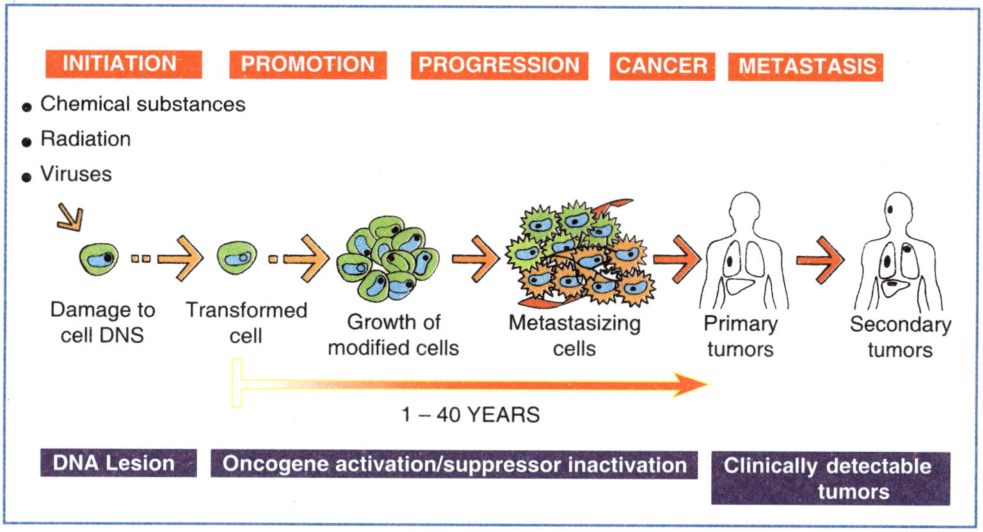

The evolution of cancer from initiation to metastasis.

Initiation (the planting of the seed) depends largely on our genes and on toxins (radiation, carcinogens, etc.).

Promotion (the growth of the seed) depends on having the right survival conditions: favorable soil, water, and sun.

The good news is that promotion is controllable & reversible!. Simply by changing the tumor's environment, you can prevent it from spreading. Diet plays a role – probably a big role – in the creation of a favorable vs. unfavorable tumor environment.

We have the longest & biggest window of opportunity during this stage. This process, which might take place over several years (even several decades), offers a large therapeutic window for blocking the development of cancer.

Preventing cancer by blocking development of these precancerous cells is extremely important because even healthy people have a certain number of latent tumors in their tissues.

Studies of people who died from causes unrelated to cancer have shown that 30% to 50% of women aged 40 to 50 years had premalignant microscopic breast tumors, and 40% of similarly aged men had precancerous cells in the prostate.

Even more striking, virtually every person (98%) had small latent tumors in the thyroid, although these tumors are only very rarely observed in the clinic.

It thus seems that the spontaneous formation of small tumors happens frequently over a lifetime, but that in most cases the growth of these small tumors is tightly controlled by our natural defense mechanisms, and they remain in a microscopic and harmless state.

The appearance of clinically detectable cancer thus implies that precancerous cells have overwhelmed these defenses and acquired the ability to grow and invade the host tissues.

Progression – The uncontrolled and wild spreading:

In their landmark study, Doll and Peto showed that 75% to 80% of all cancers diagnosed in the United States in 1970 might have been prevented by altering lifestyle factors, such as smoking and diet.

Subsequently, their conclusions were confirmed by a large number of studies. Researchers currently estimate that diet could account for approximately 30% of cancer deaths, similar to the number accounted for by smoking.

The close relationship between diet and cancer is suggested by the large variation in rates of specific cancers in different countries and by the spectacular changes observed in the incidence of cancer in migrating populations.

For example, studies have shown that Asians have a 25-fold lower incidence of prostate cancer and a 10-fold lower incidence of breast cancer than inhabitants of Western countries do, but that rates of these cancers dramatically increase following migration to the West.

The importance of lifestyle factors in the development of cancer was also shown in studies of mono-zygotic twins (who share all genes). Inherited genetic factors were shown to be responsible for only about 15% of all cancer cases.

These observations indicate that most cancers are not of hereditary origin and that lifestyle factors, such as dietary habits, have a profound influence on their development. Many epidemiologic studies have consistently linked abundant consumption of foods of

plant origin, such as fruit, vegetables, whole grains, legumes, nuts, seeds, and tea, with decreased risk of developing several types of cancers, up to the extent of 80 per cent.

Anti-cancer properties of plant-based food:

There is now considerable evidence that the chemo-preventive properties of plant-based food are related to their ability to block the progression of latent micro-tumors.

These properties arise from the high content of phytochemicals, molecules that target several key events in the development of cancer.

Intensive research conducted over the last few years has shown that phytochemicals derived from the diet interfere with tumor progression by acting directly on tumor cells as well as by modifying the tumor's microenvironment (stroma) and creating physiologic conditions that are hostile to tumor growth.

Several phytochemicals also inhibit tumor growth by directly inducing cancer cell death by apoptosis. For example, phenethyl isothiocyanate from cruciferous vegetables, curcumin from turmeric, and resveratrol from grapes have all been shown to possess strong pro-apoptotic activity against cells isolated from a variety of tumors.

Anti-angiogenic properties:

Angiogenesis is the process by which tumor cells stimulate formation of new blood vessel networks that sustain the development of cancer by providing oxygen and nutrients to tumor cells.

Work from laboratory has shown that several phytochemicals possess strong anti-angiogenic activity and that this effect likely plays an important role in their chemo-preventive properties.

For example, epigallocatechin-3-gallate (EGCG), an abundant polyphenol found in green tea, potently inhibits vascular endothelial growth factor receptor-2, a key receptor involved in tumor angiogenesis.

There is growing evidence that the anti-angiogenic effects of these phytochemicals play a crucial role in their chemo-preventive activity by preventing latent tumors from acquiring the blood vessel network necessary to sustain their growth and permit them to invade host tissues.

Daily intake of food rich in anticancer molecules could thus be compared to a preventive, non-toxic version of

> *"Almost everyone has cancer cells present at times in our bodies. If our immune system is working properly, these cells are killed or reabsorbed by our defense system before they begin to grow and threaten our health.*
> *The only real defense against cancer is the immune system"*
>
> *...Dr. George C Pack, MD, a cancer specialist Cornell*

chemotherapy that is harmless to the physiology of normal tissue and stops micro-tumors from attaining a stage that would allow them to have pathologic consequences.

Based on these considerations, there is no doubt that all patients, particularly those who have family history of cancer, should be strongly encouraged to change their dietary habits to include at least 5 to 10 servings daily of plant-based food, especially food with the highest content of anticancer phytochemicals.

In the eighteenth century, British physician Percival Pott made the first link between cancer and environmental agents when he noted a high incidence of scrotal cancer among chimney sweeps. He hypothesized that it was caused by exposure to coals and tars.

TUMORS THAT ARE NOT CANCER

Not all tumors are cancerous. Tumors that aren't cancer are called benign. Benign tumors can cause problems – they can grow very large and press on healthy organs and tissues. But they cannot grow into (invade) other tissues. Because they can't invade, they also can't spread to other parts of the body (metastasize). These tumors are almost never life threatening.

If we accept cancer as a process, arising in health and, if unperturbed, resulting in illness, disability, and death, then the strategy for cancer control must address the process, not just the disease.

CHAPTER 2

Humbling with Herbs

"I dig up the plant of Herbs the most potent by whose power rival women are overcome and husbands are obtained."

... Atharva Veda quotes

HUMBLING WITH HERBS AND SPICES

Herbs and spices play an important role in enhancing the appealing and healing powers of food. You may be surprised they have unparalleled concentration of cancer-fighting nutrients.

Thousands of studies are going on in the world on these tiny miracles of nature's very own pharmacy. Results are amazing and astounding, to say the least.

Cinnamon's power to regulate sugar and Turmeric capacity to kill the cancer cells are some of the recent discoveries.

The powers of Herbs and Spices were fully utilized by our wise ancestors and old cultures. They have the power to turn off the "master switch" that triggers cancer genes.

As very aptly said by Charlemagne, the eighth-century king, conqueror and spice lover, that "Spices, the friend of physicians and pride of cooks."

ENHANCING THE POWER

When it comes to increasing the yum factor of food, nothing does the trick better than Herbs and Spices.

The best way to use them for maximum release of flavors and enhancing the Anti-Cancer benefits is to add dried Herbs and Spices in the beginning of the cooking process instead of sprinkling them in the last.

> *"The human body heals itself and nutrition provides the resources to accomplish the task."*
>
> -Roger Williams Ph.D.

Heating, especially in combination with small quantity of right type of fat like extra virgin Olive Oil, extracts the maximum amount of beneficial antioxidant nutrients in the Herbs and Spices and transfers them to the dishes.

So it is good to add Cumin seeds, or Coriander seeds, or Turmeric, or Black Cumin seeds, etc., in the beginning of the cooking process.

It is best to add fresh herbs like Coriander, Cilantro, Mint, Parsley, Green Chilies, Fresh Ginger, etc. at the end of cooking, to retain maximum color and flavors.

Garnishing the dishes with a generous use of fresh Herbs and Spices is a very healthy practice.

FLAVORFULLY HEALTHY

Herbs and Spices are intrinsically associated with Indian cuisine and its aroma and color can make an ordinary dish into a sublime feast. Spices are used in meals to create a state of wellness. Cooking foods with spices is the oldest form of aromatherapy, thus stimulating gastric secretions that create appetites.

> *"The Herbs (medicines) while descending down from heaven to earth proclaimed those who eat us, are never destroyed"*
>
> – Yajur Veda

Many of the spices that are popular today are indigenous to India, where they have been savored for thousands of years.

Ayurveda, the ancient system of healing from India, has been singing praises of Herbs and Spices as "wonder-foods" for thousands of years. The sacred Ayurvedic texts, which were formulated before 1000 B. C., dealt with matters of health and medicine, make frequent reference to the use of them.

For the maximum medicinal benifits we should follow the world's best practices in selecting, storing and serving of herbs and spices.

SELECTION

Whole v. Powdered: Everyone prefers the freshly made food. The "fresh" taste which we seek from Herbs and Spices actually come from their aroma. This aroma is due to the volatile component present in them.

Aroma can be lost during harvesting, storing, processing or handling. For some spices, the fresh forms have different flavor profiles than the dried forms; examples include ginger, cilantro or basil.

Whole spices, when freshly ground, give prepared foods a fresh taste. Fresh spices provide crunchy, crispy textures and colorful appeal.

Fresh whole spices also become very aromatic when they are roasted or fried in oil, and their aroma transfers to the food. This is especially true of whole or cracked seeds and leaves, such as bay leaf, cumin, coriander and mustard seeds, etc.

Full flavor is intact in the whole spices and is more slowly released as compared to ground spices. It can be speeded up, when subjected to preparation techniques such as frying or roasting, during which time, the whole spice slightly cracks open.

Most spices such as cumin, coriander and cardamom give more aroma and flavor when freshly ground than when bought as a pre-ground spice.

Although buying pre-ground spices is certainly convenient, but for the full aromas freshly ground herbs and spices are certainly is a much better option. You are also protected against contamination, adulteration, artificial colors and preservatives.

When you create your own spice blends, you control the ingredients, including salt, which is often one of the main ingredients in store-bought spice mixes. Look for fresh, whole spices that you can buy in bulk and grind yourself.

STORING

Store the freshly ground spices in an airtight container. Use the ground spices for up to one month. Ground spices should be stored in tightly closed containers and should not be exposed to light, high temperatures or humidity. Spices need to be stored at 50°F to 60°F (10°C to 15°C).

SERVING

High flavor with low labor - Heating some of the spices before adding them to the main dishes enhances the flavors many folds, by releasing the volatile aromas present in them. The process is called toasting.

HOW TO TOAST SPICES

- Add whole spices to a cold, dry (no oil) frying pan. You can do this in any type of frying pan, but it's easiest in a heavier pan which won't get the hot/cold sections that can result in burning. You do not have to use a non-stick pan here, as these will not stick.

- Heat the pan over medium and as the pan heats and the spices become fragrant, stir or shake the spices often. They may pop and jump a bit, this is OK.

- Once the spices just start to brown, transfer them immediately out of the pan into a waiting bowl – their residual heat will keep the cooking and toasting process going a little bit longer. If you wait until they are very toasted in the pan, they will become burnt and bitter once off the heat.

- Powder them manually, or in coffee grinder, or with a mortar and pestle. The total toasting time generally is between 3 and 4 minutes.

TIPS

Do not toast different spices in the same pan at the same time. The spices will toast and brown at different speeds, and so you're either left with some that aren't toasted or some that are burnt!

Spices that benefit from toasting include: cumin seed, fennel seed, cinnamon, Cardamom, coriander seed, star anise, and mustard seed.

❍ Bottom Line

1. The fresh-ground Herbs and Spices are definite winner for their superior aroma, vibrancy, and roundness of flavor.
2. Buy in small quantity or keep them in fridge.
3. Lightly toast them, do not ROAST them.

BASIL

"Tulasi Daivam Mahathmeeyam" (Sanskrit) – St. Vyasa Maha Muni.

(Basil in it-self is God, and the values are innumerable by counts)

Some call it "the Garden of Youth" and some call it "the Herb of Kings". Whatever you want to say, it is one of the oldest and popular herbal plants rich in many notable health benefiting phytochemicals. This highly prized plant is revered as "holy herb" in many traditions all over the world.

The Hindu name for holy basil is "Tulsi" which means "the incomparable one." Medicines are made from the leaves, stems, and seeds. Basil is originally native to India and other tropical regions of Asia, having been cultivated there for more than 5,000 years.

It is worshipped as "**Goddess Tulsi**" in India and it is planted in most of the Indian homes and around shrines. It is kept in every "pooja" (worship) and for every "shubh karya" (happy and good occasion.)

Basil is also a very popular herb in Italian cooking, particularly in pesto. This fragrant and flavorful herb, a relative of peppermint, is an excellent, nutritious addition to pasta sauce, soup and salad.

RICH SOURCE

Basil is an excellent source of vitamin K and a very good source of iron, calcium and vitamin A. In addition, basil is a good source of dietary fiber, manganese, magnesium, vitamin C and potassium.

Research studies on basil have shown unique health-protecting effects in two basic areas: basil's flavonoids and volatile oils.

ANTI-CANCER BENEFITS

The unique array of active constituents called flavonoids found in basil provides protection at the cellular level. "Orientin" and "Viceninare" are two water-soluble flavonoids that have been of particular interest in basil.

In the studies conducted on human white blood cells, these components of basil protect cell structures as well as chromosomes from radiation and oxygen-based damage.

In addition, basil has been shown to provide protection against unwanted bacterial growth. These anti-bacterial properties of basil are associated with its volatile oils, Lab studies show the effectiveness of basil in restricting growth of numerous bacteria including *Listeria monocytogenes, Staphylococcus aureus, Escherichia coli*.

Basil's seed oil has shown promise in the initial research, done on animals, in slowing down the progression of certain type of cancers and improve their survival rates. Researchers think this benefit may be explained by the oil's ability to act as an anti-oxidant.

"THE GUARD"

Basil may help lower cholesterol, fight cancer and enhance the immune system, according to a study published in the September 2010 "Taiwan Journal of Obstetrics and Gynecology."

According to Ayurveda, basil is helpful in fighting cancer. It claims that by simply consuming 20 basil leaves with water every day, many cancers can be prevented and cured.

Cervical Cancer: A chemical constituent of basil, known as caffeic acid, was tested in the study, conducted at Chung Shan Medical University, Taichung, Taiwan, and found to be effective against cervical cancer.

Skin Cancer: Research has shown that a kitchen spice rack may hold the cure to skin cancer. When Indian researchers induced cancer cells in laboratory rats and tested nine commonly used spices and vegetables against the cancers they found out two effective herbs against skin cancer.

In the study, published in Food and Chemical Toxicology in November 1992, the researchers noted that the cumin seeds and basil leaves significantly decreased the incidence of skin cancer.

Liver, Stomach and Lung Cancers: Laboratory studies in India found that the anti-oxidant activity in basil has "the potential to block or suppress" liver, stomach, and lung cancers. (Source book 'Healing Spices' by Dr. Bharat B. Aggarwal)

SELECTION

Basil plant can be grown in a pot in the backyard so that fresh leaves are readily available for use whenever the need arises.

In the herb store, choose fresh organic basil over the dried form of the herb since it is superior in quality and flavor. Fresh basil leaves should feature deep green in color and free from dark spots or yellowing.

Dry basil leaves and seeds can be found in stores, however, sun-dried as well as radiation-treated basil leaves may contain significantly decreased vitamin C and carotenoids levels.

STORAGE

Fresh basil herb should be stored in the refrigerator set at appropriate humidity. Dried basil should be kept in a tightly sealed glass container in a cool, dark and dry place where it will keep fresh for up to six months.

SERVING

Wash fresh basil leaves in cold running water or rinse for few minutes to remove any dust or pesticide residues. In order to keep the fragrance and flavor intact, it is generally added at the last moment in the cooking recipes, since prolonged cooking results in evaporation of its essential oils.

Basil has a natural affinity with tomato. Its assertive flavors go well with other equally assertive flavors, such as dry-roasted tomatoes, roasted peppers, and olive oil.

Basil leaves are used to flavor any vegetable, poultry, or meat dish. Basil is also often used in tomato and egg dishes, stews, soups, and salads.

A very simple way to add basil to your life is to add along with the tea leaves while preparing your daily cup of tea.

Bottom Line

A man taking basil from a woman will love her always."

Sir Thomas Moore

1. Not only keeping a basil plant at home is a good omen, but it can also keep many diseases away, including mosquitoes.
2. Researchers believe that more than 30 varieties of basil are available in the world, but all of them contain same amount of uniquely health protecting and promoting nutrients.
3. The herb of kings should have some place in your garden of youth.

2/52

BLACK CUMIN SEED

"The seeds of blessing"

Prophet Mohammed, founder of Islam, once said, "Black cumin can cure every disease except death". It is a culinary herb used in many Middle Eastern, Asian, Indian and Eastern European dishes. Due to its myriad uses the Black Cumin Seed has also earned the approbation "the seed of blessing".

Black Cumin Seeds are the most revered medicinal seeds in history. The best seeds come from Egypt where they grow under almost perfect conditions in oasis where they are watered until the seed pods form. Egyptians consider them as a panacea for everything from colds to toothaches, to headaches.

Black Cumin Seeds have a history of 2500 years. This makes black seed one of the safest plant extracts for human consumption. Black seed has the ability to increase the resistance of the human body, protecting it against various diseases.

Clinical trials have shown that Black Seed Oil controls Blood Sugar and Cholesterol apart from many other diseases and is considered to be one of the greatest healing herbs of all times. Nearly 70% of all traditional Ayurvedic formulas contain a special blend of ingredients, which includes Black Cumin Seeds.

The seeds are frequently referred to as black cumin In English-speaking countries with large immigrant populations; it is known as kaljeera or kalonji. It is also known as Black Caraway and many other names. Its botanical name is *Nigella sativa*.

Though it is the oil that is most often used medicinally, the seeds are a bit spicy and are often used whole in cooking—curries, pastries, and Mediterranean cheeses.

RICH SOURCE

Black Cumin (*Nigella sativa*) Seed is rich in nutritional values. It is a valuable source of protein, carbohydrates, essential fatty acids, vitamins A, B1, B2, C and niacin as well as minerals such as calcium, potassium, iron, magnesium, selenium and zinc.

ANTI-CANCER BENEFITS

Though black cumin seeds are mentioned in the Bible as well as in the words of the Prophet Mohammed, they were not carefully researched until about forty years ago. Since this time, more than 200 studies have been conducted in different universities.

The reason might be found in the complex chemical structure of the seeds. These little seeds have over one hundred different chemical constituents, including abundant sources of all the essential fatty acids.

Black Cumin Seeds protect healthy cells and stimulate production of Natural Interferon. Interferon is essential to the immune system and helps protect us from the daily exposure to millions of germs that can lead to serious infection.

The first major study of black cumin seeds in cancer prevention and treatment was performed by scientists at Cancer Immuno-Biology Laboratory of Hilton Head Island, South Carolina.

They concluded that a healthy immune system will detect and destroy cancer cells before the cancer endangers the patient. The immune system does this by supporting increased production of immune cells, bone marrow cells, and B-cells that produce antibodies. Black cumin stimulates this activity.

Aggressive Cancers: In animal studies, while none of the subjects in the control group survived, two-thirds of the mice that had been given black cumin seed oil were still alive 30 days after deliberate efforts to cause cancer in the subject groups. Black cumin is particularly useful in aggressive cancers whose growth depends on angiogenesis (Cancer feeding roots).

The seeds protect the normal body cells against any damage due to infection and viral ailments. They increase the interferon production and hence help in destroying tumor cells.

BLACK CUMIN GUARDS

Cervical Cancer: Researchers at the Institute of Genetics and Hospital for Genetics at Hyderabad, India, tested an extract from the powder of Black Cumin seeds against cervical cancer cells – and it killed them. The Black Cumin Seeds is a "potential therapeutic against cervical cancers" they concluded in Cancer Cell International.

Liver, Stomach & Eye Cancers: Black cumin seeds are a rich source of beta-sterol, an anti-tumor sterol that helps in fighting the tumors of liver, stomach and eyes. The constituents of the seeds, including TQ(thymoquinone), reduced the growth and size of tumors in rats.

Pancreatic Cancer: An anti-inflammatory herbal extract from black cumin may inhibit pancreatic cancer, U.S. researchers say.

TQ is the major constituent of the oil extract from black cumin seed. It reduces the release of inflammatory mediators in pancreatic cancer cells.

Dr Hwyda Arafat of the Jefferson Medical College of Philadelphia USA, who was the study leader, says TQ almost completely abolished the expression of several inflammatory cytokines.

The herb also inhibited the activation and synthesis of NF-kappaB, a transcription factor that has been implicated in inflammation associated with cancer. It is like switching off the master switch of the cancer activation.

"These are very exciting and novel results," Arafat said in a statement.

He further observed that "These potent effects show promise for the herb as a potential preventive and therapeutic strategy for pancreatic cancer. More importantly, the herb and oil are safe when used moderately, and have been used for thousands of years without reported toxic effects."

While the studies are in the early stages, the findings suggest TQ may eventually have some use as a preventive strategy in patients who have gone through surgery and chemotherapy or in individuals who are at a high risk of developing cancer.

Prostate Cancer: Researchers in the Hematology/Oncology at the Henry Ford Hospital in Michigan studied prostate cancer cells. They found that TQ blocked the cellular receptors for androgen, the hormone that powers the growth of prostate tumor.

"We conclude that TQ, a naturally occurring herbal product, may prove to be effective in treating prostate cancer", wrote the researchers in Cancer Research Journal. They further concluded that TQ can be safely used in preventing prostate cancers.

SELECTION

Black Cumin seeds are not easy to find and many times you end up with the wrong product. You may find them on the internet. Ensure that their correct botanical name is "*Nigella sativa*". In India they also come by the name Kalonji and Shahi Jeera. Black Cumin Seed oil is also available as a dietary supplement.

STORAGE

Toasting black cumin seeds also helps to bring out the nutty flavor of this spice. Store in a dry place, and keep container tightly sealed to protect the natural aroma and flavor.

SERVING

Black cumin seeds are small. They can be used to make tea by simply pouring hot water over the seeds and letting the brew steep for 10 minutes, about a tablespoon makes a nice cup of tea, but it is better to keep the cup covered until ready to drink so as to prevent the aroma from escaping.

Some people add a few seeds to their favorite tea or coffee. The seeds can also be added to casseroles or breads, used in canning, or extracted in wine or vinegar.

Some people grind the seeds and mix them with honey or sprinkle them on salads. They make a nice addition to salad dressings and even stir fry dishes, especially when combined with lemon, cilantro, and tahini.

Black cumin seeds mixed with honey and garlic are excellent tonics for people with asthma or coughs as well as those who want to enhance their immunity during cold and flu season or when an infection is setting in.

Grind black cumin seeds and use them to give a flavor to salads, casseroles, bread and stir-fry dishes.

Bottom Line

1. Black Cumin Seeds oil is a good alternative to seeds.
2. A few herbs have the ability to cure cancers to common cold.
3. Let our homes are blessed with these "seeds of blessing".

BLACK PEPPER

"Black pepper is an antioxidant powerhouse"

Black pepper is not just a spice accompanying salt in your dining table. Incredibly black pepper often referred as "king of spice" is a popular spice known to the world since ancient times.

The peppercorn plant is native to tropical evergreen rain forest of South Indian state, Kerala, from where it spread to rest of the world. The pepper fruit, also known as peppercorn, is actually a berry obtained from this plant.

Peppercorns contain impressive list of plant derived chemical compounds that are known to have disease-preventing and health-promoting properties. Peppers have been in use since ancient times for its anti-inflammatory, carminative and anti-flatulent properties.

RICH SOURCE

Black peppers contain good amount of minerals like potassium, calcium, zinc, manganese, iron, and magnesium. They are also excellent source of many vital B-complex groups of vitamins such as Pyridoxine, riboflavin, thiamin and niacin. Peppercorns are rich source of many anti-oxidant vitamins such as vitamin C and vitamin A.

Piperine, the real health nutrient, is found in all the peppercorns, but it's most abundant in black peppers.

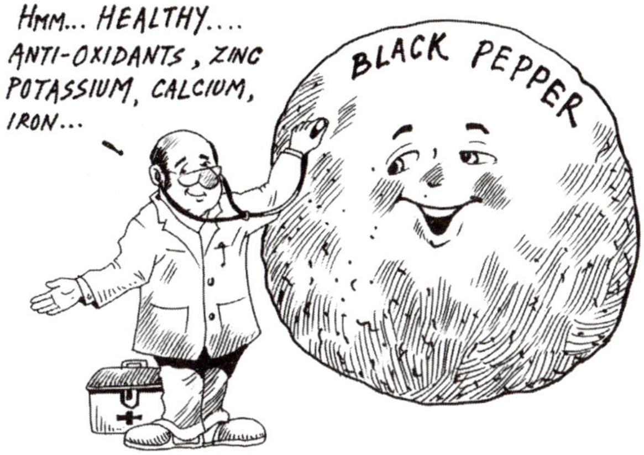

ANTI-CANCER BENEFITS

Black pepper's anti-oxidant compounds help the body remove harmful free radicals and help protect from cancers and diseases. Black peppers have a unique ability of increasing the bioavailability of nutrients from other herbs and spices. While black pepper improves digestion and frees nutrients for absorption, its piperine compound operates through several other pathways to increase the bioavailability of nutrients.

It allows nutrients to enter and remain within their target cells for longer periods of time than would normally be the case. Through these actions, piperine can turn a marginally effective therapeutic substance into a highly effective one.

Curcumin, a compound from the herb turmeric, is known for fighting cancer, pain, inflammation and infection. The action of curcumin, and thereby its effectiveness, is increased many folds when it is taken with piperine.

Colon Cancer: A study at St. Louis University in Missouri was designed to determine if black pepper, resveratrol from grapes, and cinnamaldehyde from cinnamon have anti-prolific effects on colon cancer.

Black pepper showed significant anti-proliferative activity at 24, 48 and 72 hours following administration. Black pepper inhibits the rapid growth of colon cancer cells.

Lung Cancer: Black pepper has also shown to suppress the development of colon and lung tumors in animal studies.

The average daily dietary intake of turmeric in the Indian population ranges between 2 and 2.5 grams. Black pepper was one of the first crops that was cultivated in India and is consumed together with turmeric. Rates for colorectal, prostate and lung cancers, in India are one of the lowest in the world.

Breast Cancer: Natural chemicals found in the spices turmeric and black pepper appear to stop the growth of breast tumors, according to a study conducted by researchers from the University of Michigan Comprehensive Cancer Center and published in the journal Breast Cancer Research and Treatment.

Researchers applied a solution containing both curcumin, found in turmeric, and piperine, which makes black pepper spicy, to breast cancer cells in a laboratory, using concentrations 20 times higher than those found in the human diet.

They found that the solution hampered the ability of stem to propagate but did not affect the differentiation of normal breast cells. "This shows that these compounds are not toxic to normal breast tissue, but at the same time are deadly to cancer stem cells," lead author Madhuri Kakarala observed.

Cancer stem cells are the cells in tumors that allow it to keep growing without limit. Current chemotherapy treatments are unable to affect stem cells, which is part of the reason that cancer can spread and recur even in those undergoing treatment. "If we can limit the number of stem cells, we can limit the number of cells with potential to form tumors," Kakarala said.

SELECTION

Black peppers are available year around. They are available whole, crushed or ground into powder. Since it is piperine that gives black pepper its kick, the more intense the flavor and heat, the greater the level of piperine. Pepper that comes pre-ground has lost much of its piperine.

Purchasing whole peppercorns also assures that the pepper is free of additives and other adulterated spicy powders. The peppercorns should be wholesome, heavy, round and compact. Black peppers have the highest amount of concentration of piperine as compared to white or green or pink.

STORING

Peppercorns can be stored at room temperature for many years and can be milled using hand mill as and when required. Powdered pepper should be stored in the refrigerator in airtight containers. It can be kept in the refrigerator for up to a month or so.

SERVING

Buying whole peppercorns and grinding them in a mill just before eating provides the highest level of piperine. Freshly ground whole organic peppercorns provide the greatest benefits.

Black pepper should not be added while food is being cooked, as it loses its flavor, aroma and vitamin C when heated.

In India and Pakistan, black peppercorn powder is mixed with salt, and the mixture is a common item on serving table in restaurants. The mixture is used as sprinkle over vegetable/fruit salads, chaats, lemonades, in soups, etc. Lassi (churned yoghurt) is often flavored with this spice-salt mixture in Punjab province.

Black pepper is one of the most versatile spices used in virtually all savory cooking. They can be used along with other spices and seasonings, used to marinate chicken, fish, and meat.

It is used liberally in Indian vegetarian and chicken curries. In the Middle-East, this pepper is used in meat and rice dishes.

They can be used in the preparation of soups, barbecue sauces, pickling and as main ingredient in variety of curry powders.

❍ Bottom Line

1. Next to salt, black pepper is the world's most frequently used spice
2. Sprinkling a pinch of freshly ground black pepper just before eating is the best option
3. Encourage kitchen queens to fall in love with king of spices "Black Pepper".

CARDAMOM

"Queen of Spices"

Cardamom, the queen of spices, is only second to black pepper, the king of spices. It is one of the most valued spices in the world. Cardamom is farmed in only a few places in the world, including Sri Lanka, China, Laos, Nepal, Vietnam, pockets of India, and Guatemala.

It gets its title "Queen of Spices" because of its very pleasant aroma and taste. There are mainly two types of cardamom - green cardamom and brown cardamom. Green cardamom pods are chewed as a mouth freshner from ancient times in India. They have a pleasant aroma with a characteristic, slightly pungent taste and leave a warm feeling in the mouth. It is the seeds, taken out from the fruit, which produce the warm sensation.

Brown cardamom pods are larger in size than the green cardamoms, and are hairy. In fact, they look like tiny fibrous coconuts. Brown cardamom is medicinal in flavor.

Each cardamom pod encloses several dark brown seeds which contain the entire flavor and aroma.

RICH SOURCE

The pods contain many essential volatile oils. Volatile oil makes up about 5 per cent of the seed's mass. These volatile oils have the aromatic and medicinal properties, and it is they what makes cardamom so valuable. The most medicinally active and researched, anti-oxidant oil is 'Cineole".

Cardamom is a good source of minerals like potassium, calcium, magnesium, manganese and iron. The pods are also rich in many vital vitamins including riboflavin, niacin, vitamin C that are essential for optimum health.

ANTI-CANCER BENEFITS

Research at Jawaharlal Nehru University and the American University of Sharja have labelled fennel seeds and cardamom chemo-preventives in subjects with cancer due to their ability of reducing or killing tumors and their multiplicity.

The moderate vitamin C levels found in cardamom and fennel ultimately play a role in the body's ability to heal and combat free radical damage associated with cancer. According to the University of Maryland Medical Center, vitamin C is also responsible for creating collagen, a vital protein for the growth and repair of tissues.

Both fennel and cardamom aid in alleviating cellular damage via rich amounts of the mineral manganese. According to the Linus Pauling Institute, without the anti-oxidants found in manganese, the energy structures of cells would suffer immense oxidative stress due to their over-consumption of oxygen cells in the body.

According to NutritionData.com, adding 1 tbsp. of cardamom to your lunch or dinner will offer 80 per cent of the daily value for manganese.

Breast, Ovarian and Prostate Cancers: Phytochemicals in cardamom are well-known cancer fighters, helping to specifically ward off hormone-responding cancers like of breast, ovarian and prostate. Research suggests that consuming cardamom regularly may help prevent these forms of cancer.

Colon Cancers: A study by A. Sangupta for the Department of Cancer Chemoprevention at Chittaranjan National Cancer Institute in India revealed that oral administration of cardamom was effective in inhibiting cell growth and proliferation, and even caused cell death, in human colon cancer cells.

SELECTION

The fat green pods grown in South India are considered the best in the world. Green cardamom is available in the pod form or as powder. Fresh cardamom pods as well as its powder are available in the markets year around.

Both varieties of pods are available in the markets. Fresh pods feature heavy and give sweet aroma when scratched with finger-tip. Avoid pods that appear light and contain stain or spots which may feature mould.

STORING

Store the pods in airtight containers in cool, dark place. They remain fresh for longer period when placed in the refrigerator. Powdered form should be kept in airtight containers and used as early as possible since it may lose its flavor rather quickly.

SERVING

Green cardamom – Many Indian savories and sweets are flavored with cardamom. This fragrant spice is used in rich curries and milk-based preparations.

In India, tea and coffee are sometimes spiked with cardamom. Around the world, green cardamom is used in spiced cakes and breads.

It is one of the essential ingredients in garam masala (a blend of mixed spices). The pods are chewed for freshness and digestion after the food.

Brown cardamom is well known as a spice used in Indian cooking, and is also one of the primary constituents of garam masala.

Cardamom pods are usually split and seeds are crushed using hand mill just before their use.

Bottom Line

CARDAMOM - NATURE'S TOOTH BRUSH

1. Queens always deserve special treatment and so do not boil this herb too much in cooking, add it in the last.
2. Some people call it "Mother nature's tooth brush."
3. Not only green cardamom has mouth and breath-freshening benefits, as per Aras cultures it is considered as aphrodisiac. You can please your queen with another herbal queen of spices.

5/52

CHILIES

"It is quite ironic to call a Red Hot thing as Chili."

Chilies are most widely consumed spice worldwide. We eat 20 times more chilies than any other spice. It is hard to imagine Indian cuisine without chilies. It is commonly believed that it originated in India.

Red chilies peppers are available throughout the year to add zest to flavorful dishes and health to those brave enough to risk their fiery heat.

This is the plant that puts fire on your tongue and maybe even a tear in your eyes when you eat spicy Mexican, simmering Szechuan, smoldering Indian, or torrid Thai food. Chilies pepper contains impressive list of plant derived chemical compounds that are known to have disease-preventing and health-promoting properties.

RICH SOURCE

Fresh chilies peppers, red or green, are rich source of vitamin C. 100 g fresh chilies provide about 143.7 mcg (240% of RDA). Chilies contain good amount of minerals like potassium, manganese, iron, and magnesium. Chilies are also good in B-complex group of vitamins such as niacin, vitamin B-6, riboflavin, and vitamin B-1.

Chili peppers contain a substance called capsaicin, which gives peppers their characteristic pungency, producing mild to intense spice when eaten. The hotter the chili pepper, the more capsaicin it contains.

ANTI-CANCER BENEFITS

Laboratory studies on experimental mammals suggest that capsaicin has anti-bacterial, anti-carcinogenic, analgesic and anti-diabetic properties. It is also found to reduce LDL cholesterol levels in obese individuals.

Prostate Cancer: Red chili peppers' capsaicin, the compound responsible for their pungent heat, stops the spread of prostate cancer cells through a variety of mechanisms, indicates a study published in the March 15, 2006 issue of 'Cancer Research'.

Capsaicin triggers suicide in primary types of prostate cancer cell lines, those whose growth is stimulated by male hormones and those not affected by them. In addition,

capsaicin lessens the expression of prostate-specific antigen (PSA), directly inhibits PSA transcription, causing PSA levels to plummet.

In one of the studies on men, just by taking capsaicin three times a week, in only four weeks, prostate cancer tumor growth and size decreased significantly.

Breast Cancer: According to the journal "Oncogene", capsaicin blocked human breast cancer cells in the test tube and decreased the size of tumors by 50% in test animals.

Researchers, at Cedar-Sinai-Medical Center in LA USA, observed "a potential role in treatment and prevention of breast cancer by capsaicin in future".

SELECTION

There are hundreds of different types of chili peppers that vary in size, shape, color, flavor and "hotness." Chili peppers are usually red or green in color.

Chili peppers are available year around in the markets either in the fresh, dried or powdered form. In the store, buy fresh chili peppers instead of powder, since oftentimes it may contain adulterated spicy mixtures.

Look for raw, fresh chilies featuring brilliant color (green, yellow, orange, red depending on the variety), with healthy stalk, wholesome and compact. Avoid those with spots or those spoiled tips and inflicted by molds.

Select dried chili peppers that are still vivid in color. If they've lost their color, they've probably lost their flavor as well. Both fresh and dried chili peppers are available throughout the year in most areas.

Ground chili peppers are used to make chili powder, cayenne powder and paprika. Chili peppers are used as a food and seasoning.

STORING

Place unwashed fresh peppers in paper bags or wrap in paper towels and store in the vegetable compartment of the refrigerator, where they should keep for at least one week.

1907: Thanks to his dog, Edward Fishkopp discovers the rocket drive.

Avoid storing peppers in plastic bags as this may result in moisture accumulation, which will cause them to spoil more quickly.

Dry whole red chilies are also available in the market, they can be stored at room temperature in a cool, dark place and in airtight containers for many months; can be milled to powder using hand mill as and when required.

If you want to buy dry chili powder instead, go for the authentic and branded products. Powdered chili pepper should be stored in cool place in airtight containers.

Fresh peppers can also be hung in the sunlight to dry. Once dried, they can be used to make freshly ground chili powder.

SERVING

Raw, fresh chilies should be washed in clean water before using it in cooking in order to remove any residual fungicides, sand and soil. Chilies, either fresh or powder form, can cause severe burning sensation to hands and may cause severe irritation to nasal passages, eyes, lips, skin and throat.

Therefore, it may be advised to some sensitive individuals to use thin hand gloves and face masks while handling chilies. Be very careful when you are handling and cooking fresh chili peppers. Additionally, you should wash your knife and cutting board after cutting.

Dried chili powder is an important ingredient in spice mix known as curry powder in many Asian countries. Hot chilies are used as condiment in the preparation of soups, chili-sauce, spicy water, vinegar-spice mix, etc.

Chilies, soaked in yogurt and then dried under sunlight, are used as side snacks during dinner in south Indian states. The next time you make healthy sautéed vegetables, add some chili peppers to turn up the spice volume.

Add chili peppers to your favorite corn bread recipe to give it an extra spark. Add minced chili peppers to yogurt and use as a condiment or dip and if your curry dishes need a little extra zip, try adding some chili peppers.

If you find you can't take the heat, cool off with a glass of milk or spoon of ice cream. A protein in milk called casein can help douse capsaicin's fire.

Bottom Line

1. Seeds and inner white flesh in chilies have maximum health benefiting nutrient called "Capsaicin"
2. Increase your cancer killing fire power by including more hot chilies
3. From heart disease to arthritis pains, obesity to diabetes - HOT chilies are helpful. Slowly increase your capacity and handling power.

6/52

CINNAMON

"Cinnamon bites and kisses simultaneously". – Actor Vanan Bonta

Cinnamon is one of the oldest spice known. It was mentioned in the Bible and was used in ancient Egypt not only as a beverage flavoring and medicine, but also as an embalming agent.

It was so highly treasured that it was considered more precious than gold. Cinnamon's popularity continued throughout history.

Ceylon variety cinnamon is produced in Sri Lanka, India, Madagascar, Brazil and the Caribbean, while cassia is mainly produced in China, Vietnam and Indonesia.

Cinnamon has been shown to have powerful anti-inflammatory, anti-fungal, anti-bacterial, insecticidal and anti-oxidant properties. Consumption of cinnamon has been shown to improve glucose metabolism, lowering blood sugar and reducing insulin resistance.

The spice is actually made from the inner skin of the cinnamonum verum, a shrub that belongs to the laurel family. To harvest the spice, the skin of the young plant is detached from the branch, which allows the skins to roll around themselves and dry, forming fine cinnamon sticks.

RICH SOURCE

Cinnamon is an excellent source of manganese and a very good source of dietary fiber, calcium and iron.

Besides its great taste, cinnamon also has one of the highest anti-oxidant contents of the entire vegetable world, a property that is linked in large part to the spice's huge content of complex polyphenols called proanthocyanidin.

When comparing them weight for weight, cinnamon's level of these polyphenols is 25 times higher than what is found in wild blueberries.

ANTI-CANCER BENEFITS

"More Cinnamon less Cancer" – Toronto Sun, Canada.

All types of cancer are completely reliant on blood support system, without which they cannot survive. Research recently published by a group of Americans has suggested that cinnamon could possess preventive properties, because of its ability to block this blood support system.

Spread of Cancer: In addition to the well-known health properties of turmeric and ginger, a recent study has suggested that cinnamon could be equally useful in reducing tumor growth by blocking the formation of new vessels using a process called angiogenesis.

Cancers cannot progress without being adequately fed by a network of blood vessels that provide the disease with the elements it needs to grow. This process, called angiogenesis, is caused by chemical signals secreted by cancer cells that attract nearby cells from blood vessel.

Cervical Cancer: Research by S.J. Koppikar and associates, published in the May 2010 issue of "BMC Cancer," found that cinnamon alters the growth kinetics of cervical cancer cells in a dose-dependent manner, leading the authors to conclude that cinnamon could be used as a potent chemo-preventive drug in cervical cancer.

Research by C.S Rejiya, published in the September 2009 edition of "Toxicology in Vitro," also found that cinnamon induced cervical cancer cell death. Both studies were carried out in the laboratory; human studies are needed to confirm these effects.

Blood & Bone Marrow Cancer: Cinnamon treatment has also been found to inhibit the expression of regulators of tumor progression in melanoma cells. The same

study found that cinnamon treatment enhanced the anti-tumor activities of a type of T cell whose functions include destroying tumor cells. Another study found that cinnamon extract reduced cellular proliferation of blood and bone marrow cancer.

SELECTION

Cinnamomum cassia or *Cinnamomum aromaticum*, which is also sold as cinnamon (but is considered inferior to true cinnamon), is made from the bark of a related tree. It is sometimes marketed as "Cassia," "Chinese cinnamon," "Vietnamese cinnamon," or "Indonesian cinnamon."

Cassia has a stronger (some would say harsher) flavor than cinnamon and is more toxic to the liver at lower dosages as a result of its far higher coumarin content. We should avoid cassia.

Cinnamon is available in either stick or powder form. While the sticks can be stored for longer period the ground powder has a stronger flavor. If possible, smell the cinnamon to make sure that it has a sweet smell, a characteristic reflecting that it is fresh.

Oftentimes, both Ceylon cinnamon and Chinese cinnamon (cassia) are labeled as cinnamon. If you want to find the sweeter, more refined tasting Ceylon variety, you may need to shop in either a local spice store or ethnic market since this variety is generally less available.

Just like with other dried spices, try to select organically grown cinnamon since this will give you more assurance that it has not been irradiated.

STORING

Cinnamon should be kept in a tightly sealed glass container in a cool, dark and dry place. Ground cinnamon will keep for about six months, while cinnamon sticks will stay fresh for about one year stored this way.

Alternatively, you can extend their shelf life by storing them in the refrigerator. To check to see if it is still fresh, smell the cinnamon. If it does not smell sweet, it is no longer fresh and should be discarded.

SERVING

One thing to keep in mind is that cinnamon loses its aroma quickly in powder form. So, if you want to add cinnamon to your dishes, use the sticks and grind them into a powder.

Drink cinnamon tea simply by adding cinnamon sticks in the water and boil it along with tea leaves.

Enjoy one of the favorite kids' classics—cinnamon toasts—with a healthy twist. Drizzle flax seed oil onto whole wheat toast and then sprinkle with cinnamon and honey.

Simmer cinnamon sticks with soyamilk and honey for a deliciously warming beverage. Adding ground cinnamon to black beans to be used in burritos or nachos will give them a uniquely delicious taste.

Healthy sauté lamb with eggplant, raisins and cinnamon sticks to create a Middle Eastern inspired meal. Add ground cinnamon when preparing curries.

Bottom Line

1. Select the right type of cinnamon that is Ceylon cinnamon.
2. As far as possible use fresh sticks or freshly ground.
3. Hold on to the sticks of cinnamon and safely ride through Diabetes to Cancer.

7/52

CORIANDER

"Perfume of spices"

Coriander is considered both a herb and a spice since both its leaves and seeds are used as a seasoning condiment. Fresh coriander leaves are more commonly known as cilantro and bear a strong resemblance to Italian flat leaf parsley.

Coriander seeds have a more health-supporting reputation and is high on the list of the healing spices. In parts of Europe, coriander has traditionally been referred to as an "anti-diabetic" plant.

In parts of India, it has traditionally been used for its anti-inflammatory properties. In the United States, coriander has recently been studied for its cholesterol-lowering effects.

The coriander seeds oil has found application in many traditional medicines as analgesic, aphrodisiac, anti-spasmodic, deodorant, digestive, carminative, fungicidal, weight loss, stimulant and stomachic.

RICH SOURCE

The herb is a good source of minerals like potassium, calcium, manganese, iron, and magnesium. It is also rich in many vital vitamins including folic acid, riboflavin, niacin, vitamin A, beta carotene, vitamin C and vitamin K, which are essential for optimum health.

It is rich in anti-oxidants and dietary fiber. The leaves and seeds contain many essential volatile oils. The leaves and stem tips are also rich in numerous anti-oxidant nutrients.

ANTI-CANCER BENEFITS

Many of the healing properties of coriander can be attributed to its exceptional high phytonutrient content of oils. Coriander seeds are 85% volatile oils and containing at least 26 energetic compounds, claims Dr. Bharat B. Aggarwal in his book "Healing with Spices".

Colon Cancer: Coriander showed protective benefits against colon cancer in a study published in the August 2000 issue of the "Journal of Ethnopharmacology."

In the laboratory animal study, coriander reduced cholesterol levels in blood and increased the excretion of sterol compounds and bile, which decreases toxin levels in the colon.

Based on the results of their preliminary animal study, the researchers concluded that coriander offers protective benefits against detrimental effects of lipids in the colon that can lead to colon cancer. However, further studies on humans are needed to confirm these preliminary results in colon cancer in humans.

Breast and Liver Cancers: As per Ayurveda coriander seeds are the most cooling of all the spices that significantly improve digestion and are a good choice for people high in Pitta. It is further believed coriander helps in combating breast and liver cancers.

SELECTION

Fresh cilantro leaves as well as seeds are available in the markets and herb stores all around the year. Whenever possible, buy fresh leaves over dried ones since they are superior in flavor and rich in many vital vitamins and anti-oxidants.

Fresh coriander (or cilantro) leaves should look vibrantly fresh and be deep green in color. They should be firm, crisp and free from yellow or brown spots.

SERVING

Once at home, wash it in clean water, discard roots, old or any bruised leaves. Since it is highly perishable, fresh coriander should always be stored in the refrigerator. If possible, it should be stored with its roots still attached by placing the roots in a glass of water and covering the leaves with a loosely fitting plastic bag.

If the roots have been removed, wrap the coriander leaves in a damp cloth or paper towel and place them in a plastic bag. Whole coriander will last up to one week, while coriander leaves will last about three days.

For best results, always buy whole coriander seeds instead of coriander powder. Since coriander seeds are super rich in volatile oils they lose their flavors and health benefits, very quickly. Coriander seeds can be easily ground with a mortar and pestle.

Coriander seeds and coriander powder should be kept in an opaque, tightly sealed glass container in a cool, dark and dry place. Ground coriander will keep for about four to six months, while the whole seeds will stay fresh for about one year.

SERVING

Coriander leaves have been used in preparation of many popular dishes in Asian and east European cuisine since ancient times. Along with other spicy items, it is being used to enhance the flavor and taste of vegetable, chicken, fish and meat dishes.

While in the kitchen, it is generally used just before preparing recipes in order to keep the fragrance and aromatic flavor intact.

The herb has also been used in the preparation of soups and sauces. Popular Mediterranean cilantro pesto is a great addition on pasta, in sandwiches or as a marinade to fish, poultry, etc., dishes. Freshly chopped and sautéed coriander leaves are a great addition to green salad.

Coriander seed powder is one of the main ingredients used in the preparation of curry powder. You may wish to first soak them in cold water for ten minutes and then drain them, as this process will revive their fragrant aroma.

Put coriander seeds in a pepper mill and keep on the dinner table so that you and your family can use them at any time.

Bottom Line

1. Whole coriander seeds have maximum health benefits.
2. Coriander seeds are super rich health benefiting volatile oils, so grind them just before using them
3. Slowly accommodate perfume of spices , as your spice of life.

8/52

CUMIN

"Known for distinctive flavor and strong, warm aroma"

One of the special spices known for their distinctive aroma, cumin seeds are popular in North African, Middle Eastern, Western Chinese, Indian, Cuban and Northern Mexican cuisines. This spicy item is native to middle-east Asian region and now grown all over the world for its flavorful seeds.

Cumin seeds contain numerous phyto-chemicals that are known to have anti-oxidant, carminative and anti-flatulent properties. Distinctive flavor and strong, warm aroma of cumins is due to its essential oil content.

RICH SOURCE

Cumin is an excellent source of minerals like iron, copper, calcium, potassium, manganese, selenium, zinc and magnesium. It also contains very good amounts of B-complex vitamins such as thiamin, vitamin B-6, niacin, riboflavin, and other vital anti-oxidant vitamins like vitamin E, vitamin A and vitamin C. The seeds are an excellent source of dietary fiber.

The seeds are also rich source of many anti-oxidant nutrients. Its main constituent and important aroma compound is cumin-aldehyde.

Freshly ground cumin seeds contain greater flavoring power, when used in recipes because grinding exposes more of cumin's volatile oils and they have not been lost during storage.

ANTI-CANCER BENEFITS

Cumin belongs to the parsley family of herbs and spices, the same family that contains anise, caraway, coriander, dill, fennel, and parsley. The parsley family contains some unique phytochemicals which show cancer-protective activity and anti-inflammatory properties. Cumin has a unique ability to eliminate cancer causing substances.

Stomach & Liver Cancer: Cumin seeds may also have anti-carcinogenic properties. In one study, cumin was shown to protect laboratory animals from developing stomach or liver tumors. This cancer-protective effect may be due to cumin's potent free radical scavenging abilities as well as the ability it has shown to enhance the liver's detoxification enzymes.

Skin & Liver Cancer: Skin cancer research has shown that a kitchen spice rack may hold the cure to skin cancer. When Indian researchers induced skin and liver tumors, in the laboratory rats and tested nine commonly used spices and vegetables against the cancers, they found that cumin seeds, basil leaves and poppy seeds were all effective at fighting cancer.

In the study, published in Food and Chemical Toxicology in November 1992, the researchers noted that the cumin seeds and basil leaves significantly decreased the incidence of both cancers.

Cervical Cancer: In one study on animals it was observed that cumin reduced the incident of cervical cancer by 82% , as compared to animals not receiving cumin.

SELECTION

Cumin spice is available year around in the markets both in the form of seeds and in the powdered form. Good quality cumin releases peppery flavor when squeezed between index and thumb fingers.

Buy whole seeds instead of powder, since oftentimes it may contain adulterated spicy powders or might have lost some of its flavors and health benefiting volatile oils.

STORING

Cumin seeds and cumin powder should be kept in a tightly sealed glass container in a cool, dark and dry place. Ground cumin will keep for about six months, while the whole seeds will stay fresh for about one year.

Whole cumin seed can keep its flavor for years stored in a dark, dry pantry in an airtight jar or other container. Powdered cumin, however, will lose flavor quickly once you open the bottle, particularly if you expose it to heat and sunlight.

The shelf life of ground cumin and similar aromatic spices is four weeks or less because the essential oils quickly evaporate, advises Meena Pathak, author of "Complete Indian Cooking." The finer the grind, the more quickly your cumin will discolor and lose flavor.

The seeds can be stored in cool, dry, dark place, in airtight containers for many months and can be milled using hand mill as and when required.

SERVING

In order to keep the fragrance and flavor intact, cumin is generally grounded just before preparing dishes or whole seeds are lightly toasted before using them in a recipe. The seeds can be easily ground with a mortar and pestle.

Cumin seeds are widely used as flavoring agent in chicken, fish and meat dishes. Seasoning healthy sautéed vegetables with cumin will give them a North African flair.

Practically all Indian vegetarian (jeera daal, jeera rice) and chicken curries and rice dishes (biriyani) contain cumin and in the Middle East it is used in meat and rice dishes.

As the taste of cumin is a great complement to the hearty flavor of legumes such as lentils, garbanzo beans and black beans, add this spice when preparing a recipe with these foods. Take plain brown rice and magically give it special pizzazz by adding cumin seeds, dried apricots and almonds.

Bottom Line

1. Freshly toasted and grounded cumin seeds have significantly high health benefits.
2. Cumin is one of the most frequently used spice, due to its large demand, its quality cannot be ensured always, so buy respected brands or buy the seeds instead of powder.
3. Whenever I have to please my wife I prepare her food tempered with Jeera (Cumin seeds). She loves it... of course food.

FENNEL

"Puritans referred fennel as the 'meeting seed' as they would chew it during their long church services"

Fennel symbolizes longevity, courage and strength. In addition to its use as medicinal values, fennel has many health benefiting nutrients essential compounds, anti-oxidants, dietary fiber, minerals and vitamins.

RICH SOURCE

Fennel seeds are concentrated source of minerals like copper, iron, calcium, potassium, manganese, selenium, zinc, and magnesium. They are rich in insoluble dietary fiber - great and easy way to ease constipation.

Fennel seeds indeed are storehouse of many vital vitamins. Vitamin A, vitamin E, vitamin C as well as many B-complex vitamins like thiamin, pyridoxine, riboflavin and niacin are all concentrated in the fennel seeds.

ANTI-CANCER BENEFITS

The most fascinating potential anti-cancer compound in fennel is anethole—the primary component of its volatile oil. In animal studies, the anethole in fennel has repeatedly been shown to reduce inflammation and to help prevent the occurrence of cancer.

"The inclusion of fennel seeds in the diet is likely to reduce the risk of cancer in the human population", concluded the researchers in Food and Chemical Toxicology.

Liver Cancer: Researchers have also proposed a biological mechanism that may explain these anti-inflammatory and anti-cancer effects. This mechanism involves the shutting down of a intercellular signaling system called tumor necrosis factor (or TNF)-mediated signaling.

By shutting down this signaling process, the anethole in fennel prevents activation of a potentially strong gene-altering and inflammation-triggering molecule (NF-kappaB). The volatile oil has also been shown to be able to protect the liver of experimental animals from toxic chemical injury.

Colon Cancer: As a very good source of fiber, fennel seeds may help to reduce elevated cholesterol levels. And since fiber also removes potentially carcinogenic toxins from the colon, fennel seeds may also be useful in preventing colon cancer.

SELECTION

Fennel seeds are available year around in the markets either in the form of seeds or in processed powder form. In the store, buy whole fennel seeds instead of powder since oftentimes it may contain adulterated spicy powders.

STORING

Store dry fennel seeds as you do in case of other seeds like caraway, dill etc. Place whole seeds in a clean air-seal container and store in cool, dry, dark place.

Ground and powdered fennel should be stored in the refrigerator in airtight containers and should be used as early as possible since it loses its flavor quickly.

SERVING

Fennel seed is widely used as a savory spice. It is principally added in cooking as a condiment and flavoring base. They are widely used in fish dishes, cheese spreads, and vegetable dishes.

In India, its seeds are being used as part of curry powder (Bengali panch phoron). In addition, sugar-coated seeds (saunf) are used as after food chewing condiment to improve digestion in India, Pakistan and Bangladesh.

Like caraway, fennel seeds are used to flavor breads, dough, cakes, biscuits, and cheese.

1. Fennel seeds have made Italian sausages and pepperoni pizza world famous; richly deserve a place in your cooking.
2. Great way to have nutrition, digestion, prevention and mouth freshener, is by chewing one teaspoon of fennel seeds after lunch and dinner.
3. Move over Chingum, Chiclets and Bubble Gums – a new healthy, tasty and reliable option is now available.

GARLIC

"The herb is affectionately called 'the stinking rose' in light of its numerous therapeutic benefits"

Whether it is making food taste better or scaring vampires away, garlic is something that never seems to disappoint.

It is one of the most diverse ingredients in the culinary world. Garlic is featured in many types of cuisine, from Chinese to Italian to Indian.

Garlic's healing powers are acknowledged by the Egyptians and cherished by the Romans. Many books are written about garlic's health benefits.

For a small vegetable, garlic sure has a big, and well deserved reputation. It is guaranteed to transform any meal into a bold, aromatic, and healthy culinary experience. Garlic is a member of the Lily family and is a cousin to onions, leeks and chives.

RICH SOURCE

Garlic is a way to add flavor to food without adding calories or fat. One clove of garlic has only 4 calories. Garlic is a good source of calcium, phosphorus, selenium, vitamin C, vitamin B-6 and manganese.

Garlic is also rich in a variety of powerful sulfur-containing compounds. While these compounds are responsible for garlic's characteristically pungent odor, they are also the source of many of its health-promoting effects.

ANTI-CANCER BENEFITS

Garlic has many important anti-cancer properties. Interestingly, intake of garlic has been found to lower the risk of virtually all types of cancer.

National Cancer Institute of USA is of the view that the " Protective effects from garlic may arise from its antibacterial properties or from its ability to block the formation of cancer-causing substances, halt the activation of cancer-causing substances, (enhance DNA repair), reduce cell proliferation or induce cell death".

Colon Cancer: The Iowa Women's Study is a large prospective study investigating whether diet, distribution of body fat, and other risk factors are related to cancer incidence in older women. Findings from the study showed a strong association between garlic consumption and colon cancer risk.

Women who consumed the highest amounts of garlic had a 50 per cent lower risk of cancer of the colon as compared with women who had the lowest level of garlic consumption.

A compound in garlic shrinks tumors from human colon cancer cells transplanted into mice, a Penn State study of USA has found. The finding adds to a growing body of evidence that garlic can suppress human cancer cells in lab cultures and in test animals.

Researchers John Milner & Sujatha Sundaram were to find out the mechanism, how an oil-soluble sulfur compound in processed garlic shut down or killed human colon cancer cells in mice.

In the study, mice with transplanted tumor cells from human colon cancer were treated with 1 milligram of DADS (Sulphur compound from garlic extract) dissolved in corn oil three times a week for three weeks. The treatment shrank tumors started by the cells by 60 per cent. By contrast, similar tumors grew steadily in mice treated with just corn oil.

"There is also epidemiological evidence that links garlic consumption with a lower risk of colon cancer," he said. "Our latest studies support these findings. It appears that garlic can be beneficial in therapies that either prevent or treat chemically induced cancers."(Author: Scott Turner, Penn State Department of Public Information USA)

Colon, Lung and Skin Cancers: In previous research, Sundaram and Milner described how DADS killed tumor cells grown in lab cultures of human colon, lung, and skin cancers. "Our latest study confirms these earlier observations about DADS and related oil-soluble compounds in garlic," Milner says. "We extended use of DADS from lab cultures to animals and it still suppressed tumors."

"Our body of research indicates that there is more than one mechanism by which garlic compounds can inhibit either carcinogen-induced tumors or cancer cell growth," Milner said.

Breast Cancer: Milner and colleagues also described how water-soluble substance in processed garlic, S-allylcysteine (SAC), inhibited both a carcinogen's binding to rat breast cells and the incidence of breast tumors in rats.

One especially interesting area of research on garlic and cancer prevention involves meat cooked at high temperatures. Heterocyclic amines (HCAs) are cancer-related substances that can form when meat comes into contact with a high-temperature cooking surface (400F/204C or higher).

One such HCA is thought to be one reason for the increased incidence of breast cancer among women who eat large quantities of meat because it is rapidly transformed into DNA-damaging compounds.

One of the many sulfur-containing compounds in garlic has been shown to inhibit the transformation of HCAs into carcinogens.

In addition, a study in France found that increased garlic consumption was associated with a statistically significant reduction in breast cancer risk.

Stomach, Colorectal, Colon, and Esophagus Cancers: Several population studies show an association between increased intake of garlic and reduced risk of certain cancers, including cancers of the stomach, colon, esophagus, pancreas, and breast. An analysis of data from seven other population studies showed that the higher the amount of raw and cooked garlic consumed, lower the risk of stomach and colorectal cancer.

Several population studies conducted in China centered on garlic consumption and cancer risk. In one study, investigators found that frequent consumption of garlic and various types of onions and chives was associated with reduced risk of esophageal and stomach cancers, with greater risk reductions seen for higher levels of consumption.

Three randomized clinical trials have evaluated the effect of garlic intake on gastric cancer risk. In one such 5 years long study, which involved over 5,000 Chinese men and women at high risk for stomach cancer, the risk for all tumors combined was reduced by 33 per cent and the risk for stomach cancer was reduced by 52 per cent.

Pancreatic Cancer: Evidence also suggests that increased garlic consumption may reduce pancreatic cancer risk. A study conducted in the San Francisco Bay area found that pancreatic cancer risk was 54 per cent lower in people who ate larger amounts of garlic compared with those who ate lower amounts.

Intestinal Cancer: The European Prospective Investigation into Cancer and Nutrition (EPIC) is an ongoing multinational study involving men and women from 10 different countries. This study is investigating the effects of nutrition on cancer. In the study, higher intakes of onion and garlic were associated with a reduced risk of intestinal cancer.

Skin Cancer: The results of a small, non-randomized study indicate that the application of garlic extracts to some skin tumors may be beneficial. In the study, which involved 21 persons with skin cancer, the application of ajoene (sulfurous chemical found in garlic) to the skin for 1 month markedly decreased the size of cancer in 17 patients. Changes in tumor size, with an overall median reduction of 47 per cent.

Prostate Cancer: Similarly, in another study, the consumption of allium vegetables, especially garlic and onions, was linked to a reduced risk of stomach cancers. In a third study, greater intake of allium vegetables (more than 10 g per day vs. less than 2.2 g per day), particularly garlic and scallions, was associated with an approximately 50 per cent reduction in prostate cancer risk.

As per renowned Dr. Beliveau laboratory research (Canada), crude garlic extract is able to inhibit cancer cell growth in case of Colon, Brain, Lung, Prostate, and Breast cancers to the extent of 100 per cent.

SELECTION

Fresh, dried and powdered garlic are available in markets throughout the year. For maximum flavor and nutritional benefits, always purchase fresh garlic. Although garlic in flake, powder, or paste form may be more convenient, you will derive less culinary and health benefits from these forms.

Purchase garlic that is plump and has unbroken skin and gently squeeze the garlic bulb between your fingers to check that it feels firm and is not damp.

Avoid garlic that is soft, shriveled, and moldy or that has begun to sprout. Size is often not an indication of quality. If your recipe calls for a large amount of garlic, remember that it is always easier to peel and chop a few larger cloves than many smaller ones.

The NCI (National Cancer Institute, USA) does not recommend any dietary supplement for the prevention of cancer, but recognizes garlic as one of several vegetables with potential anti-cancer properties.

NCI states that "Because all garlic preparations are not the same, it is difficult to determine the exact amount of garlic that may be needed to reduce cancer risk. Furthermore, the active compounds present in garlic may lose their effectiveness with time, handling, and processing."

STORING

Best way to store fresh garlic is to keep it in either an uncovered or a loosely covered container in a cool, dark place away from exposure to heat and sunlight. It is not necessary to refrigerate garlic. Some people freeze peeled garlic; however, this process reduces its flavor profile and changes its texture.

Depending upon its age and variety, whole garlic bulbs will keep fresh for about a month if stored properly. Inspect the bulb frequently and remove any cloves that appear to be dried out or moldy. Once you break the head of garlic, it greatly reduces its shelf life to just a few days.

SERVING

The World Health Organization (WHO) guidelines for general health promotion for adults are a daily dose of 2 to 5 g of fresh garlic (approximately one clove, or any other formulations that are equal to 2 to 5 mg of allicin)

Increasing the Power: You can increase the power of garlic many folds, simply by chopping or crushing it and waiting for minimum 5 minutes, before using it in the cooking. This process stimulates the production of allicin – the real health benefiting compound of garlic.

Do not microwave garlic, as according to the research on garlic preparation methods, it only takes 60 seconds of microwaving whole cloves to lessen some of garlic's health benefits.

The first step to using garlic is to separate the individual cloves. An easy way to do this is to place the bulb on a cutting board or hard surface and gently, but firmly, apply pressure with the palm of your hand at an angle. This will cause the layers of skin that hold the bulb together to separate.

The Healthiest Way of Cooking Garlic: If it is a cooked dish you are preparing and you cannot tolerate raw garlic, add chopped garlic towards the end of the cooking time to retain maximum flavor and nutrition. Too much heat for too long will reduce the activity of the health-promoting sulfur compounds.

If you would like to combine garlic with oil, avoid high-temperature heating of this oil-garlic mixture. Keeping the heat at 250 F/121 C or lower will help preserve the health benefits of both the garlic and the oil. This same precaution should be taken while the oven roasting of garlic bulbs. Once again, lower the temperature, the better it is.

❍ Bottom Line

1. Garlic salts, flakes, capsules or oils etc. have very doubtful health benefits.
2. Crush, chop and wait for 5 minutes, before consuming or cooking it.
3. Stinking Rose has the power to blossom your life's garden.

11/52

GINGER

Aromatic, pungent and spicy, ginger adds a special flavor and zest to Asian stir fries and many fruit and vegetable dishes. Modern scientific research has revealed that health benefits of ginger are endless.

Apart from being used for cooking, the benefits of ginger also include serving as an important ingredient in many of the cures related to alternative medicines like Ayurveda, Naturopathy, Aroma therapy and Herbal therapy.

RICH SOURCE

Ginger contains essential oils, protein, calcium, phosphorus, iron, vitamin C, choline, folic acid, inositol, manganese, panthotenic acid, silicon, and a small amount of vitamin B3.

Ginger is known to have more than twelve types of anti-oxidants, making it useful for treatment of many disorders. Like other spices, it has aphrodisiac properties and is used widely for medicinal purposes.

ANTI-CANCER BENEFITS

Ginger has been used as a natural remedy for many ailments for centuries. Now, science is catching up and researchers around the world are finding that ginger works wonders in the treatment of everything from cancer to migraines. Ginger has got anti-oxidant, anti-inflammatory and anti-cancer properties.

Colorectal Cancer: Gingerols, the main active components in ginger and the ones responsible for its distinctive flavor, may also inhibit the growth of human colorectal cancer cells, suggests research presented at the Frontiers in Cancer Prevention Research, a major meeting of cancer experts that took place in Phoenix, AZ, USA.

In this study, researchers fed mice specially bred to lack an immune system, a half milligram of gingerol three times a week before and after injecting human colorectal cancer cells into their flanks. Control mice received no gingerol.

Tumors first appeared 15 days after the mice were injected, but only 4 tumors were found in the group of gingerol-treated mice compared to 13 in the control mice, plus the tumors in the gingerol group were smaller on average. Even by day 38, one mouse in the gingerol group still had no measurable tumors.

Ovarian Cancer: Lab experiments presented at the 97th Annual Meeting of the American Association for Cancer, by Dr Rebecca Lui and her colleagues from the University of Michigan, showed that Gingerols, the active phytonutrients in ginger, kill ovarian cancer cells by inducing programmed cell death (apoptosis) and self-digestion (auto-phagocytosis).

Ginger extracts have been shown to have anti-oxidant, anti-inflammatory and anti-tumor effects on cells. To investigate the latter, Dr Liu examined the effect of a whole ginger extract containing 5% gingerol on a number of different ovarian cancer cell lines. Exposure to the ginger extract caused cell death in all the ovarian cancer in line with the research done.

Liu and her colleagues believe that ginger may be of special benefit for ovarian cancer patients because cancer cells exposed to ginger do not become resistant to its cancer-destroying effects. Whereas repeated chemotherapy can actually lose its effectiveness over time as the cancer builds a resistance to the repetitive treatment.

Ovarian cancer is often deadly since symptoms typically do not appear until late in the disease process, so by the time ovarian cancer is diagnosed, it has spread beyond the ovaries. More than 50% of women who develop ovarian cancer are diagnosed in the advanced stages of the disease. Including ginger in the daily meals is a good idea.

Skin Cancer: In a recent study by Indian researchers, ginger was tested on human skin cancer (Epidermoid carcinoma A431 cells). It was found to inhibit growth of A431 cells by producing molecules that damaged the cells, leading to cell death (apoptosis).

In the study, published in May 2009 in Chemico-Biological Interactions, researchers stated that their data strongly suggests that this component of ginger can be an effective treatment against skin cancer.

Colorectal Cancer: A study at the University of Minnesota also found that ginger may slow the growth of colorectal cancer cells.

Research associate professor Ann Bode noted, these results strongly suggest that ginger compounds may be effective chemo-preventive agents for colorectal cancers. Ginger may also slow the metastasis of a non-operable tumor.

SELECTION

Whenever possible, choose fresh ginger over the dried form of the spice since it is not only superior in flavor but contains higher levels of gingerol as well as ginger's active protease (its anti-inflammatory compound).

Fresh ginger root is sold in the produce section of markets around the year. When purchasing fresh ginger root, make sure it is firm, smooth and free of mold.

Ginger is also available in several other forms including crystallized, candied and pickled ginger.

STORING

Fresh ginger can be stored in the refrigerator for up to three weeks if it is left unpeeled. Stored unpeeled in the freezer, it will keep for up to six months.

Dried ginger powder should be kept in a tightly sealed glass container in a cool, dark and dry place. Alternatively, you can store it in the refrigerator where it will enjoy an extended shelf life of about one year.

SERVING

To remove the skin from fresh mature ginger, peel with a paring knife. The ginger can then be sliced, minced or julienned. The taste that ginger imparts to a dish depends upon when it is added during the cooking process.

Added at the beginning, it will lend a subtler flavor while added near the end, it will deliver a more pungent taste.

Ginger lemonade simply combine freshly grated ginger, lemon juice, cane juice or honey and water.

Add fresh grated ginger to tea along with tea leaves.

Add extra inspiration to your rice side dishes by sprinkling grated ginger or Add grated ginger to your favorite stuffing for baked apples Spice up your healthy sautéed vegetables and lintels (Dals) by adding freshly minced ginger.

> *Home Grown Ginger: Take fresh ginger root and break off a piece at least 2 inches long. Place it in a pot filled with sandy soil. Water occasionally to keep it slightly moistened. The root will start growing in 4-5 weeks time. Whenever you need fresh ginger, dig up the root, break off a small portion. The main root will continue to grow. – Source Book, 'Healing with Spices', Dr. Bharat B. Aggarwal*

❍ Bottom Line

1. Use fresh ginger than the powdered variety.
2. One teaspoon of fresh ginger paste for the day good enough.
3. From love life to migraine free wife ginger can be of help.

12/52

MINT

"Mint is known for both Seasoning and a Medicine for Centuries."

Mint is one of the world's most popular and recognizable flavors. It is part of soft drinks, candies, cocktails, jellies, syrups, cakes, ice teas to name a few, in short it is all over.

Besides these common uses, mint is also used in cosmetics, insecticides and aromatherapy. Mint is a storehouse of medicinal properties. It is an air freshener, mouth freshener, antacid, helps in digestive problems, soothes frayed nerves and may even cure cancer.

RICH SOURCE

Mint is an excellent source of minerals–potassium, calcium, iron, manganese and magnesium. It is also rich in many anti-oxidant vitamins including vitamin A, beta carotene, vitamin C and vitamin E.

The leaves of mint also contain many important B-complex vitamins like folate, riboflavin and pyridoxine (vitamin B-6); and the herb is also an excellent source of vitamin K.

ANTI-CANCER BENEFITS

There are over one dozen test tubes and animal studies showing mint can be effective against cancer. A phytochemical in mint leaves has been found to demonstrate powerful anti-angiogenesis effects, meaning that it cuts off the blood supply to cancer tumors.

Pancreatic, Mammary and Liver Cancers: Mint oil contains Perillyl alcohol, a phytonutrient rich source of amonoterpene. In animal studies, this phytonutrient has shown to stop the growth of pancreatic, mammary, and liver cancers.

Colon, Skin and Lung cancers: It has also been shown to protect against cancers of colon, skin, and lungs. These animal-based studies have yet to be matched by equally sound human studies; however the prospects are very bright.

" AN AFTER - GRAZING PRODUCT "

SELECTION

Whenever possible, choose fresh mint over the dried form of the herb since it is superior in flavor. The leaves of fresh mint should look vibrant and be a rich green color. They should be free from dark spots or yellowing.

Just like with other dried herbs, when purchasing dried mint try to select organically grown mint since this will give you more assurance that it has not been irradiated.

STORAGE

To store fresh mint leaves, carefully wrap them in a damp paper towel and place inside a loosely closed plastic bag. Store in the refrigerator, where it should keep fresh for several days.

Dried mint should be kept in a tightly sealed glass container in a cool, dark and dry place, where it will keep fresh for about nine to twelve months.

SERVING

A cup of fresh mint tea can help to soothe your stomach and your nerves.

Toss cubes of cooked eggplant with chopped mint leaves, plain yogurt, garlic and cayenne. For a quick and easy salad, combine fennel, onions, oranges and mint leaves.

Give fruit salad a unique perk by adding some fresh mint leaves to it.

Add chopped mint leaves to gazpacho or other soups that feature tomatoes as the freshness of the mint complements the sweet acidity of tomatoes very well.

Mint Chutney –In a food processor, combine one cup of cilantro, one cup mint leaves, half teaspoon of chili pepper, one teaspoon of salt, one cup onions and half cup tamarind juice. Process it for 2-3 minutes to make a fine paste, adding enough water to achieve a thick sauce consistency:

❍ Bottom Line

1. Fresh green leaves are better than the dried ones.
2. Mint Green Chutney is a simple and great way to eat mint on daily basis.
3. Mint is bartender's greatest friend, from making over 50 drinks to mitigating the effects after serving large after drinks.

OREGANO

"Oregano is the spice of Life" – Henry J. Tillman

You cannot find a pizza parlor or Italian restaurant which does not use Oregano. This spice is life of an Italian food. Garlic bread, Lasagna, or pizza would not be considered Italian without oregano.

A Family Favorite! - Warm, balsamic and aromatic flavor of oregano makes it the perfect addition to Mediterranean and Mexican cuisines. This popular herb whose name means "mountain joy" is available throughout the year. It is a darling spice of Turkish food also.

Of all the dried herbs, oregano has one of the highest anti-oxidant levels. Just one teaspoon of dried oregano leaves has as many anti-oxidants as three ounces (100 gm) of almonds.

RICH SOURCE

Oregano is an excellent source of vitamin K and a very good source of iron, manganese and dietary fiber. In addition, oregano is a good source of calcium, magnesium, vitamin A, vitamin C and omega-3 fatty acids.

ANTI-CANCER BENEFITS

Oregano contains numerous phytonutrients – including thymoland rosmarinic acid – that have shown to function as potent anti-oxidants that can prevent oxygen-based damage to cell structures throughout the body.

Additionally, on a per gram fresh weight basis, oregano has demonstrated 42 times more anti-oxidant activity than apples, 30 times more than potatoes, 12 times more than oranges and 4 times more than blueberries.

Breast, Ovarian and Endometrial Cancers: Oregano contains quercetin, which has strong anti-oxidant properties and may be especially protective against breast, ovarian and endometrial cancers.

Colon Cancer: "Oregano is widely used in Mediterranean diet, which is associated with very low incident of colon cancer", said an Italian researcher, in the journal 'Nutrition and Cancer'.

Experts believe that high fiber content in oregano may also help in reducing the risk of colon cancer. It has been found that fibers can help in binding cancer-causing toxins and bile salts together and help in eliminating them from the body, thereby treating colon cancer.

Lung, Blood and Uterus Cancers: As per latest findings "Test tube and animal research on carvacrol and other compounds of oregano" have shown promising results in slowing down the growth cancers of the lungs, blood, and uterus.

SELECTION

Oregano is easily grown at home in the yard or in planters, so hopefully you have fresh oregano at your beck and call. Many stores now carry fresh oregano in the produce department.

Purchased fresh oregano branches should be rich green in color and not the least bit limp. You can also buy dried oregano from the grocery store.

STORING

You can store fresh oregano in a plastic bag in the refrigerator for up to 3 days. If you place a slightly damp paper towel in the bag with the oregano and leave some air in the bag, it may extend the life up to 1 week.

To dry fresh oregano, tie sprigs into a bunch and hang in a cool, dark place with good ventilation. Once dried, seal tightly and store away from sunlight.

As with all dried herbs, dried oregano should be kept in a cool, dark place in a tightly-sealed container and used within 6 months for freshest flavor. It will not spoil if kept longer, but its potency will deteriorate greatly with time.

SERVING

Oregano, either in its fresh or dried form, should be added toward the end of the cooking process since heat can easily cause a loss of its delicate flavor. It is such a great spice! You can add it to almost anything including soups, pizza, sandwiches, and eggs.

Next time you enjoy a slice of pizza, garnish it with some fresh oregano. Adding a few sprigs of fresh oregano to a container of olive oil will infuse the oil with the essence of the herb.

Fresh oregano makes an aromatic addition to omelets and frittatas. Sprinkle some chopped oregano onto home-made garlic bread. Add oregano to salad dressings.

❍ Bottom Line

1. Just one teaspoon of dried oregano leaves has as many anti-oxidants as three ounces (100 gm) of almonds.
2. Oregano is happily married with tomatoes, you can spice any tomato-based dish with it.
3. Oregano has the potential to heal liver diseases, heart ailments and cancers – there is no harm in becoming little Italian.

14/52

TURMERIC

"Indian Yellow GOLD"

Nature's most powerful healer, Turmeric has lo2ng been used as a powerful anti-inflammatory in both the Chinese and Indian systems of medicine. Turmeric was traditionally called "Indian saffron" because of its deep yellow-orange color and has been used throughout history as a condiment, healing remedy and textile dye.

" If I had only one single herb to depend upon for all possible health and dietary needs, I would choose the Indian spice turmeric", said Dr. David Frawley, founder and director of the American Institute for Vedic Studies in Santa Fe, New Mexico.

As a folk remedy, it has been used to treat some 60 maladies–from measles, chicken pox, colic to colds, gum disease, flatulence, indigestion, and stress.

"There is no spice under more scientific scrutiny in the USA and around the world–and no spice offering more promise for better health – than turmeric," says Dr. Bharat B. Aggarwal, Professor of the Department of Experimental Therapeutic, at the University of Texas, M. D. Anderson Cancer Center, USA.

Turmeric has a peppery, warm and bitter flavor and a mild fragrance and is best known as one of the ingredients used to make curry powder.

RICH SOURCE

100 g of turmeric provides (% of RDA per 100 g), 53 % of dietary fiber, 138 % of vitamin B-6, 32% of niacin, 43 % of vitamin C,21 % of vitamin E, 54 % of potassium, 517 % of iron, 340 %of manganese and 40 % of zinc and that too with 0% cholesterol.

This incredible wonder herb is economical, readily available and contains one of the highest anti-oxidant strength known for any herb or spice.

ANTI-CANCER BENEFITS

Known as a staple in the Indian diet, turmeric and its powerful derivative compound curcumin have rapidly gained attention as a potent anti-oxidant compound that is used to prevent and treat many forms of cancer. Curcumin accounts for about 5% of the total weight of turmeric powder.

Curcumin is taking its rightful place among a small handful of agents that fight cancer at all levels. The spice has demonstrated efficacy in more than 240 peer reviewed research studies over the past year alone. Scientists continue to provide conclusive evidence that indicates most health-minded adults should include the spice as part of their regular diet.

Publishing in the AAPS Journal, researchers found that curcumin is an inexpensive natural compound that fights cancer at its root cause by derailing the initiation phase of different pathways used by the disease to multiply and spread throughout the body.

Over 1000 researches and studies done on turmeric demonstrate the different stages in which it can fight cancer:

1. Inhibit the activation of genes that trigger cancer
2. Inhibit the spread of tumor cell
3. Inhibit the transformation of a normal cell into cancer cell
4. Kill cells that mutate to cancer
5. Shrink tumor cells
6. Prevent tumors from spreading to other organs
7. Prevent the development of the blood supply necessary for cancer cells to form and spread
8. Enhance the cancer-destroying effects of chemotherapy and radiation

Source: Book - Healing Spices by Dr. Bharart B. Aggarwal, Professor at M. D. Anderson Cancer Center, USA.

Throat & Food Pipe Cancers: Research groups are investigating curcumin's ability to prevent oral cancer. As per the latest research by a team of doctors at the Cork Cancer Research Centre, UK, curcumin can destroy Throat & Food Pipe (gullet) cancer cells in the lab. Cancer experts said the findings in the British Journal of Cancer could help doctors find new treatments.

Dr Sharon McKenna and her team further found that curcumin started to kill cancer cells within 24 hours by digesting themselves, after the curcumin triggered lethal cell death signals.

Breast Cancer: Epidemiological studies have linked the frequent use of turmeric to lower rates of breast, prostate, lung and colon cancer; laboratory experiments have shown curcumin can prevent tumors from forming.

Curcumin's most remarkable results have been against breast cancer, and it's showing promise against even the most drug resistant form of the disease. Research conducted at the University of Texas suggests that even when breast cancer is already present, curcumin can help slow the spread of breast cancer cells to the lungs in mice.

Cervical Cancer: Curcumin has been found to kill human papilloma-virus, the leading cause of cervical cancer. It has also been found to fight the precancerous cellular changes that often precede the disease.

Lung Cancer: Turmeric has been found to be effective against the lung cancer cells. Several animal studies have found that curcumin may protect against tobacco induced lung cancer.

In one study, 16 smokers took 1500 mg of curcumin (app. 30gm or one oz of turmeric) a day. Only after 30 days urine samples showed they had excreted significantly more tobacco-related toxins than 6 other smokers who didn't take curcumin.

Colon Cancer: Numerous animal studies have found that curcumin can help prevent and delay the onset of colon cancer, and human studies are beginning to show the same results.

Turmeric's anti-oxidant actions enable it to protect the colon cells from free radicals damage. Colon cell turnover is quite rapid, because of their frequent replication, mutations in the DNA of colon cells can result in the formation of cancerous cells much more quickly.

Turmeric and Onions May Help Prevent Colon Cancer. Curcumin, a phytonutrient found in the curry spice turmeric, and quercetin, an anti-oxidant in onions, reduce both the size and number of precancerous lesions in the human intestinal tract, shows research published in the August 2006 issue of Clinical Gastroenterology and Hepatology.

Prostate Cancer: Researchers at Rutgers University, USA, found out that if turmeric is teamed up with cauliflower, it halts the prostate cancer.

Prostate cancer, the second leading cause of cancer death in American men with 500,000 new cases appearing each year, is a rare occurrence among men in India, whose low risk is attributed to a diet rich in brassica family vegetable cauliflower and the curry spice, turmeric.

Pancreatic Cancer: Early clinical trials at the University of Texas are now also looking into curcumin's chemo-preventive and therapeutic properties against pancreatic cancer.

Both human and animal studies have found that curcumin holds promise against pancreatic cancer. In one study, 34 patients with advanced pancreatic cancer – normally lethal within one year – were given high doses of curcumin. In 64% of the patients, the spice slowed the expected progression of the disease.

Leukemia: Reduced risk of childhood Leukemia, research presented at a recent conference on childhood leukemia, held in London, provides evidence that eating foods spiced with turmeric could reduce the risk of developing childhood leukemia.

Skin Cancer: Research groups are investigating curcumin's ability to prevent multiple myeloma.

Studies done at M. D. Anderson Cancer Center, USA, on mice have shown very promising results against skin cancer. Eating curcumin or applying paste externally on the cancerous lesions has halted the progression of skin cancer. The more curcumin they added to the melanoma (skin cancer) the more the cancerous cell died.

Lowest rates of Cancers: Studies found that cancer rates are the lowest in countries with highest dietary intake of turmeric. Most common cancers – lung breast, colon, and prostate– are 10 times lower in turmeric loving country India, as compared to USA, where turmeric is hardly known.

SELECTION

"Most of the world's turmeric comes from two places in India: Alleppey and Chennai. As per the research Alleppey turmeric contains two times more curcumin than the variety from Chennai. Alleppey turmeric is also deeper in color (bright yellow) and has a mellow flavor", say Dr. Bharat B. Aggarwal in his book 'Healing with Spices'.

For the adequate quantity of curcumin, be sure to use turmeric rather curry powder study analyzing curcumin content in 28 spice products described as turmeric or curry powders found that pure turmeric powder had the highest concentration of curcumin, averaging 3.14% by weight. The curry powder samples, with one exception, contained very small amounts of curcumin.

STORING

Turmeric is highly susceptible to light; it is usually packed in airtight tins. Store the tin in a cool, dark place. Turmeric will begin to lose its potency after about six months, even sooner if exposed to light and/or heat.

Fresh turmeric rhizome should be kept in the refrigerator. If you are able to find turmeric rhizomes in the grocery store, you can make your own fresh turmeric powder by boiling, drying and then grinding it into a fine consistency.

SERVING

Be careful when using turmeric since its deep color can easily stain. To avoid a lasting stain, quickly wash any area with which it has made contact with soap and water. To prevent staining your hands, you might consider wearing kitchen gloves while handling turmeric.

Add turmeric to egg salad to give it an even bolder yellow color. Mix brown rice with raisins and cashews and season with turmeric, cumin and coriander.

Although turmeric is generally a staple ingredient in curry powder, some people like to add a little extra of this spice when preparing curries, which is a good way to increase curcumin in your recipe.

Turmeric is delicious and can be added to practically all the vegetables, meats, lentils and gravies. One teaspoon of turmeric per day, as consumed by most Indians, is able to provide you with most of the health benefits.

You can increase the bio-availability of turmeric by the addition of black pepper. For details read T+B = 1000 chapter in this book.

If you cannot eat turmeric or you have serious illness and large amount of curcumin is needed, then you can consider taking one Curcumin 500 mg capsule a day.

Bottom Line

1. Turmeric is one of the world's best healers and most economical and reliable, insurance against plethora of diseases.
2. One teaspoon of yellow gold turmeric is enough for a day.
3. From skin care to cancer cell repair, Indian Yellow Gold has got no match. It is prudent to make yellow beauty turmeric your health partner.

T + B = 1000

Turmeric & Black Peppers in their own capacities are powerful potential cancer inhibitors and their combination is proving to be even more deadly.

The average dietary intake of turmeric in the Indian population ranges between half teaspoon to one teaspoon per day. Pepper was one of the first crops that was cultivated in India and is consumed together with turmeric.

It is worth noting that rates for colorectal, prostate and lung cancers in India are one of the lowest in the world.

ANTI-CANCER BENEFITS

In 1998 researchers at St. John's Medical College, Bengaluru, India, combined piperine with curcumin to test the bioavailability (absorption) of curcumin in rats and healthy human volunteers. In rats the bioavailability was increased by 154%.

In the human volunteers, curcumin taken with 20 mg of piperine increased the bioavailability (absorption) of curcumin by 2000%.The researchers concluded that piperine enhances the serum (blood) concentration, extent of absorption and bioavailability of curcumin in both rats and humans with no adverse effects.

This means that a low dose of curcumin (or turmeric for that matter) could have a greater effect in terms of health benefits when combined with piperine than a large dose of curcumin or turmeric would.

Breast Cancer: As per another research finding, "Adding black pepper to turmeric or turmeric-spiced food enhances curcumin's bioavailability by 1,000 times, due to black pepper's hot property called piperine".

For several years now, Madhuri's lab at the University of Michigan has been studying the effect on breast cancer of curcumin -- one of the most active substances in turmeric -- and piperine, which is a substance active in black pepper.

In her latest study she demonstrates that concentrations of curcumin and piperine which can be obtained through diet or from dietary supplements are capable of eliminating breast cancer stem cells, without causing any damage to the normal breast cells.

Deadly Combination: The levels of curcumin found to be effective in laboratory studies are much higher than those your body can absorb, according to the Linus Pauling Institute. Curcumin and other components of turmeric are degraded rapidly in your intestines.

Piperine, a chemical found in black pepper, inhibits the enzymes that break down curcumin. By allowing curcumin to persist in the intestines, a larger amount of curcumin is absorbed into your blood, according to a 1998 study in "Planta Medica."

Turmeric and pepper, can be taken as part of a normal diet, are practically never toxic in any way, it is perfectly reasonable to recommend that all of us regularly consume a teaspoon of turmeric every day, with a pinch of pepper. You can use this combination in practically all the daily cookings.

Bottom Line

1. Look for Alleppey deeper color, bright yellow turmeric which has got two times more curcumin.
2. Increase the curcumin's healing power 1000 fold by just simply adding pinch of freshly ground black pepper. – "made for each other".
3. Marry the young, beautiful, bright yellow color looking, "Turmeric" with the hot, round black color "Black Pepper", in your kitchen and enjoy the life long health benefits.

Some other Books on Cancer

BOOK — **Jungle Diet**

AUTHOR — **Dr Daphane Miller, *M.D.***

The healthiest diets from around the world - why they work and how to make them work for you. That's the subtitle of Dr Miller's fascinating book. Dr Miller's book is filled with inspiring stories from her patients who healed themselves by choosing to eat different foods and from her extensive travel adventures.

She identifies "cold spots" around the world - areas where there is little or no incidence of a certain disease such as diabetes, bowel trouble or breast cancer.

Cameroon: A cold spot for colon cancer

The five "F's" of colon cancer prevention:

1. Fiber. High-fiber grains such as millet, sorghum, teff, maize, plantain and brown rice.
2. Less flesh. Meat is used sparingly, mostly in stews. Protein most often comes from grains and legumes, such as peanuts and black beans.
3. Fermented foods. Cultured sour milk and yogurt, pickled or fermented corn, manioc and millet are high in gut-friendly bacteria.
4. Foraged foods. Wild greens are rich in folate and anti-oxidants.
5. Select fats. Saturated fats, from animal products, can promote colon cancer. Omega-3 fats, found in fish and grains, protect against it.

Okinawa: A cold spot for breast and prostate cancer

The last leg of Miller's journey was Okinawa, Japan, a cold spot for breast and prostate cancers. She met beautifully preserved older Okinawans and delved into markets with a rainbow of colorful fruits and vegetables such as yams, squash, cabbages, greens, papayas, and melons.

Miller observed that people drink three cups of green tea per day. A variety of sea vegetables, fish, and soy foods are staples. And surprisingly, pork is popular.

"In Okinawa, the elderly population has surprisingly low breast and prostate cancer rates," she says. "They don't even do mammograms in older women there. When you walk through the markets, you see so many foods likely to help maintain a healthy glandular system, such as seaweed and soy.

There is a soy controversy in the U.S. over whether it causes cancer, but in Okinawa, they were eating a lot of real soy in the unrefined form, like edamame. There is a link between more refined soy products and cancer promotion, while eating the whole soy is likely to have a cancer-blocking effect."

She continues: "It was also fascinating to see how pig is revered in that culture. Pork is in all meals, but they use just a little bit as flavor. The pigs are fed wild yam, so they've eaten healthfully. These free-range pigs have a healthier fat composition with higher omega-3 fatty acid content."

CHAPTER 3

Vital Vegetables

"Please understand the reason why Chinese vegetables taste so good. It is simple. The Chinese do not cook them they just threaten them'

... ...Jim Smith

VITAL VEGETABLES

Vegetables talk to us. It takes time to learn their hidden language, which they only speak when they're really, really fresh.

When they are at peak of flavor, nutrition, and color, it sounds like symphony at farmers market: Pick me! Pick me! Please!

Seasonal, fresh and local vegetables are visually very stimulating foods. Vegetables are bursting with phytochemicals that do every thing from protecting our bodies from wear and tear to combat cancer.

Raw, steaming, sautéing, baking.... There are so many quick and simple ways to make these delights part of our every day delicious meals.

We should gracefully accept incredible bounty of anti-cancer properties that veggies willingly offer up, with their heart-felt thanks.

16/52

BEETROOT

"Russian Secret of Long Life"

Beetroot is a root vegetable which is very nutritious and has heaps of health benefits. It tastes salty and sweet at the same time.

Remember all those legendary Russian centenarians? Beets, frequently consumed either pickled or in borscht, the traditional Russian soup, may be one reason behind their long and healthy lives. These colorful root vegetables contain powerful nutrient compounds that help protect against heart disease, birth defects and certain cancers, especially colon cancer.

The color of red/purple beetroot is due to a variety of betalain pigments in it. The roots and leaves both have medicinal uses.

RICH SOURCE

Beets are loaded with vitamins A, B1, B2, B6 and C. They are also an excellent source of calcium, magnesium, copper, phosphorus, sodium and iron.

Sweet beetroot has a remarkable source of choline, folic acid, iodine, manganese, organic sodium, potassium, fiber and carbohydrates in the form of natural digestible sugars.

Its iron content, though not high, is of the highest and finest quality that makes excellent food that is blood building.

ANTI-CANCER BENEFITS

The compound that gives beets their rich colors and potent anti-cancer powers is called *betacyanin*.

The combination of anti-oxidant and anti-inflammatory molecules in beets makes this food a highly likely candidate for risk reduction of many cancer types. Eventually, we expect to see large-scale human studies that show the risk-reducing effect of dietary beet intake.

In recent lab studies on human tumor cells, betanin pigments from beets have been shown to lessen tumor cell growth through a number of mechanisms, including inhibition of pro-inflammatory enzymes (specifically, cyclooxygenase enzymes).

Colon, Stomach, Nerve, Lung, Breast, Prostate and Testicular Cancers: The tumor cell types tested in these studies include tumor cells from colon, stomach, nerve, lung, breast, prostate and testicular tissue. The results of these studies are encouraging researchers to look more closely than ever at the value of betanins and other betalains in beets for both prevention and treatment of certain cancer types.

Lung Cancer: From 1950, Alexander Ferenczi, MD, a Hungarian cancer therapist, at the Department for Internal Diseases at the district hospital at Csoma, Hungary, began putting patients on a diet of red beetroot (raw or juiced) which they ate in addition to their normal diet.

Patients ate up to 1 kg daily (2 pounds). The patients he worked with had all previously received chemotherapy and radiation but were, at the time he started to treat them with beetroot juice, mostly at the final stage.

"BEET ROOT BOND"

He advocates, "If you have a large cancer, start with small quantities of beetroot, and gradually increase them until you start to feel unwell, and then back off the amount. You may get a fever if your liver is being asked to work too hard".

Brief details of this treatment were reprinted in the Australian International Clinical Nutrition Review for July 1986. One case study he reported was a 50-year-old man referred to as D. S., who had a lung tumor. "After 6 weeks of treatment the tumor had disappeared...After 4 months of treatment he gained 10 kg (22 lbs.) in weight. The improvement lasted for about 6 months." All other tests confirmed that he had the symptoms of a clinical recovery. However, he discontinued taking the beetroot, the cancer returned and no further treatment could save him.

From this, two lessons must be taken on board. People with cancer should start the beetroot therapy as early as they can, perhaps building up slowly from 250 grams a day to a kilo, reducing the intake in the event of nausea, but maintaining the beetroot intake for years as a maintenance regime.

SELECTION

Choose small or medium-sized beets whose roots are firm, smooth-skinned and deep in color. Smaller, younger beets may be so tender that peeling won't be needed after they are cooked.

Avoid beets that have spots, bruises or soft, wet areas, all of which indicate spoilage. Shriveled or flabby should also be avoided as these are signs that the roots are aged, tough and fibrous.

While the quality of the greens does not reflect that of the roots, if you are going to consume this very nutritious part of the plant, look for greens that appear fresh, tender, and have a lively green color.

STORING

Cut the majority of the greens and their stems from the beetroots, so they do not pull away moisture from the root. Leave about two inches of the stem attached to prevent the roots from "bleeding."

Do not wash beets before storing. Place in a plastic bag and wrap the bag tightly around the beets, squeezing out as much of the air from the bag as possible, and place in refrigerator where they will keep for up to 3 weeks.

Store the unwashed greens in a separate plastic bag squeezing out as much of the air as possible. Place in refrigerator where they will keep fresh for about four days.

SERVING

Health benefits such as curing cancer are greatly reduced by cooking. Studies show beets' concentration of phytonutrients, such as betalains, is diminished by heat.

Juicing beetroots is the best options. By this method you include large quantity of beet-roots and also you avoid heating beetroots.

If you really must cook them, leave 1 inch - 2 inch (up to 50 mm) of stem attached and leave dangling roots intact when cooking fresh beets to prevent loss of color. Cook beets lightly.

The skins slip off easily after cooking. The cooked beets are excellent served as a hot vegetable or cooled and added to salads.

Better still; eat them raw without peeling them. Grate them for a salad, or blend them into a fruit and vegetable drink or marinate steamed beets in fresh lemon juice, extra virgin olive oil, and fresh herbs.

Consumption of beets can cause urine to become red or pink in color. This condition called "beeturia" is not considered harmful. About 5-15% of U.S. adults are estimated to experience beeturia following consumption of beets in everyday amounts.

It's possible for beet consumption to bring a red color into your bowel movements as well, although this outcome tends to be more common in children than adults. Once again, the production of a reddish color in the stool due to beets is not considered harmful.

Bottom Line

1. Beetroot is considered good for liver, healthy for heart and a purifier of blood.
2. Juicing is one of the best options. It can also be combined with many other vegetable carrot etc.
3. Beat your diseases with roots of beet more often.

17/52

BELL PEPPERS

"Bright and Beautiful"

Red, yellow and green bell peppers have a sweet and tangy flavor and offer a bounty of health benefits.

They are named for their bell-like shape. They are sometimes ambiguously known simply as "pepper" or "capsicum". Bell peppers can help in reducing the risk of heart disease, stroke, some cancers, cataracts, and alleviate symptoms of arthritis and asthma.

Because bell peppers can be grown in a variety of climates and are popular in cuisines throughout the world, they can frequently be found on small farms in North America, Central America, South America, Europe, Africa, the Middle East, and parts of Asia.

Bell peppers are green while developing and then ripen to a variety of colors, of which red and yellow are the most common but purple and orange are also found. They all have a mild, sweet flavor and crisp juicy flesh.

RICH SOURCE

Bell peppers are packed with several nutrients. They are a good source of vitamin C, thiamine, vitamin B6, beta carotene, and folic acid. Bell peppers also contain a large amount of phytochemicals that have exceptional anti-oxidant activity.

When comparing the nutrient values of the different bell peppers, studies have shown that red bell peppers have significantly higher levels of nutrients than green.

In fact compared to green ones, red ones have three times as much vitamin C and 11 times as much beta carotene. Red bell peppers also contain lycopene, which is a carotene that helps to protect against cancer and heart disease.

ANTI-CANCER BENEFITS

As a food that is rich in anti-oxidant and anti-inflammatory nutrients, bell peppers are expected to provide us with important anti-cancer benefits.

Alongside of this anti-oxidant/anti-inflammatory component of bell peppers' potential anti-cancer benefits is expected from the metabolism of sulfur compounds in bell peppers, and in particular the sulfur-containing amino acid cysteine.

Digestive tract Cancers: Based on preliminary studies on animals and in the lab, cancers of the digestive tract (including gastric cancer and esophageal cancer) may be areas in which bell peppers end up showing a special potential for support.

Several recent studies have taken a close look at the presence of enzymes in bell peppers called cysteine S-conjugate beta-lyases and their role in a sulfur-containing metabolic pathway called the thiomethyl shunt.

These enzymes and this pathway may be involved in some of the anti-cancer benefits that bell pepper has shown in some preliminary animal and lab studies.

They may be the basis for some of the anti-cancer benefits shown by green, yellow, red and orange vegetable intake in recent studies, including a recent study on risk reduction for gastric cancer and esophageal cancer.

Colon, Cervical, Bladder, Prostate and Pancreatic Cancers: "Lycopene along with vitamin C and lots of fiber in red bell peppers may offer protection against colon, cervical, bladder, prostate and pancreatic cancers" claims the book "The World's Healthiest Foods".

Lung Cancer: The vitamin A-promoting carotenoid beta-cryptoxanthin works wonders against lung cancer prevention as claimed by Rebecca Katz in her latest book "The Cancer Fighting Kitchen". Red peppers contain beta-cryptoxanthin.

One study, in Cancer Epidemiology Biomarkers and Prevention, followed more than 63,000 people in China and found that those eating the most cryptoxanthin-rich foods had 27% lower risk for lung cancers.

SELECTION

Their skin should be firm without any wrinkles, and the stem should be fresh and green. Avoid peppers with sunken areas, slashes or black spots.

You don't want them to be overly ripe to the point of getting too soft, wrinkly, or blemished. Over-ripe peppers may lose more than 25% of vitamin C.

So the golden rule is, whether green, red, yellow, or orange, optimally ripe bell peppers will have deep, vivid colors, should be heavy for their size (reflecting their thick, well-formed and well-hydrated walls). And firm enough so that they will only yield slightly to a small amount of pressure.

STORING

Unwashed sweet peppers stored in the vegetable compartment of the refrigerator will keep for approximately 7-10 days. Bell peppers need to be still well hydrated and are very sensitive to moisture loss, including a damp cloth or paper towel in the vegetable compartment to help the peppers retain their moisture.

Do not cut out the bell pepper stem prior to storage in the refrigerator. Bell peppers are especially sensitive to moisture loss through this stem portion and are more susceptible to chilling injury if the stem is removed. Green bell peppers will stay fresh a little longer than the yellow and red ones.

SERVING

Before coring and/or cutting the pepper, wash it under cold running water. If the pepper has been waxed, you should also scrub it gently but thoroughly with a natural bristle brush. A recent study has shown that bell peppers retain more of their total antioxidant capacity when washed under cold versus hot water.

They are edible even in the raw and unripe stage. You can easily bake, broil, grill, roast, and stew them. Bell peppers match well with anchovies, basil, chilies, coriander, corn, garlic, lemon, meat, olive oil, onions, rice, tomatoes, and vinegar.

Red ones are often heated over a fire, such as a gas range, to remove the skins it would add distinctive smokey flavor in the final dish.

Bell peppers are commonly added to pizza, stir-fry, and sweet and sour vegetables. They can also be opened at the top and deseeded, then stuffed with boiled mashed potatoes and baked.

For general usage: Slice in half lengthwise, then remove the stem, core, seeds, and retain the white veins. The pulpy white inner cavity of the bell pepper is rich in flavonoids and can be eaten, even though some people have a personal preference for removing this section.

Light cooking or sautéing in a wok with minimum oil is one of the healthiest ways to eating bell peppers. You can add finely chopped bell peppers to practically all green, tuna or chicken salads.

1. All bell peppers start green, change colors with time and finally they end up turning red.
2. Do not remove the stem during storing for a long shelf life.
3. Give me red bell pepper since it has the maximum amount of cancer fighting nutrients.

18/52

BROCCOLI

"If I could un-invent anything, I would un-invent Hitler's mum, guns and broccoli"
– Dominic Monaghan

Woe to those who dislike the taste of broccoli. When health experts compare different beneficial vegetables side by side, broccoli wins hands down. It is the celebrity of the nutrition world.

It regularly finds its way to the "top ten" lists of healthy foods compiled by many nutritionists and health experts according to Dr. Jonny Bowden author of the book "The 150 Healthiest Foods on Earth".

Broccoli is one of the most powerful anti-cancer foods in the world: it contains phyto-chemicals so effective that given a chance every drug company would like to patent them. Adjust the taste for the super blast of nutrition broccoli offers.

RICH SOURCE

Broccoli is an excellent source of vitamin C, anti-inflammatory vitamin K, heart-healthy folate.

It is a very good source of vitamin A, manganese and molybdenum; digestive-health-supporting fiber; potassium and vitamin B6; and vitamin B2 and phosphorus.

It is a good source of vitamin B1, vitamin B3, vitamin B5, protein, and iron; magnesium and calcium; and anti-oxidant-supportive vitamin E and selenium.

Broccoli is also concentrated in phytonutrients. In one particular phytonutrient "glucosinolates", broccoli is simply outstanding. The "glucosinolates" are the key to broccoli's cancer-preventive benefits.

ANTI-CANCER BENEFITS

The unique combination of anti-oxidant, anti-inflammatory, and pro-detoxification components in broccoli makes it a unique food in terms of cancer prevention.

It offers a vast array of cancer-fighting compounds, including antiangiogenesis phytochemicals that help "starve" tumors so they die, all without harming healthy cells.

In a way that might be unique among foods, the nutrients found in broccoli are able to change this set of connections between inflammation, oxidative stress, detox and cancer. In fact, it would be fair to describe broccoli as containing anti-inflammatory nutrients, anti-oxidant nutrients, detox-support nutrients, and anti-cancer nutrients as well!

If cancer development is compared to a 3-legged stool, the anti-oxidant benefits of broccoli can be viewed as weakening one leg of the stool, namely the leg called "oxidative stress."

The glucosinolates and omega-3 fats in broccoli can be viewed as helping to weaken a second leg of the stool (chronic inflammation).

Iso-thio-cyanate-s (ITCs) made from the glucosinolates in broccoli are well-documented modifiers step in detoxification, thus breaking the third leg of the stool (inadequate detoxification).Source: book "The World's Healthiest Foods" by George Mateljan

Breast and Cervical Cancer: Broccoli has a chemical component called indole-3-carbinol that can combat breast cancer by converting a cancer-promoting estrogen into a more protective variety. Source book "The 150 Healthiest Foods on Earth" by Jonny Bowden, Ph.D., C.N.S.

Colon, Rectal and Lung Cancers: Broccoli has the phytochemical sulforaphane, a product of glucoraphanin - believed to aid in preventing cancer of colon and rectal. Bitterer the broccoli is the more glucoraphanin it has got.

A good intake of vitamin C is associated with a reduced risk of colon cancer and broccoli has plenty of it.

In 2008 a couple of American researchers reported evidence that eating raw cruciferous veggies – broccoli and cauliflower fall into this group – lowered the risk of developing lung cancer in smokers and former smokers: and the range of risk reduction was fairly significant ranging from a 20 to 55%.

Now scientists have uncovered one of the chemicals in broccoli that plays a part in this preventive puzzle. Sulforaphane, a phytochemical found in high quantities in cruciferous vegetables, has for the first time been shown to selectively target and kill cancer cells whilst leaving normal cells healthy and unaffected.

Lung, Breast and Colon Cancers: Fung-Lung Chung and colleagues showed in previous experiments that substances called iso-thio-cyanate-s (or ITCs) -- found in broccoli, cauliflower, watercress, and other cruciferous vegetables -- appear to stop the growth of cancer.

But nobody knew exactly how these substances work, a key to developing improved strategies for fighting cancer in humans. The tumor suppressor gene p53 appears to play a key role in keeping cells healthy and preventing them from starting the abnormal growth that is a hallmark of cancer. Researchers say these mutations are found in about half of all human cancers.

The scientists studied the effects of certain naturally-occurring ITCs on a variety of cancer cells, including lung, breast and colon cancer, with and without the defective tumor suppressor gene.

They found that ITCs are capable of removing the defective p53 protein but apparently leave the normal one alone. Big potential for the drug companies to extract or make ITCs in future.Source: ACS' *Journal of Medicinal Chemistry.*

Prostate, Colon, Breast, Bladder and Ovarian Cancers: In another research the broccoli has shown strongest results in decrease of cancer of prostate, colon, breast, bladder and ovarian. Researchers strongly feel it is not long before risk of other cancers will also show reduction from regular consumption of broccoli.

In a study of 252 cases of bladder cancer that developed in population of 47,909, over 10 years period, it was observed that people who eat 5 or more serving of cruciferous vegetable, particularly broccoli and cabbage, reduced their chances of getting bladder cancer by 50%, as compared to the ones who took 1 or less than 1 serving per week. Source: book "Foods to Fight Cancer" by Richard Beliveau Ph.D

SELECTION

Choose broccoli with floret clusters that are compact and not bruised. They should be uniformly colored, either dark green, sage or purple-green, depending upon variety, and with no yellowing.

In addition, they should not have any yellow flowers blossoming through, as this is a sign of over-maturity. The stalk and stems should be firm with no slimy spots appearing either there or on the florets. If leaves are attached, they should be vibrant in color and not wilted.

STORING

Place broccoli in a plastic bag, removing as much of the air from the bag as possible. Store in the refrigerator where it will keep for 10 days. Do not wash broccoli before storing because exposure to water encourages spoilage.

Partial heads of broccoli should be placed in a well-sealed container or plastic bag and refrigerated. Since the vitamin C content starts to quickly degrade once broccoli has been cut, it is best to use it within a couple of days.

Broccoli that has been blanched and then frozen can stay up to a year. Leftover cooked broccoli should be placed in tightly covered container and stored in the refrigerator where it will keep for a few days.

SERVING

Broccoli, prepared correctly, is an extremely potent cancer-fighting agent.

Ms. Elizabeth Jeffery, professor of nutrition, says that "many people destroy myrosinase by overcooking their broccoli and others who use Broccoli powder supplements in recipes to boost their nutrition are also missing out. These supplements often do not contain this necessary enzyme".

Recent studies have also provided us with a much better idea about the amount of broccoli that we need to lower our cancer risk. At the lower end of the spectrum, it looks like an average of 1/2 cup of broccoli per day is enough to provide some measurable benefits.

2-cup serving twice a week would also meet this minimum average amount. There is no reason to shy away from 2-3 cup servings of broccoli when enjoying this cruciferous vegetable, especially if you want to optimize its cancer-preventing benefits.

As per the study published in the January 2011 issue of *Nutrition and Cancer*, ""Steaming broccoli for two to four minutes is the perfect way to protect both the enzyme and the vegetable's nutrients."

You can further enhance the powers by sprinkling broccoli sprouts on your steamed broccoli or make a mustard sauce to serve with broccoli.

Other similar beneficial vegetables that contain sulforaphane and can be teamed with broccoli to boost its benefits are mustard, radishes, arugula, cabbage and cauliflower.

Bottom Line

1. Super star in fight against cancer.
2. Light steaming is the best option.
3. Broccoli supplements are like second wife, generally good in looks but bad in virtues.

18A/52

BRUSSELS SPROUTS

Brussels sprouts are a vegetable that looks like a mini-cabbage, with a diameter of about 1 inch. They grow in bunches of 20 to 40 on the stem of a plant that grows from two to three feet tall.

What do broccoli, cauliflower, Brussels sprouts, kale, cabbage, and bokchoy have in common? They're all members of the cruciferous, or cabbage, family of vegetables.

Brussels sprouts are now cultivated throughout Europe and the United States. In the U.S., almost all Brussels sprouts are grown in California.

And they all contain phytochemicals, vitamins and minerals, and fiber that are important to your health (although some have more than others). In fact, health agencies recommend that we eat several servings per week of cruciferous vegetables -- and for good reason.

RICH SOURCE

Brussels sprouts are excellent source of vitamin C and vitamin K. They are a very good source of numerous nutrients including folate, vitamin A, manganese, dietary fiber, potassium, vitamin B6 and vitamin B1 and a good source of omega-3 fatty acids, iron, phosphorus, protein, magnesium, vitamin B2, vitamin E, copper and calcium.

In addition to these nutrients, Brussels sprouts contain numerous disease-fighting phytochemicals including sulforaphane, indoles, glucosinolates, isothiocynates, coumarins, dithiolthiones, and phenols.

For total glucosinolate content, Brussels sprouts are now known to top the list of commonly eaten cruciferous vegetables. Their total glucosinolate content has been shown to be greater than the amount found in mustard greens, turnip greens, cabbage, kale, cauliflower, or broccoli.

ANTI-CANCER BENEFITS

You'll find nearly 100 studies in PubMed (the health research database at the National Library of Medicine in Washington, D.C.) that are focused on Brussels sprouts, and over half of those studies involve the health benefits of this cruciferous vegetable in relationship to cancer.

This connection between Brussels sprouts and cancer prevention should not be surprising since Brussels sprouts provide special nutrient support for three body systems that are closely connected with cancer development as well as cancer prevention.

These three systems are (1) the body's detox system, (2) its anti-oxidant system, and (3) its inflammatory/anti-inflammatory system.

Among all types of cancer, prevention of the following cancer types is most closely associated with intake of Brussels sprouts: bladder, breast, colon, lung, prostate, and ovarian cancer.

All cruciferous vegetables contain glucosinolates, but Brussels sprouts deliver all the four types of glucosinolates found in this cruciferous vegetable: glucoraphanin, glucobrassicin, sinigrin, and gluconasturtiian and that too in a special combination.

DNA–Cancer: Evidence in the Netherlands suggests that Brussels sprouts keep the body free from cancer by promoting healthy DNA. DNA is responsible for cell division in the body. When DNA gets damaged, cells may begin to replicate much more rapidly than normal, which can cause a cancerous tumor to begin to form.

Researchers compared two groups of healthy men. Half of these men ate 300 grams (2 cups) of Brussels sprouts daily, while the other men didn't have any cruciferous vegetables in their diet. After three weeks, the men who ate their daily dose of Brussels sprouts had 28% decrease in measured DNA damage.

Colon Cancer: The phytonutrients in Brussels sprouts have been shown to protect against heterocyclic amines, which are the carcinogenic compounds found in grilled and charbroiled meat. These carcinogens are particularly associated with colon cancer.

The study, published in Carcinogenesis, found that animals that were given Brussels sprout juice and heterocyclic amine carcinogen were less likely to develop the cancer.

The animals given Brussels sprouts had a reduction in pre-cancerous cells of 41-52% in the colon and drastically diminished the size (85-91%) of pre-cancerous lesions in the liver. These amazing results seem to be a result of Brussels sprouts potent ability to detoxify the body and clear out the colon.

Brussels sprouts are also packed with fiber, which nourishes the cells lining the walls of the colon and prevents colon problems including cancer.

Bladder Cancer: Bladder cancer is diagnosed in more than 300,000 people internationally every year and is the fourth most common cancer in men and the eighth most common in women.

Research published in the International Journal of Cancer shows that Brussels sprouts protect against bladder cancer. The diets of 697 people who were recently diagnosed with bladder cancer were compared with 708 people with the same age, gender and ethnicity who were healthy.

The average daily intake of Brussels sprouts and other cruciferous vegetables was significantly lower in those with bladder cancer than in their healthy counterparts. Those who had the highest intake of Brussels sprouts and cruciferous vegetables had a 29% lower risk of bladder cancer than those who ate the least.

The benefits of these vegetables were highest in those who had the highest risk of bladder cancer, including men, smokers and older individuals.

Brussels sprouts' bladder cancer properties appear to come from their high levels of isothiocyanates, which are potent anti-carcinogens. Isothiocyanates travel through the bladder to be excreted, making them particularly powerful against this form of cancer.

The researchers led by New Zealand scientist Dr. Rex Munday discovered that an extract of broccoli sprouts can halve the incidence of bladder cancer in an animal model.

Breast Cancer: Sulforaphane is released by Brussels sprouts and has been proven to trigger the liver to produce enzymes that detoxify the body of cancer-causing chemicals; they have been shown to inhibit chemically-induced breast cancers in animal studies.

Research published in the Journal of Nutrition shows that Sulforaphane can halt the proliferation of breast cancer cells, even in the later stages of their growth.

Prostate Cancer: Research at FredHutchinson Cancer Research Center in Seattle studied 1,000 men. It was shown that eating 28 servings of different vegetables a week reduced their risk of prostate cancer by 35%.

But those who ate 3 or more servings of cruciferous vegetables each week had a 44% lower prostate cancer risk.

SELECTION

Good quality Brussels sprouts are firm, compact, and vivid green. Choose those of equal size to ensure that they will cook evenly.

STORAGE

Keep unwashed and untrimmed Brussels sprouts in the vegetable compartment of the refrigerator. Stored in a plastic bag, they can be kept for 10 days. If you want to freeze Brussels sprouts, blanch them first for between three to five minutes. They will keep in the freezer for up to one year.

SERVING

Before washing Brussels sprouts, remove stems and any yellow or discolored leaves. Wash them well under running water or soak them in a bowl of water to remove any insects that may reside in the inner leaves.

Brussels sprouts are usually cooked whole. To allow the heat to permeate throughout all of the leaves and better ensure an even texture, cut an "X" in the bottom of the stem before cooking.

While Brussels sprouts are usually served as a side dish, they also make a nice addition to cold salads. Perfectly cooked Brussels sprouts have a crisp, dense texture and a slightly sweet, bright, and "green" taste.

It is very important not to overcook Brussels sprouts. Not only do they lose their nutritional value and taste but they will begin to emit the unpleasant sulfur smell associated with overcooked cruciferous vegetables.

Steam Brussels sprouts for maximum nutrition and flavor. Fill the bottom of a steamer pot with 2 inches of water. While waiting for the water to come to a rapid boil cut Brussels sprouts into quarters. Steam for 5 minutes and toss with our Honey Mustard sauce to add extra flavor and nutrition.

Since cooked Brussels sprouts are small and compact, they make a great snack food that can be simply eaten as it is or seasoned with salt and pepper to taste.

Many people claim to not enjoy eating Brussels sprouts. If you are not a fan of this incredible food, try chopping them up into tiny pieces and sprinkling them over a salad. You won`t even be able to taste them but you will still get the health enhancing benefits and defend your body against disease.

At a minimum, include cruciferous vegetables as part of your diet 2-3 times per week, and make the serving size at least 1-1/2 cups–more the merrier.

Bottom Line

1. Brussel Sprouts can be called mini nutritional bomb very efective against war on cancer.
2. Cut them, keep them for 5 minutes and lightly steamed. You can replace cabbage with Brussel sprouts.
3. Your family may not like it to begin with but slowly Brsussel sprouts would become Baby Darling of the house.

19/52

CABBAGE

Green Cabbage

Red Cabbage

Savoy Cabbage

> *"Having a good wife and rich cabbage soup, seek not other things"*
> – Russian Proverb

One of the most popular vegetables in the world, Cabbage is a sturdy, strong and abundant vegetable. Hardy and easy to grow, it is almost universally available in all countries and cultures.

Cabbage belongs to the all-important family of cruciferous vegetables, with a long history of being used as food and medicine. The members of this family of vegetables are so named for their cross-shaped (crucifer) flower petals. Other members of the family include cauliflower, broccoli, collards and brussels sprouts.

The cheap, humble looking and lowly cabbage can work miracles in your life; it is the darling of nutritionists. It is widely used throughout the world, eaten cooked or raw as salad. Cabbage has the reputation of being a big cancer fighter.

There are three major types of cabbage: green, red, and Savoy. Red and green cabbage has a more defined taste and crunchy texture as compared to Savoy cabbage's more delicate nature.

RICH SOURCE

Cabbage is an excellent source of vitamin K and vitamin C. It is also a very good source of fiber, manganese, folate, vitamin B6, potassium and omega-3 fatty acids. Cabbage is also a good source of vitamin B1, vitamin B2, calcium, magnesium, vitamin A, and protein.

It's worth making a special note about the omega-3s found in cabbage. Cabbage is not a fatty food! But among the little bit of fat it contains, there is a surprising amount of one particular omega-3 fatty acid called alpha-linolenic acid, or ALA.

There is actually far more ALA in 100 calories of cabbage than there is in 100 calories of salmon! While fish like salmon do contain most of their omega-3s in the form of EPA or DHA rather than ALA.

The past 5 years' research on cruciferous vegetables and inflammation points to the omega-3 content of cruciferous vegetables as a potentially critical component of their unique health benefits.

Cabbage is also a unique source of several types of phytonutrients. Its overall anti-oxidant activity is most likely due to its unusual polyphenol content. Cabbage is also unique for its rich supply of glucosinolates. These phytonutrients have special detoxification and anti-cancer properties.

Red cabbage has more phytonutrients than the green cabbage. The vitamin C content of red cabbage is 6-8 times higher than that of the green cabbage. Red cabbage contains anthocyanin (red pigment/color) an anti-oxidant that can help protect brain cells, thus can help prevent Alzheimer's disease also.

ANTI-CANCER BENEFITS

More than 475 studies have examined the role cabbage vegetable in cancer prevention treatment. The uniqueness of cabbage in cancer prevention is due to the three different types of nutrient richness found in it - (1) anti-oxidant richness, (2) anti-inflammatory richness, and (3) richness in glucosinolates.

The anti-oxidant richness of cabbage is partly responsible for its cancer prevention benefits. Without sufficient intake of anti-oxidants, we can experience oxidative stress. Chronic oxidative stress can be a risk factor for development of cancer.

Lung, Stomach, Colon and Prostate Cancers: Cabbage may lower the incidence of cancer, especially in the lung, stomach, colon and prostate while green cabbage is the most commonly eaten variety of cabbage; we highly recommend trying red cabbage because of its added nutritional benefits and its robust hearty flavor. We don't think you will be disappointed.

The rich red color of red cabbage reflects its concentration of anthocyanin polyphenols, which contribute to red cabbage containing significantly more protective phytonutrients than green cabbage.

A recent study showed that a 100 gram (about 3 ounces) serving of raw red cabbage delivers 196.5 milligrams of polyphenols, of which 28.3 milligrams are anthocyanins. For the same quantity green cabbages yielded much less–45 milligrams–of polyphenols including 0.01 milligram of anthocyanins. Red cabbage is one of the most nutritious and best tasting vegetables around.

Breast Cancer: The phytochemicals in cabbage, called indoles, are also being studied for their ability to convert estradiol, an estrogen-like hormone that may play a role in the development of breast cancer, into a safer form of estrogen. Here also the red cabbage scores better due its higher content of polyphenols.

The anthocyanins found in red cabbage are well-documented anti-inflammatory compounds, and make red cabbage a standout anti-inflammatory food for this reason. However, all types of cabbage do contain significant amounts of polyphenols that provide anti-inflammatory benefits.

We have seen one study, from Poland, showing impressive reduction of breast cancer risk in women consuming large amounts of cabbage.

In this particular study, this reduction in risk was associated with consumption of at least 4 cabbage servings per week, in comparison with the once-per-week serving consumed by women with higher breast cancer risk.

Cabbage contains another compound, Sulforaphane, which has been shown to block cancer by stepping up the production of tumor-preventing enzymes in the body.

In a pioneering study at Johns Hopkins University in Baltimore, scientists exposed 145 laboratory animals to a powerful cancer-causing chemical.

Twenty-five of the animals had not received any special treatment, while the rest had been fed high doses of Sulforaphane. Fifty days later, 68 per cent of the unprotected animals had breast tumors, compared with only 26 per cent of those given high doses of Sulforaphane.

In one study, researchers gave a group of Israeli women about a third of a head of cabbage a day for three months. After five days of eating the fortified diet, the women's levels of harmful hormones dropped significantly.

Bladder, Breast, Colon and Prostate Cancers: Glucosinolates are cabbage's trump card with regard to "anti-cancer" benefits. The glucosinolates found in cabbage can be converted into isothiocyanate compounds that are cancer preventive for a variety of different cancers, including bladder cancer, breast cancer, colon cancer, and prostate cancer.

Sulforaphane makes this super vegetable a particularly prized fighter in the battle against colon cancer, because it stimulates levels of an enzyme called glutathione in the colon, which researchers believe sweeps toxins out of the body before they have a chance to damage the delicate cells lining the intestinal wall.

Eating any kind of cabbage on a regular basis will probably lower your risk for cancer. To get the best possible protection, however, you can't do better than the Savoy variety, say researchers. Savoy contains not only I3C and Sulforaphane but also four other tongue-twisting phytonutrients, beta-sitosterol, pheophytin-a, nonacosane, and nonacosanone, that studies show are powerful contenders against potential cancer-causing agents.

SELECTION

Even though the inside of cabbage is usually clean since the outer leaves protect it, you still may want to clean it. Remove the thick fibrous outer leaves and cut the cabbage into pieces and then wash under running water.

If you notice any signs of worms or insects, which sometimes appear in cabbage, soak the head in salt water or vinegar water for 15-20 minutes first. To preserve its vitamin C content, cut and wash the cabbage right before cooking or eating it. Since phytonutrients in the cabbage react with carbon steel and turn the leaves black, use a stainless steel knife to cut.

STORING

Keeping cabbage cold will keep it fresh and help it retain its vitamin C content. Put the whole head in a plastic bag in the crisper of your refrigerator. Red and green cabbage will keep this way for about 2 weeks while Savoy cabbage will keep for about 1 week.

If you need to store a partial head of cabbage, cover it tightly with plastic wrap and refrigerate. Since the vitamin C content of cabbage starts to quickly degrade once it has been cut, you should use the remainder as soon as possible.

SERVING

Finally, it's important to remember that we can allow myrosinase enzymes in cabbage to do their natural work by slicing, shredding, or chopping raw cabbage and letting it sit for 5-10 minutes before cooking.

Once the cells in cabbage have been broken apart through slicing, shredding, or chopping, the myrosinase enzymes in those cells can become active in converting the glucosinolates in cabbage into isothiocyanates (ITCs).

One of the best healthy methods of cooking cabbage is Sauté. It provides the greatest flavor and is also a method that allows for concentrated nutrient retention.

To Healthy Sauté cabbage, heat 5 TBS of broth (vegetable or chicken) or water in a stainless steel skillet. Once bubbles begin to form add shredded cabbage, cover, and Healthy Sauté for 5 minutes.

Turn off the heat and let sit for 2 more minutes before transferring to a bowl and tossing with Mediterranean Dressing. Ginger is a great addition to your Healthy Sautéed cabbage; you can also add rice vinegar and sesame seeds.

Combine shredded red and green cabbage with fresh lemon juice, olive oil, and seasonings such as turmeric, cumin, coriander, and black pepper to make coleslaw with an Indian twist.

❍ Bottom Line

1. Cabbage is a mine full of cancer fighting nutrients.
2. Enhances the cancer fighting spirit by washing, chopping and waiting for 10 minutes before cooking cabbage.
3. Threatens to cook it (like sauté), never over, cook it.

20/52

CARROTS

"If your husband is old and weak you must have him to drink the juice from two big carrots and one firm celery" – An old Polish saying

Carrots are one of the most popular root vegetables in the U.S. - and widely enjoyed in many other countries as well. Carrots almost feel like an old friend for many people who are looking for just the right crunchy snack or addition to a salad.

In today's commercial marketplace, China currently produces about one-third of all carrots bought and sold worldwide. Russia is the second largest carrot producer, with the U.S. following a close third.

The health benefits of carrot include reduced cholesterol, prevention from heart attacks, warding off certain cancers and many other diseases. Most of the benefits of carrot can be attributed to its beta carotene and fiber content.

RICH SOURCE

Carrots are good source of immune-supportive vitamin C; bone-building vitamin K; and heart-healthy dietary fiber and potassium. They are a good source of heart-healthy vitamin B6, niacin, folate, and vitamin E; enzyme-supporting manganese and molybdenum; and energy-supportive vitamin B1, vitamin B2 and phosphorus.

A single carrot can supply all your vitamin A needs for the whole day. It's also a great food to nibble, being a much healthier pastime than grazing on potato chips.

Research has also shown that this vegetable has a protective effect against ultraviolet light (in other words they will help you look younger and live longer).

Carrots are perhaps best known for their beta-carotene content. While they can be an outstanding source of this phytonutrient, carrots actually contain a fascinating combination of phytonutrients.

ANTI-CANCER BENEFITS

The anti-cancer benefits of carrot have been best researched in the area of colon cancer. Some of this research has involved actual intake of carrot juice by human participants, and other research has involved the study of human cancer cell types in the lab.

Colon Cancer: The study results to date have been encouraging. Lab studies have shown the ability of carrot extracts to inhibit the grown of colon cancer cells, and the poly-acetylenes found in carrot have been specifically linked to this inhibitory effect.

In studies of carrot juice intake, small but significant effects on colon cell health have been shown for participants who consumed about 1.5 cups of fresh carrot juice per day.

In a study, researchers found that eating only one fiber-rich carrot a day reduced the risk of colon cancer by as much as 24 per cent.

Lung Cancer: Beta-carotene consumption has been linked to reduced risk of several cancers, notably lung cancer. British researchers discovered that increasing beta-carotene consumption from 1.7 to 2.7 milligrams a day reduced lung cancer risk more than 40 per cent. The average carrot contains about 3 milligrams of Beta-carotene.

A total of 417 lung cancer cases and 849 controls were interviewed on their life-long tobacco usage and their current intake of four food items rich in retinol or carotene.

The study was a hospital-based case control where 'cases' were lung cancer patients diagnosed during the period 1979/80 at seven hospitals in the Lombardy region (90% pathologically confirmed) and controls were patients admitted to the same hospitals for causes unrelated to tobacco smoking.

Current smokers who did not consume carrots showed a three-fold risk of developing lung cancer compared with those who ate them more than once a week.

Breast Cancer: Another study shows that women who ate raw carrots were five to eight times less likely to develop breast cancer than women who did not eat carrots.

What Kills the Smokers: "Camels or Carrots or It is the carotene in the vitamin tablets". A recent study is very critical, of beta-carotene in dietary supplements. The study authors wrote, "High-dose beta-carotene supplementation appears to increase the risk of lung cancer among current smokers."

A team of researchers, from the University of Newcastle upon Tyne in England and Denmark, found the natural pesticide "falcarinol", found in carrots, reduced the risk of cancer developing in rats by one-third.

The study results, published in the Journal of Agricultural and Food Chemistry, are significant as they could contribute to healthy eating advice for consumers and recommendations for growers and may eventually aid the development of anti-cancer drugs.

The research team carried out tests on 24 rats with pre-cancerous tumors in laboratory conditions. They divided them into three groups and fed them different diets.

The team found that, after 18 weeks, rats who ate carrots (the popular orange variety) along with their ordinary feed and the group which consumed falcarinol with their feed - in a quantity equal to that contained in the carrots - were one-third less likely to develop full-scale tumors than the rats in the control group.

Dr Kirsten Brandt, a senior lecturer with Newcastle University's School of Agriculture, Food and Rural Development, carried out the research with the University of Southern Denmark and the Danish Institute of Agricultural Sciences.

She said: "We already know that carrots are good for us and can reduce the risk of cancer but until now we have not known which element of the vegetable has these special properties."

We now need to take it a step further by finding out how much falcarinol is needed to prevent the development of cancer. Dr Brandt, who says she eats "more carrots than most" and grows her own organic varieties, recommended that consumers should eat one small carrot every day, together with other vegetables and fruits, to benefit from their health-giving properties.

SELECTION

Carrot roots should be firm, smooth, relatively straight and bright in color. The deeper the orange-color, the more beta-carotene is present in the carrot. If the green tops are attached, they should be brightly colored, feathery and not wilted.

Avoid carrots that are excessively cracked or forked as well as those that are limp or rubbery. In addition, if the carrots do not have their tops attached, look at the stem end and ensure that it is not darkly colored as this is also a sign of age.

STORAGE

Research has shown that the especially valuable beta-carotene is well-retained in carrots if stored properly. Carrots are hardy vegetables that will keep longer than many others if stored properly. The trick to preserving the freshness of carrot roots is to minimize the amount of moisture they lose.

Since the sugars are concentrated in the carrots' core, generally those with larger diameters will have a larger core and therefore be sweeter- the slimmer carrots are healthier!

To do this, make sure to store them in the coolest part of the refrigerator in a plastic bag or wrapped in a paper towel, which will reduce the amount of condensation that is able to form. They should be able to keep fresh for about two weeks.

Carrots should also be stored away from apples, pears, potatoes and other fruits and vegetables that produce ethylene gas since it will cause them to become bitter.

If you purchase carrot roots with attached green tops, the tops should be cut off before storing in the refrigerator since they will cause the carrots to wilt prematurely as they pull moisture from the roots.

SERVING

Wash carrot roots and gently scrub them with a vegetable brush right before eating. Unless the carrots are old, thick or not grown organically, it is not necessary to peel them.

If they are not organically grown, peel them; most all conventionally grown carrots are grown using pesticides and other chemicals. If the stem end is green, it should be cut away as it will be bitter.

Depending upon the recipe or your personal preference, carrots can be left whole or julienned, grated, shredded or sliced into sticks or rounds.

Carrots are delicious eaten raw or cooked. While heating can often damage some of the delicate phytonutrients in vegetables, the beta-carotene as found in carrots has been shown to be surprisingly heat-stable.

Chinese medical practitioners recommend eating carrots to give your liver more energy.

In fact, carrots' beta-carotene may become more bioavailable through well-timed steaming. Still, be careful not to overcook carrots if you want your carrots to retain their maximum flavor and strong overall nutritional value.

Cooking carrots by steaming is a healthy way to eat them. To Healthy Steamed carrots, fill the bottom of the steamer with 2 inches of water and bring to a rapid boil. Slice carrots ¼-inch thick and steam for 5 minutes. Transfer to a bowl. For more flavor, toss carrots with some mustard dressing.

Shredded raw carrots and chopped carrot greens make great additions to salads. Combine shredded carrots, beets and apples, and eat as a salad.

For quick, nutritious soup that can be served hot or cold, purée boiled carrots and potatoes in a blender or food processor, and add herbs and spices to taste.

Spiced carrot sticks are a flavorful variation on an old favorite at parties or at the dinner table. Soak carrot sticks in hot water spiced with cayenne, coriander seeds and salt. Allow to cool, drain and serve.

Bottom Line

1 Lightly steamed "Slim" bright red carrots are the best option. Peel them if they are not organically grown.

2. Smokers should eat at least two carrots a day. Dietary supplement of beta-carotene is believed to increase chances of cancer.

3. For a long younger looking life, no harm in dangling some bright red slim carrots before you on daily basis.

21/52

CAULIFLOWER

"Cauliflower is nothing but cabbage with a college education'

– Mark Twain

Packed with rich nutrients, cauliflower or cabbage flower is one of the commonly used flower-vegetables. Its creamy white flower heads are favored in variety of delicacies world-wide.

Cauliflowers are available all around the year in the markets; however they are at their best during winter months. Include cauliflower as one of the cruciferous vegetables on a regular basis, to receive the fantastic health benefits provided by the cruciferous vegetable family.

Like broccoli, cauliflower is made up of tightly clustered florets that are begin to form but stopped at bud stage. This cool season vegetable prefers fertile rich adequate moisture in the soil to flourish.

RICH SOURCE

Cauliflower is an excellent source of vitamin C, vitamin K and folate. It is a very good source of vitamin B5, potassium, dietary fiber, manganese, and molybdenum. Additionally, it is a good source of protein, phosphorus, magnesium, vitamin B1, vitamin B2, vitamin B3, and iron.

The cauliflower heads contain numerous health-benefiting phytonutrients such as indole-3-carbinol, Sulforaphane etc that help prevent prostate, ovarian and cervical cancers.

ANTI-CANCER BENEFITS

The detox support provided by cauliflower includes anti-oxidant nutrients to boost detoxification activities and sulfur-containing nutrients to further support detoxification. Cauliflower also contains phytonutrients called glucosinolates that can help activate detoxification enzymes and regulate their activity.

As an excellent source of vitamin C, and a very good source of manganese, cauliflower provides us with two core conventional anti-oxidants.

As an excellent source of vitamin K, cauliflower provides us with one of the hallmark anti-inflammatory nutrients. Vitamin K acts as a direct regulator of our inflammatory response.

Bladder, Breast, Colon, Prostate and Ovarian Cancers: Cauliflower contains several anti-cancer phyto-chemicals like Sulforaphane and plant sterols such as indole-3-carbinol which appears to function as an anti-estrogen agent.

There are several dozen studies linking cauliflower-containing diets to cancer prevention, particularly with respect to the following types of cancer: bladder cancer, breast cancer, colon cancer, prostate cancer, and ovarian cancer, by virtue of their cancer cell growth inhibition, cytotoxic effects on cancer cells.

Breast and Prostate Cancer: Curry and cauliflower could halt prostate cancer. Rutgers (USA) researchers have found that the curry spice turmeric holds real potential for the treatment and prevention of prostate cancer, particularly when combined with certain vegetables.

The discovery was announced in the journal Cancer Research by Kong and his colleagues at Rutgers' Ernest Mario School of Pharmacy.

Prostate cancer is the second leading cause of cancer death in men in the United States, with a half-million new cases appearing each year. The incidence and mortality of prostate cancer have not decreased; this is because advanced prostate cancer cells are barely responsive even to high concentrations of chemotherapeutic agents or radiotherapy.

Cauliflower or other cruciferous vegetables like broccoli protect against cancer. Sulforaphane — one of the primary phytochemicals in these vegetables — has been shown for the first time to selectively target and kill cancer cells while leaving normal prostate cells healthy and unaffected.

The authors noted that in contrast to the high incidence of prostate cancer in the United States, the incidence of this disease is very low in India. This has been attributed to the dietary consumption of large amounts of plant-based foods rich in phytochemicals. (cauliflower, cabbage etc.)

Scientists in the Linus Pauling Institute at the Oregon State University discovered another important step forward for the potential use of Sulforaphane in cancer prevention and treatment.

It appears that Sulforaphane, which is found at fairly high levels in broccoli, cauliflower and other cruciferous vegetables, is an inhibitor of histone deacetylase, or HDAC enzymes.

HDAC inhibition is one of the more promising fields of cancer treatment, and is being targeted from both a pharmaceutical and dietary approach, scientists say. Clinical prevention trials are under way for its use in these areas, particularly prostate and breast cancer.

SELECTION

When purchasing cauliflower, look for a clean, creamy white, compact curd in which the bud clusters are not separated. Spotted or dull-colored cauliflower should be avoided, as well as those in which small flowers appear.

Heads that are surrounded by many thick green leaves are better protected and will be fresher. As its size is not related to its quality, choose one that best suits your needs.

STORING

Store uncooked cauliflower in a paper or plastic bag in the refrigerator where it will keep for up to a week. To prevent moisture from developing in the floret clusters, store it with the stem side down.

If you purchase pre-cut cauliflower florets, consume them within one or two days as they will lose their freshness after that. Since cooking causes cauliflower to spoil quicker, consume it within two to three days of placing in the refrigerator after cooking.

SERVING

Cauliflower florets are the part of the plant that most people eat. However, the stem and leaves are edible too and are especially good for adding to soup stocks.

Cauliflower contains phytonutrients that release odorous sulfur compounds when heated. These odors become stronger with increased cooking time. If you want to minimize odor, retain the vegetable's crisp texture, and reduce nutrient loss, cook the cauliflower for only a short time.

Some phytonutrients may react with iron in cookware and cause the cauliflower to take on a brownish hue. To prevent this, add a bit of lemon juice to the water in which you washed the cauliflower.

Cooking cauliflower, healthy way is by Sauteing. It provides the greatest flavor and is also a method that allows for concentrated nutrient retention.

Begin by cutting cauliflower florets into quarters and let it sit for at least 5 minutes to enhance its health-promoting benefits. Add little oil in the wok and sauté cauliflower for 5 minutes, along with turmeric, dash of black peppers, potatoes and peas.

Puree cooked cauliflower, add fennel seeds and your other favorite herbs and spices and serve as soup. Because of its shape and taste, cauliflower florets make wonderful crudite for dipping in sauces.

Bottom Line

1. Cauliflower along with turmeric is a deadly cancer killing combination.
2. Wait for 5-10 minutes after cutting the cauliflower for enhancing phytonutrient power.
3. Do not over-cook sautéing for less than 5 minutes is good method of cooking.

22/52

ONIONS

Red Onion

Shallot

Scallion or Green

What would be life and what would a kitchen be without the distinctively pungent smell and taste of onions filling out the flavors of almost every type of cuisine imaginable?

Onions were highly regarded by the Egyptians. Not only did they use them as currency to pay the workers who built the pyramids, but they also placed them in the tombs of kings, such as Tutankhamen, so that they could carry these gifts bestowed with spiritual significance with them to the afterlife.

Onions (*Allium cepa*) belong to the lily family, the same family as garlic, leeks, chives, scallions and shallots. There are over 600 species of Alliums, distributed all over Europe, North America, Northern Africa and Asia.

The onion has been used as an ingredient in various dishes for thousands of years by many cultures around the world. World onion production is steadily increasing so that onion is now the second most important horticultural crop after tomatoes.

Onions range in size, color, and taste depending upon their variety. Onions are a major source of polyphenols in general, and also of many flavonoids. They vary greatly in their polyphenols and flavonoids content. In general, red onions are higher in total flavonoids than white onions, (with yellow onions falling somewhere in between).

Scallion, commonly known as green onions, spring onion, or salad onion, is a small onion with long leaves that are considered a necessity in Chinese recipes, as well as in teas, wine, vinegar, honeys, garlic, and ginger. The green onion's medicinal part is its stem.

Onion extracts are also recognized by World Health Organization (WHO) for providing relief in the treatment of coughs and colds, asthma and bronchitis.

Founder of The Food Doctor, author, broadcaster and health journalist Ian Marber comments: "The term super foods tends to be applied to nearly

> *Onion skin contains another phytonutrient quercetin, a potent natural anti-histamine and anti-inflammatory compound. According to Dutch researchers, Onions contain three times as much Quercetin as Kale – the next-richest source – and 10 times as much as Broccoli.*

everything these days, but the humble onion does offer far more benefits than most vegetables owing to its potent anti-oxidant and probiotic effects."

Onions also contain very high levels of chromium which helps maintain a positive hormone balance that can help combat PMS symptoms.

RICH SOURCE

Onions are often overlooked as a health food in favor of more typically health-lauded vegetables as tomatoes or broccoli, but the onion is a powerhouse of valuable nutrients and vitamins to help your body. The onion's greatest strength lies in the wide variety of sulfur compounds it contains.

Onions are a rich source of potassium and also contain other minerals, like magnesium, calcium, zinc, selenium, copper, manganese and iron. They are especially rich in vitamin niacin and also contain vitamin B6, thiamin, riboflavin, pantothenic acid and folate. Additionally, there are small vitamins C, E, A and K present in them.

Compounds such as flavonoids and phenolics are also found in great quantities in onions, according to Vegetarianism & Vegetarian Nutrition. These compounds have anti-tumor properties and anti-proliferative activity, which slows tumor growth. These compounds also have strong anti-oxidant capabilities; in general, the stronger the flavor of the onion, the greater the concentration of beneficial compounds.

Onions, like garlic, are members of the Allium family, and both are rich in sulfur-containing compounds that are responsible for their pungent odors and for many of their health-promoting effects. They are primarily responsible for the onion flavor and the eye-irritating induced tears.

The total polyphenols content of onion is not only higher than its fellow allium vegetables, garlic and leeks, but also higher than tomatoes, carrots, and red bell pepper.

ANTI-CANCER BENEFITS

Onions are one of those vegetables chock-full of anti-cancer chemicals. Phenols and flavonoids found in different onions, like other anti-oxidants, help prevent cancer by mopping up cell-damaging free radicals and inhibiting the production of reactive substances that could damage normal cells. Studies done at USA and China are very encouraging.

Colon Cancer: Shallots, Western Yellow, pungent yellow and Northern Red onions are particularly high in these compounds as well as more effective in inhibiting liver and colon cancer cell growth than other common varieties, according to a new study by Cornell-USA, food scientist.

Colon cancer cells treated with extracts from the 10 onion varieties. The Liu group found that pungent yellow and Western Yellow onion extracts provided the strongest anti-proliferation protection against colon cancer cells.

Liver Cancer: RuiHai Liu, M.D., Ph.D., associate professor of food science at Cornell, led the study to determine the potential health benefits of common onions. He found that Western Yellow, shallots and pungent yellow onions were particularly effective against liver cancer cells.

The Western Yellow, shallots and pungent yellow extracts provided the strongest anti-proliferation protection against liver cancer cells.

Prostate Cancer: Men, you may want to spice up your meals. A diet rich in onions and garlic cuts men's risk of prostate cancer in half, according to a large study in China funded by the U.S. government's National Cancer Institute (NCI). Scallions provided the most protection; men who ate the most of these green onions slashed their risk of getting cancer by a whopping 70 per cent.

Men in China have the lowest rate of prostate cancer in the world, and a diet rich in garlic, scallions and onions may be one of the reasons.

The study is based on interviews with 238 men with prostate cancer and 471 men who were free of the disease. Men in the study, all residents of Shanghai, were asked how frequently they ate 122 food items.

The results showed that those who ate more than a third of an ounce a day from the allium food group were about 50 per cent less likely to have prostate cancer than those who ate less of those foods.

Scallions (Green Onions) seemed to be the most protective. Men who ate about a tenth of an ounce or more a day reduced their prostate cancer risk about 70 per cent. For garlic consumption of the same amount, the risk was cut by about 53 per cent.

Ann Hsing, M.P.H., Ph.D., an NCI epidemiologist and the lead author of the study, advises eating raw alliums when possible; cooking them at high temperatures reduces their cancer-fighting properties.

Stomach Cancer: Onion extracts, rich in a variety of sulfides, provide some protection against tumor growth. In central Georgia where onions are grown, mortality rates from stomach cancer are about one-half the average level for the United States. Studies in Greece have shown a high consumption of onions, garlic and other allium herbs to be protective against stomach cancer.

Chinese with the highest intake of onions, garlic, and other Allium vegetables have a risk of stomach cancer 40 per cent less than those with the lowest intake. Elderly Dutch men and women with the highest onion consumption (at least one-half onion/day) had one-half the level of stomach cancer compared with those consuming no onions at all.

Onion has repeatedly been shown to lower our risk of several cancers, even when we consume it in only moderate amounts. "Moderate" generally means 1-2 times per week.

Colorectal cancer, laryngeal cancer, and ovarian cancer are the cancer types for which risk is reduced along with moderate amounts of dietary onion. For other cancer types, however, you have to eat them on more regular basis.

SELECTION

Red onions have one of the richest concentrations of flavonoids and phenolics, providing them with the greatest anti-oxidant and anti-proliferative activity of 10 onions tested.

The mild-tasting White variety onions had the lowest anti-oxidant content and lowest anti-proliferative activity. The consumer trend to increasingly purchase the less pungent, milder onion varieties may not be the best, since the onions with a stronger flavor and higher astringency appear to have superior health-promoting properties.

Choose onions that are clean, well shaped, have no opening at the neck, and feature crisp, dry outer skins.

Avoid those that are sprouting or have signs of mold. In addition, onions of inferior quality often have soft spots, moisture at their neck, and dark patches, which may all be indications of decay.

Purchase organically grown varieties whenever possible.

When purchasing Green Onions or scallions, look for those that have green, fresh-looking tops that appear crisp yet tender. The base should be whitish in color for two or three inches. Avoid those that have wilted or yellowed tops.

STORING

Onions should be stored in a well ventilated space at room temperature, away from heat and bright light. With the exception of green onions, do not refrigerate onions.

Place them in a wire hanging basket or a perforated bowl with a raised base so that air can circulate underneath. The length of storage varies with the type of onion. Those that are more pungent in flavor, such as yellow onions, should keep for about a month if stored properly. They will keep longer than those with a sweeter taste, such as white onions, since the compounds that confer their sharp taste help to preserve them.

Green onions should be stored in a plastic bag in the refrigerator where they will keep for about one week. All onions should be stored away from potatoes, as they will absorb their moisture and ethylene gas, causing them to spoil more readily.

Store cut onions by placing in a sealed container; use them within a day or two since they tend to oxidize and lose their nutrient content rather quickly.

SERVING

The flavonoids in onion tend to be more concentrated in the outer layers of the flesh. To maximize your health benefits, peel off as little of the fleshy, edible portion as possible when removing the onion's outermost paper layer. Even a small amount of "over-peeling" can result in unwanted loss of flavonoids. For example, a red onion can lose about 20% of its quercetin and almost 75% of its anthocyanins if it is "over-peeled."

When onions are simmered to make soup, their quercetin does not get degraded. It simply gets transferred into the water part of the soup. By using a low-heat method for preparing onion soup, you can preserve the health benefits of onion that are associated with this key flavonoid.

Cut onions into 1/4-inch slices to cook them evenly and quickly. Let them sit for at least 5 minutes to help enhance their health-promoting benefits. Green onions' white stem contains a lot of glucose and allylsulfides, generously include them in your dishes.

While many people love to eat onions, most dread cutting them since this process usually brings a tear or two to the eyes. The substance that causes the eyes to burn is a special gas that has been named lachrymatory factor (LF).

If cutting onions irritates your eyes, there are a few tricks that you can employ. Use a very sharp knife and always cut the onions while standing; that way your eyes will be as far away as possible.

Consider cutting onions by an open window. If cutting onions really makes you cry, consider wearing glasses or goggles.

Chill the onions in the refrigerator for an hour or so before cutting; this practice can slow down the onion's metabolism and thereby lessen the rate of LF gas production. Cutting onions under cold, running water is a method that is often used to cut back on eye irritation, but it's a method we view as a second-best choice since some of the nutrients found in onion can be lost into the flow of water.

Onions can be used in variety of ways but they are more often used as a seasoning.

Combine chopped onions, tomatoes, avocado, and jalapeno for an all-in-one guacamole salsa dip.

To perk up plain rice, top with green onions (scallions) and sesame seeds.

Healthy Sauteed chopped onions can enhance the flavor of almost any vegetable dish.

Enjoy a classic Italian salad dish of sliced onions, tomatoes, and mozzarella cheese drizzled with olive oil.

To bring out the sweet flavor of onions we recommend Sauteing onions for just 7 minutes. Cut onions into slices of equal 1/4-inch thickness to help them cook more evenly. The thinner you slice the onions the more quickly they will cook. Let them sit for at least 5 minutes to enhance their health-promoting properties.

Bottom Line

1. Common red and green onions have maximum health benefits.
2. Target eating 2 medium size raw red onions a day.
3. We always have some reason of not including onions in our meals - breath, religion and tears in the eyes, are some of the common ones. After knowing the immense health benefits it offers from common cold to cancer let us decide to include RAW onions in our daily meals. .... hope my wife is listening.

23/52

PUMPKIN AND SEEDS

"Men are like pumpkins. It seems like all the good ones are either taken or they've had everything scraped out of their heads with a spoon."

Delicious and perfumed taste, the pumpkin is a favorite for many people. Whether age-old remedies have ultimate healing powers or not, the nutrients present in just one serving of pumpkin are a testament to the health benefits of this timeless fruit.

The bright orange color of pumpkin is a dead giveaway that pumpkin is loaded with an important anti-oxidant beta-carotene. Beta-carotene is one of the plant carotenoids converted to vitamin A in the body. In the conversion to vitamin A, beta carotene performs many important functions in overall health.

Pumpkin helps the body in its process of regeneration, slowing down the aging process. Current research indicates that a diet rich in foods containing beta-carotene may reduce the risk of developing certain types of cancer, offers protection against heart disease and are good for eyes.

It is one of the vegetables which has very low calories; just 26 calories per 100 g and contains no saturated fats or cholesterol; but is a rich source of dietary fiber, anti-oxidants, minerals, vitamins. It is recommended by many dieticians for cholesterol controlling and weight reduction.

Pumpkin is one of the most popular vegetables that are grown as commercial field crops all over the world including the USA. It is a vegetable with many uses: used as a basis for food, an ingredient for sweets and medicine.

Pumpkin is well known because of Halloween, when it is carved in the shape of a face and lit with candles to banish evil spirits. Pumpkins vary greatly in shape, size and colors. Giant pumpkins generally weigh 4–6 kg with the largest capable of reaching a weight of over 25 kg.

RICH SOURCE

Pumpkin is incredibly a rich storehouse of vital anti-oxidants and vitamins such as vitamin A, vitamin C and vitamin E. It is a very good source of minerals like copper, calcium, potassium and phosphorus.

This humble backyard vegetable is very low in calories yet excellent source of anti-oxidants like lutein, xanthins and carotenes.

In structure, the pulp feature golden-yellow to orange color depending upon the poly-phenolic pigments in it. The fruit has hollow center, with numerous small, off-white colored seeds interspersed in the net-like structure.

Pumpkin seeds are a great source of protein, vitamins and omega-3 fatty acids. Pumpkin seeds are a very good source of the minerals–phosphorus, magnesium and manganese. They are also a good source of other minerals including zinc, iron and copper.

ANTI-CANCER BENEFITS

Pumpkin is a super cancer food that has been said to prevent cancer. Packed with anti-oxidants alpha-carotene and beta-carotene, pumpkins help boost the immune system and block potential cancerous cells.

Anti-oxidants are found in pumpkins, and are typically higher in vegetables and fruits that are of brighter colors. In fact, beta-carotene is what gives pumpkins their orange-red color.

Pumpkin seeds contain the strongest therapeutic effects. These help in eliminating intestinal parasites, cleaning blood vessels, adjusting cholesterol level and stimulating kidney activity.

In treating cancer, leukemia, sclerosis, or various diseases which are hard to cure, pumpkin seeds have an energizing role. The carotenoids and the omega-3 fats found in pumpkin seeds are also being studied for their potential prostate benefits.

Lung and Oral Cavity Cancer: Vitamin A is a powerful natural anti-oxidant and is required by body for maintaining the integrity of skin and mucus membranes. It is also an essential vitamin for vision. Research studies suggest that natural foods rich in vitamin A help protect body against lung and oral cavity cancers.

Research shows that people who eat a diet rich in beta-carotene are less likely to develop certain cancers than those who fail to include beta-carotene-rich foods in their diet. Pumpkin also has another carotenoid, beta-cryptoxanthin, which may decrease the risk of lung cancer in smokers.

Prostate Cancer: There have been many researches linking the pumpkin seed to a healthy prostate. But what is so special about these little green seeds one might ask.

The protective compounds present within the seed of the pumpkin, called phytosterols, may be responsible for shrinking the prostate. They also contain chemicals that may prevent some transformation of testosterone into dihydrotestosterone (DHT). High levels of DHT are associated with enlarged prostate.

The fact that pumpkin seeds are a good source of zinc may also contribute to the role of pumpkin seeds in support of the prostate.

For BPH (Benign Prostatic Hyperplasia or enlarged prostate) prevention, eating a handful (about 1 ounce) of shelled pumpkin seeds three times a week is recommended.

SELECTION

Pumpkins are readily available in the markets year around. Buy well grown whole pumpkin instead of sections. Look for mature product that feature fine woody note on tapping, heavy in hand and stout stem. Avoid the one with wrinkled surface, cuts and bruises.

For maximum health benefits choose the darkest deep yellow or the orange variety.

Pumpkin seeds are generally available in prepackaged containers as well as bulk bins.

STORING

Once at home, fully ripen pumpkin can be stored for many weeks at cool, well ventilated place at room temperature. However, cut sections should be placed inside the refrigerator where they keep well for few days.

Pumpkin seeds should be stored in an airtight container in the refrigerator. While they may stay edible for several months, they seem to lose their peak freshness after about one to two months.

SERVING

Some hybrid varieties are usually subjected to insecticide powder or spray. Therefore, wash them thoroughly in running water in order to remove dust, soil and any residual insecticides/fungicides.

Cut the stem end and slice the whole fruit into two equal halves. Remove central net-like structure and set aside seeds. Then cut into desired sizes. In general, small cubes are used in cooking preparations.

Almost all the parts of the pumpkin plant–fruit, leaves, flowers and seeds–are edible. Pumpkin can be used in variety of delicious recipes either baked, stew fried; but eaten best by steam cooking in order to get maximum nutrients.

In China, the leaves of this plant are consumed as cooked greens or in soups. In the Indian subcontinent where it is popular as "sitaphal", it is used in the preparation of "sabzee", sweet dishes, soups, curries, etc.

It can also be used in the preparations of pies, pancakes, custard, ravioli, etc. Golden nugget pumpkins are used to make wonderful souffles, stuffing, soups, etc. Roasted Pumpkin seeds (pepitas) can be used as snack.

❍ Bottom Line

"WELL THAT SHOULD FIX YOUR EXCUSES"

1. Choose the deep yellow or orange variety.
2. Snack on pumpkin seeds.
3. Pump up the pumpkin – economical and energizing.

24/52

SOYBEANS

Edamame

Soybeans

Soy Flour

"If I could only have one type of food with me, I would bring soy sauce. The reason being that if I have soy sauce, I can flavor a lot of things"
–Martin Yan

Soybeans originated in China over 13,000 years ago and the Chinese name for soybeans means "greater bean" and this amazing legume could not deserve a more fitting title. After all, what could be greater than a bean that offers such a wealth of nutritional value in addition to its culinary versatility?

Like other beans, soybeans grow in pods, featuring edible seeds. While we most often think of them as being green, the seeds can also be yellow, brown or black.

The texture of soybeans is so adaptable that they can be processed in a host of different ways making it easy for you to enjoy them in your daily diet. There are fresh soybeans (also known as Edamame), dried soybean seeds, soymilk, soy nuts, tofu, tempeh, soy flour, natto; miso...the list goes on and on.

Soy is the original health food. Soy is a heart-healthy, cancer-fighting, and immune-boosting food. Comparing the overall health of high soy-consuming cultures, such as the Japanese, and low soy-eating folk, like Americans, provides the first clue that soy has health-building properties.

RICH SOURCE

Soybean is truly a nutrient-dense food. Few foods contain as much nutritional bang for the buck as this bountiful bean. Ounce for ounce, calorie for calorie, the soybean gets top-billing as a rich source of protein, unsaturated fats, fiber, B-vitamins, folic acid, potassium, calcium, zinc, and iron - and it's cholesterol-free.

"There is no other single food that supplies so much nutrition in such a tiny package. While TV and print ads tout milk as the perfect food, the soybean actually deserves this title".

Soybeans are also excellent source of molybdenum, manganese, phosphorus, magnesium, copper and omega-3 fatty acids.

Soy contains cancer-fighting phytonutrients. The phytonutrient most prominent in soy products is genestein and isoflavones. The anti-cancer properties of soy seem to be more associated primarily with the non-fermented soy products, such as tofu and soymilk.

ANTI-CANCER BENEFITS

The average Japanese person eats 2 to 3 ounces (50 to 80 grams) of soy food daily in various forms, such as miso, tempeh, and soy milk. The average American eats a scant 5 grams of soy, and that mostly in the form of oils (often hydrogenated) hidden in high-fat foods.

Comparing Japanese and American health: The Japanese enjoy a longer lifespan and lower rates of cancer (especially colon, lung, breast, and prostate) and have a much lower incidence of heart disease.

Prostate Cancer: The incidence of prostate cancer is much lower in Asian than Western populations, and soy foods may be one important reason why, suggests research published in Cancer Epidemiological Biomarkers and Prevention.

A 9-year Japanese study involving 43,509 men ranging in age from 45 to 74 years found that those eating the most soy food and miso had a significantly lower risk of localized prostate cancer.

Among the men who were older than 60, the protective effect was strongest. Men whose diets provided the most soy products had a 48% reduced risk of localized prostate cancer compared to men food delivered the least.

Research suggests that isoflavone phytonutrients found in soybeans may protectively alter men's metabolism of estrogen, Yes, real men produce some estrogen, and in men, the prostate is the primary locus of estrogen production.

In epidemiological studies of genestein, naturally occurring isoflavones found chiefly in soybeans, has been consistently linked to lower incidence of prostate cancer.

A study published in Cancer Epidemiological Biomarkers that evaluated 398 Chinese men (men with prostate cancer as well as residential community matched controls) found that those consuming the most tofu had a 42% lower risk of developing prostate cancer compared to those consuming the least.

Colon Cancer: High-fiber soybeans may be able to help reduce the risk of colon cancer. As a matter of fact, in areas of the world where soybeans are eaten regularly, rates of colon cancer, as well as some other cancers, including breast cancer, tend to be low.

A study published in the Journal of Nutrition suggests that colon cancer may be a hormone-responsive cancer, and that soy protein can not only help prevent its occurrence but can have a very positive effect on the number and size of tumors that do occur.

In this study, female laboratory animals whose ovaries had been removed to limit their sources of estrogen were exposed to an agent that causes colon tumors, then fed five different diets designed to compare the effects of specific ingredients, and followed for a year. While the diet containing most soy products was the most effective in preventing colon cancer and the worst were animals fed with milk protein diets.

Casein is a protein found in milk and other dairy products. In his book, The China Study, Dr. T. Colin Campbell reports how he discovered, over many years of cancer research, a possible link between animal protein intake and cancer development.

Dr. Campbell discovered that casein, which comprises 85% of the protein in cow's milk, promoted cancer in all stages of its development; he also found that feeding the animals the same levels of plant based protein (gluten and soy) did not at all promote cancer growth.

The researchers gathered data on 367 variables, across 65 counties in China and 6,500 adults. The research was conducted over a 10-year period and was funded by both the Chinese and the United States government.

Breast Cancer: In addition to its fiber, soy's isoflavones also contribute to its protective effect against breast and prostate cancer.

Research involving nearly 22,000 Japanese women—the Japan Public Health Center-Based Prospective Study on Cancer and Cardiovascular Diseases—shows that a diet high in isoflavone-rich soy foods, particularly miso, is linked to a significantly lower risk of breast cancer.

The women, who ranged in age from 40 to 59 years, filled out a dietary questionnaire that included questions about soy consumption and were followed for 10 years.

Whether pre- or postmenopausal, women who reported eating three or more cups of miso soup per day had a 40% lower risk of developing breast cancer compared to women who reported consuming less than one cup per day.

Women with the highest intakes of soy products had a 54% lower risk of developing breast cancer compared to those whose intakes were the lowest. The average intake of isoflavones among participants in this study was calculated to be about 700 times higher than that of Caucasians in the United States.

Endometrial Cancer: Soy foods may also reduce risk of endometrial cancer. Research conducted in Shanghai and published in the British Medical Journal suggests that eating soy foods may be one reason why Asian women have the lowest incidence in the world of endometrial cancer (cancer affecting the lining of the uterus).

The study included over 800 women with endometrial cancer, aged 30-69 years, and a disease-free, matched control group of over 800 women. For five years, all subjects answered food frequency questionnaires.

When the data was evaluated, a significant inverse association was found between frequency of eating soy foods and endometrial cancer risk. Compared to women who ate the least soy foods, endometrial cancer risk was reduced from 7% to 15% to 33% as soy food intake increased. Minimally processed soy foods are rich in dietary fiber, which has also been shown to lower estrogen levels.

Canned soybeans can be found in many markets. Unlike canned vegetables, which have lost much of their nutritional value, there is little difference in the nutritional value of canned soybeans and those you cook yourself.

SELECTION

Dried soybeans are generally available in prepackaged containers. Make sure that there is no evidence of moisture or insect damage, and that the beans are whole and not cracked.

On the other hand, beans require a long time to cook whether they are canned or you cook them yourself.

Therefore, if enjoying canned beans is more convenient for you, by all means go ahead and enjoy them. We would suggest looking for those that do not contain extra salt or additives.

Edamame (fresh soybeans) should be deep green in color with firm, un-bruised pods. Edamame can be found in many supermarkets as well as in natural food stores and Asian markets.

It is usually available in the frozen food section, although during its peak season you can find it in the produce aisle of many natural food stores and Asian markets. Some stores offer pre-cooked Edamame in their refrigerated display cases.

STORING

Store dried soybeans in an airtight container in a cool, dry and dark place where they will keep for up to 12 months. Cooked soybeans will keep fresh in the refrigerator for about three days if placed in a covered container.

Fresh Edamame should be stored in the refrigerator and eaten within two days. Frozen Edamame will keep fresh for a few months.

SERVING

Before washing dried soybeans, spread them out on a dark colored plate or cooking surface to check for and remove small stones, debris or damaged beans. After this process, place the beans in a strainer and rinse them thoroughly under cool running water.

To shorten their cooking time and make them easier to digest, dried soybeans should be presoaked. There are two basic methods for presoaking. For each, start by placing the beans in a saucepan and adding two to three cups of water per cup of beans.

The first method is to boil the beans for two minutes, take pan off the heat, cover and allow to stand for two hours. The alternative method is to simply soak the beans in water for eight hours or overnight, placing pan in the refrigerator so that the beans will not ferment.

Before cooking the beans, regardless of method, drain the soaking liquid and rinse the beans with clean water.

To cook soybeans, you can either cook them on the stovetop or use a pressure cooker. For the stovetop method, add three cups of fresh water or broth for each cup of dried beans. The liquid should be about one to two inches above the top of the beans.

Bring the beans to a boil and then reduce to a simmer, partially covering the pot. If any foam develops, simply skim it off during the simmering process. Soybeans generally take about one to one and a half hours to become tender using this method.

They can also be cooked in a pressure cooker where they take about 40 minutes to prepare. Regardless of cooking method, do not add any seasonings that are salty or acidic until after the beans have been cooked since adding them earlier will make the beans tough and greatly increase the cooking time.

Replace some of the wheat flour in your favorite baked goods recipe with soybean flour and increase the protein content of your cookies, cakes, muffins and breads. Mix sprouted soybeans into salads or use as toppings for sandwiches.

Frozen Edamame is simple to prepare and makes a great snack or appetizer. Just add the soybean pods to slightly salted water and boil for approximately 10 minutes. Add soybeans to vegetable stews and soups.

A study published in Carcinogenesis suggests that not only is the cancer-preventive ability of soy foods markedly reduced in highly purified soy products and supplements, but that such processed foods can stimulate the growth of pre-existing estrogen-dependent breast tumors.

Use soymilk in place of cow's milk as a beverage and cereal topper.

A large percentage of the conventionally grown soybeans in the United States come from genetically modified (GM) seeds. If you are looking your exposure to GM foods, choose organically grown soybeans (and foods such as tofu, tempeh and miso made from it.

Practical Tips: Protect your prostate health by making soy foods a staple part of your healthy way of eating. Not a fan of tofu? Soy milk is now an available option, even at most espresso stands.

You can take packets of miso to work with you, just as you would any dehydrated soup mix. Miso not only makes a delicious broth on its own, but can be sprinkled like seasoning over brown rice or any grain, any soup, or sautéed vegetable to add great flavor. Try a tofu burger for lunch. Soy nuts can also go with you to the office for a quick snack.

Whole or Purified: In the animals given minimally processed soy flour, a form of soy comparable to the whole soy foods consumed in the Asian diet, tumors neither grew nor regressed. But in the animals given dietary soy products containing isoflavones in more purified forms, the tumors grew.

These products are similar to the materials used in isoflavone-containing dietary supplements, which is how many Americans consume these compounds.

The take-home message for women, especially post-menopausal women with estrogen-responsive breast cancers, who are looking for alternatives to HRT:

Avoid processed soy products and supplements that contain isoflavones in more purified forms. Choose minimally processed whole soy foods such as Edamame, whole soy flour, tofu or tempeh.

Bottom Line

1. Cancer to cholesterol there is no match for whole soy products, tested, tried and enjoyed in China and Japan, for centuries.
2. Isolates, refined, genetically modified and processed soy may have none of health benefits and on the other hand may increase chances of diseases.
3. Do as the Japanese or Chinese do, you would be safe, secure and healthy eat whole Soya foods.

25/52

SPINACH

"Green beauty"

Bright, vibrant-looking spinach leaves are not only more appealing to the eye but more nourishing as well. Low in calories and high in vitamins, spinach is one of the most nutrient-dense foods in existence.

Spinach is thought to have originated in ancient Persia (Iran). Spinach made its way to China in the 7th century when the king of Nepal sent it as a gift to this country. Spinach grows well in temperate climates. Today, the United States and the Netherlands are among the largest commercial producers of spinach.

The iron content in spinach is twice that of other greens. Spinach is also one of the most alkaline foods. This makes it useful in helping to regulate the body's pH balance. Spinach also contains one of the richest dietary sources of lutein.

Therefore, it is effective in promoting healthy eyesight and preventing macular degeneration and cataracts. Spinach, like other chlorophyll and carotene containing vegetables, contains anticancer properties.

Other health benefits of spinach include, lower blood pressure, strengthens muscles, atherosclerosis and heart attack, neurological benefits, bone mineralization, anti-ulcerative, anti-cancerous property, skin protection, fetus development, protein rich for infant's proper growth.

RICH SOURCE

Among the world's healthiest vegetables, spinach comes out at the top of our ranking list for nutrient richness. Rich in vitamins and minerals, it is also concentrated in health-promoting phytonutrients such as carotenoids (beta-carotene, lutein, and zeaxanthin) and flavonoids to provide you with powerful anti-oxidant protection.

Spinach is an excellent source of bone-healthy vitamin K, magnesium, manganese, and calcium; heart-healthy folate, potassium, and vitamin B6; energy-producing iron and vitamin B2; and free radical-scavenging vitamin A (through its concentration of beta-carotene), vitamin C and vitamin E.

It is a very good source of digestion-supportive dietary fiber; muscle-building protein; energy-producing phosphorus and vitamin B1; and the anti-oxidants copper, zinc, and E. In addition, it is a good source of anti-inflammatory omega-3 fatty acids, and heart-healthy niacin and selenium.

While this mixture of conventional nutrients gives spinach a unique status in the anti-oxidant and anti-inflammatory department, it is the unusual mixture of phytonutrients in spinach that "seals the deal" in terms of its anti-oxidant and anti-inflammatory components.

ANTI-CANCER BENEFITS

Even though virtually all vegetables contain a wide variety of phytonutrients—including flavonoids and carotenoids—spinach can claim a special place among vegetables in terms of its phytonutrient content.

Researchers have identified more than a dozen different flavonoid compounds in spinach that function as anti-inflammatory and anti-cancer agents. These elements neutralize free radicals in the body and thus help to prevent cancer.

The anti-cancer properties of these spinach flavonoids have been so impressive that researchers are prompted to create specialized spinach extracts that could be used in controlled laboratory studies.

Prostate Cancer: In a recent study on the relationship between risk of prostate cancer and vegetable intake–"including the vegetables spinach, broccoli, cauliflower, cabbage, brussels sprouts, mustard greens, turnip greens, collards, and kale".

Only spinach showed evidence of significant protection against the occurrence of aggressive prostate cancer. "Aggressive prostate cancer" was defined as stage III or IV of prostate cancer.

Stomach, Skin and Breast Cancer: Spinach extracts have been shown to slow down cell division in human stomach cancer cells (gastric adenocarcinomas), and in studies on laboratory animals, to reduce skin cancers (skin papilloma).

A study on adult women living in New England in the late 1980s also showed regular intake of spinach to reduce incidence of breast cancer.

Excessive inflammation, of course, typically emerges as a risk factor for increased cancer risk. Particularly in the digestive tract, reduced inflammation has been associated not only with the flavonoids found in spinach, but also with its carotenoids which are plenty in unusual amounts in spinach.

SELECTION

Choose spinach that has vibrant deep green leaves and stems with no signs of yellowing. The leaves should look fresh and tender, and not be wilted or bruised. Avoid those that have a slimy coating as this is an indication of decay.

STORING

Do not wash spinach before storing as the exposure to water encourages spoilage. Place spinach in a plastic storage bag and wrap the bag tightly around the spinach, squeezing out as much of the air as possible.

Place in refrigerator where it will keep fresh for up to 5 days. Avoid storing cooked spinach as it will not keep very well.

SERVING

Spinach should be washed very well since the leaves and stems tend to collect sand and soil. Before washing, trim off the roots and separate the leaves. Place the spinach in a large bowl of tepid water and swish the leaves around with your hands as this will allow any dirt to become dislodged.

Remove the leaves from the water, empty the bowl, refill with clean water and repeat this process until no dirt remains in the water (usually two to three times will do the trick). Do not leave spinach soaking in the water as water-soluble nutrients will leach into the water.

Enjoy baby spinach in your favorite salads or make a salad made exclusively of baby spinach.

Spinach is recommended for boiling to free up acids and allow them to leach into the boiling water; this brings out a sweeter taste from the spinach. Discard the boiling water after cooking; do not drink it or use it for stock because of its acid content.

Use a large pot (3 quart) with lots of water and bring to a rapid boil. Add spinach to the boiling water and boil for 1 minute. Begin timing as soon as you place the spinach in the pot.

Do not cover the pot when cooking spinach. Leaving the pot uncovered helps to release more of the acids with the rising steam. Research has shown that the boiling of spinach in large amounts of water helps decrease the oxalic acid content by as much as 50%.

Remove spinach from pot, press out liquid with a fork, place in a bowl, toss with your favorite dressing or cook as per your recipe requirements.

Add layers of steamed spinach to your next lasagna recipe. Pine nuts are a great addition to cooked spinach. Spinach salads are a classic easy and delicious meal or side dish.

Bottom Line

1. Spinach is a gold mine of nutrients and anti-cancer benefiting phytochemicals.
2. Dip spinach in a boiling water to decrease its acid content.
3. Green beauty spinach richly deserves a place in your heart and home.

26/52

TOMATOES

"A world without tomatoes is like a string quartet without violins."

–Laurie Colwin

The French sometimes refer to the tomato as pomme d'amour, meaning "love apple," and in Italy, tomato is sometimes referred to as "pomodoro" or "golden apple".

Regardless of its name, the tomato is a wonderfully popular and versatile food that comes in over a thousand different varieties that vary in shape, size, and color. There are small cherry tomatoes, bright yellow tomatoes, Italian pear-shaped tomatoes, and the green tomato, famous for its fried preparation in Southern American cuisine.

Tomatoes are widely known for their outstanding anti-oxidant content, including, of course, their oftentimes-rich concentration of lycopene. Researchers have recently found an important connection between lycopene, its anti-oxidant properties, and bone health.

RICH SOURCE

Tomatoes are also an excellent source of free radical-scavenging vitamin C and vitamin A as well as bone-healthy vitamin K. They are a very good source of enzyme-promoting molybdenum; heart-healthy potassium, and dietary fiber; blood sugar-balancing chromium and manganese; and energy-producing vitamin B1.

In addition, tomatoes are a good source of heart-healthy vitamin B6, folate, magnesium, niacin, and vitamin E; energy-producing vitamin B2, iron, pantothenic acid, and phosphorus; muscle-building protein, and bone-healthy copper.

Tomatoes are a treasure of riches when it comes to their anti-oxidant benefits. Tomatoes are super rich in many phytonutrients like lycopene, carotenoids, flavonoids, glycosides and fatty acid derivatives.

ANTI-CANCER BENEFITS

The track record for tomatoes as a cancer-protective food should not be surprising, since there is a very large amount of research on tomato anti-oxidants and anti-inflammatory nutrients.

Risk for many types of cancers starts out with chronic oxidative stress and chronic unwanted inflammation. For this reason, foods that provide us with strong anti-oxidant and anti-inflammatory support are often foods that show cancer prevention properties.

Prostate Cancer: Prostate cancer is by far the best-researched type of cancer in relationship to tomato intake. The jury verdict here is clear: tomatoes can definitely help lower risk of prostate cancer in men.

"The only nutrient that turned out to have significant preventive value (against prostate cancer) was lycopene," writes Dr. Giovannucci who also found that lycopene was most efficiently absorbed into the body when accompanied by dietary fats.

"Cooking tomatoes in oil encourages intestinal absorption and results in a two-to-threefold rise in plasma lycopene concentrations," said Dr. Giovannucci. "Tomato sauce is one of the best lycopene sources."

Eating tomatoes, ketchup, tomato sauce and tomato paste-topped pizza more than two times a week can reduce the risk of prostate cancer by 21 to 43 per cent according to Dr. Edward Giovannucci of the Harvard University School of Public Health.

Studies have shown that men who eat lycopene-rich foods have anywhere from 25-80% reduction in the risk of prostate cancer. Some of the research even suggests that boosting lycopene intake from foods may slow or stop the progression to metastatic cancer in those who have already been diagnosed with prostate cancer– writes Dr. Daphne Miller MD, in her book "The Jungle Effect".

Breast, Endometrium, Cervix, Pancreatic & Lung Cancers: Along with prostate cancer and non-small cell lung cancer, pancreatic cancer and breast cancer are the two best-studied areas involving tomatoes and cancer risk.

Research on tomatoes and breast cancer risk has largely focused on the carotenoid lycopene, and there is fairly well documented risk reduction for breast cancer in association with lycopene intake. Lycopene is a powerful inhibitor of the growth of breast, endometrium (inner lining of the uterus) and lung cancer cells.

Lycopene helps women guard against cervical intra-epithelial neoplasia, (CIN), tumorous tissue growth in the cervix according to research from the University of Illinois at Chicago, USA.

Research on alpha-tomatine has also been conducted for non-small cell lung cancer, with similar findings.

SELECTION

Choose tomatoes that have rich colors. Deep reds are a great choice, but so are vibrant oranges/tangerines, brilliant yellows, and rich purples. Tomatoes of all colors provide outstanding nutrient benefits.

Tomatoes should be well shaped and smooth skinned with no wrinkles, cracks, bruises, or soft spots. They should not have a puffy appearance since that characteristic is often associated with inferior flavor and may also result in excess waste during preparation. Ripe tomatoes will yield to slight pressure and will have a noticeably sweet fragrance.

When buying canned tomatoes, it is often better to buy those that are produced in the United States as many foreign countries do not have as strict standards for lead content in containers. This is especially important with a fruit such as tomatoes, whose high acid content can cause corrosion too, and subsequent migration into the foods of, the metals with which it is in contact.

STORING

Since tomatoes are sensitive to cold, and it will impede their ripening process, store them at room temperature and out of direct exposure to sunlight. They will keep for up to a week, depending upon how ripe they are when purchased.

To hasten the ripening process, place them in a paper bag with a banana or apple since the ethylene gas that these fruits emit will help speed up the tomato's maturation. If the tomatoes begin to become overripe, but you are not yet ready to eat them, place them in the refrigerator (if possible, in the butter compartment which is a warmer area), where they will keep for one or two more days.

Removing them from the refrigerator about 30 minutes before using will help them to regain their maximum flavor and juiciness. Whole tomatoes, chopped tomatoes and tomato sauce freeze well for future use in cooked dishes. Sun-dried tomatoes should be stored in an airtight container, with or without olive oil, in a cool dry place.

SERVING

Ketchup can be a surprisingly good source of tomato nutrients, including lycopene. But if you are going to purchase tomatoes in the form of ketchup, we recommend that you choose organic ketchup. A recent study indicates higher lycopene content in organic versus non-organic ketchup. Before serving, wash tomatoes under cool running water and pat dry.

"Cherry tomatoes contain 6 times more anti-oxidants than normal size tomatoes, mainly because cherry tomato has more skin to volume ratio", claims Daphne Miller MD, in her book The Jungle Effect. So, it is a wise step to choose smaller tomatoes than the large ones.

Target Lycopene Content 15 -20 mg per day	
Dietary Sources of Lycopene	
Food	**Lycopene Content (mg per 100 mg)**
Tomato Paste	29.3
Spagheti Sauce	17.5
Ketchup	17
Tomato Sauce	15.9
Tomato Soup	9.3
Canned Tomatoes	9.7
Tomato Juice	9.3
Guava Fruit	5.4
Watermelon	4.8
Raw tomato	3
Papaya	2
Pink grapefruit	1.5

Source: USDA Database -Carotenoid Content of selected foods,1998

If your recipe requires seeded tomatoes, cut the fruit in half horizontally and gently squeeze out the seeds and the juice. However, we encourage you to think about the recipe and consider whether the tomato could be incorporated with seeds intact. There are simply too many valuable nutrients in the seeds that you would not want to lose unnecessarily.

When cooking tomatoes, we recommend avoidance of aluminum cookware since the high acid content of the tomatoes may interact with the metal in the cookware.

Whenever possible, try to develop recipes that make use of the whole tomato. We've seen research showing higher lycopene content in whole tomato products. For example, when the skins of tomatoes are included in the making of the tomato paste, the lycopene and beta-carotene content of the paste is significantly higher according to research studies.

Tomatoes are a great addition to bean and vegetable soups.

Enjoy a classic Italian salad - sliced onions, tomatoes and mozzarella cheese drizzled with olive oil.

Combine chopped onions, tomatoes, and chili peppers for an easy-to-make salsa dip.

Puree tomatoes, cucumbers, bell peppers and scallions together in a food processor and season with herbs and spices of your choice to make the refreshing cold soup, gazpacho.

Add tomato slices to sandwiches and salads. To keep things colorful, use yellow, green and purple tomatoes in addition to red ones.

Organic varieties of tomato ketchup contain three times as much of a cancer-fighting chemical called lycopene as non-organic brands.

❍ Bottom Line

"PERFORMANCE APPRAISALS"

1. Cherry tomatoes have 6 times more cancer protecting lycopene.
2. Cooked tomatoes with little oils is the best health option.
3. Ideally one should drink one cup juice or soup of tomatoes daily.

   (As per latest research tomatoes are deliciously healthy. Including tomato ketchup or sauce or puree in our daily diets is easy and beneficial. Unlike supplemental calcium, high intakes of dietary calcium do not appear to cause kidney stones and may actually protect against their development.)

TOFU

"The cheese of Asia"

Discovered over 2000 years ago by the Chinese, tofu is sometimes called "the cheese of Asia," because of its physical resemblance to a block of farmer's cheese. It can also be called "Soy Paneer" from plant kingdom.

Tofu is made in much the same way as cheese, except that it is made from soya-beans rather than milk. It is sometimes referred to as bean curd also. It is entirely plant-based, which means that it is an ideal food for vegans and for people who are intolerant to dairy products.

Tofu is a highly nutritious, protein-rich food that is made from the curds of soybean milk. Off-white in color, it is usually sold in rectangular blocks. Tofu is a staple in the cuisines of many Asian countries. Tofu is its Japanese name, while in China it is known as doufu.

Although once only found in Asian food markets, this seemingly bland food can miraculously take on the flavor of its surrounding ingredients making it a highly versatile as well as highly nutritious part of a healthy diet. Tofu can now be found in your local supermarkets throughout the year.

Tofu is also extremely versatile. It can be baked, broiled, deep fried, shallow fried, marinated, stewed, scrambled, added to soups and casseroles, stuffed into tacos, made into dips ... the list goes on and on. Tofu comes in a range of consistencies that can suit a variety of different recipes.

Tofu's popularity in the West has mirrored the increasing interest in healthier foods. First gaining more widespread attention during the 1960s, tofu has been skyrocketing in popularity ever since research has begun to reveal the many significant benefits this nutrient-rich, plant-based food can provide.

RICH SOURCE

All the good news about tofu being a health-promoting food is true. Tofu is a very good source of protein, specifically soy protein, as well as numerous other nutrients necessary for good health. While a complete review of all the benefits soybeans offer could easily fill a large book.

Tofu is a very good source of manganese, iron and protein. In addition, tofu is a good source of selenium, omega-3 fatty acids, phosphorus, copper, calcium and magnesium.

ANTI-CANCER BENEFITS

Tofu contains several types of phytoestrogens — weak, non-steroidal estrogens that could help prevent both breast and prostate cancer by blocking and suppressing cancerous changes.

Selenium in the Tofu may also be responsible for the proper function of the anti-oxidant system, which works to reduce the levels of damaging free radicals in the body–selenium is an anti-oxidant, anti-cancer, anti-inflammatory trace mineral.

Breast Cancer: There are a number of isoflavones in soy products, but research has shown that genistein is the most potent inhibitor of the growth and spread of cancerous cells. It appears to lower breast-cancer risk by inhibiting the growth of epithelial cells and new blood vessels that tumors require to flourish and is being scrutinized as a potential anti-cancer drug.

Researchers from China report that soy lowers the risk of recurring breast cancers among women with estrogen-positive tumors, just the cancers that might be more sensitive to soy's tumor-promoting effects. Comparing the volunteers who ate the least amount of these foods including tofu, to those eating the most (eight times the daily dose), the researchers found that the high consumers lowered their risk of having a recurrent breast tumor by 33%.

A recent study from Korea assessed the impact of soy protein intake on the occurrence of breast cancer. For the study, the researchers compared consumption patterns of tofu and other soy products of 362 women with breast cancer with 362 women of the same age who had never been diagnosed with breast cancer.

The study reports that "high soy protein intake was associated with reduced breast cancer risk" in pre-menopausal as well as post-menopausal women. The breast cancer preventive effect was more evident in pre-menopausal women for whom the cancer risk decreased as tofu consumption increased.

A study in Singapore reported in the Lancet (1991) found that pre-menopausal females who rarely ate soy foods had twice the risk of breast cancer than those who ate soy foods frequently. All other food and lifestyle differences were taken into account. In both of these cases it was the soy alone which made the difference, not the amount of fat.

In addition to being wonderfully inexpensive, tofu is high in protein, low in fat.

Stomach Cancer: Japanese cancer researchers found that people who regularly ate tofu were at less risk for stomach cancer than those who did not.

Colon and Melanoma Cancer: There are several compounds in Tofu and other soy products that help fight cancer. Genistein inhibits angiogenesis (the formation of new blood vessels) which is necessary for a rapidly growing tumor to feed itself.

Saponins are naturally occurring compounds in soy beans. Saponins significantly reduced the growth and viability of cancerous colon cells and melanoma cells, according to A. Venket Rao of the University of Toronto in Canada.

Prostate Cancer: Another study of 8,000 Hawaiian men with Japanese ancestry published in Cancer Research in 1989 found that men who ate the most tofu had the lowest rates of prostate cancer, with other influences factored out.

SELECTION

Tofu is available refrigerated in individual packages or in bulk, or non-refrigerated in aseptically sealed containers. Packaged tofu should feature expiration dates, which you can use as a guideline for how long of a shelf life it will have.

Tofu varies in texture from soft to firm to extra-firm. Soft tofu has a smoother texture and is therefore better suited for salad dressings, sauces and desserts, while firm and extra-firm tofu are best for baking, stir-frying and grilling.

If you are selecting tofu on the basis of fat content, the firmer tofus are usually the highest in fat, and the softest tofus, often called silky or silken, are the lowest.

If you are looking for tofu with high calcium content, look for products that specifically say "calcium-precipitated" on the label or that include calcium sulfate in their ingredient list. This method of tofu manufacturing uses calcium to help coagulate the soy milk.

STORING

Packaged tofu need not be refrigerated until it is opened; all other forms of tofu should be refrigerated in their container. Once their packages are open, all types should be rinsed well, kept in a container covered with water, and placed in the refrigerator. Changing the water daily will help keep the tofu fresh for up to one week.

Tofu can also be frozen in its original packaging and will keep this way for up to five months. This process will actually alter its texture and color, making it more spongy and absorbent, and more yellowish in color. This change in physical properties is actually very suitable for certain recipe preparations.

GMO–Free: A large percentage of the conventionally grown soybeans in the United States come from genetically modified (GM) seeds.

SERVING

You can practically replace in all your favorite recipes requiring Paneer (cottage cheese) and Chicken with Tofu, without much effort and also without any family member noticing it.

Blend together soft tofu, olive oil, garlic and lemon juice to make a tofu oil dip.

Scramble soft tofu together with your favorite vegetables and the spice turmeric to give it a yellow "egg-like" coloring. This delicious dish can be served as it is or can be used as the basis for "tofu rancheros" by being wrapped in a tortilla and served with black beans and salsa.

Stir-fry firm tofu with your favorite vegetables and seasonings. Add cubes of tofu to miso soup.

Blend soft tofu with your favorite fruits (and honey or other natural sweeteners to taste) in a blender or food processor and serve for breakfast or dessert.

Bottom Line

1. Organic Tofu is much better option than the regular one.
2. Replace Cottage Cheese (Paneer) with Tofu.
3. Let us accept, acknowledge and welcome the healthy gift of Tofu, from our Japanese and Chinese brethren.

Some other Books on Cancer

BOOK — Foods That Fight Cancer
AUTHOR — Dr Richard Beliveau and Denis Gingras

How you can help prevent and fight cancer with healthy food choices. Approximately one-third of all cancers are directly related to diet. To help prevent cancer, try making some of these foods that fight cancer a regular part of your diet.

- A diet containing three or four weekly servings of broccoli, nothing too excessive, was shown to be sufficient to protect individuals from colon polyps.
- **Cruciferous vegetables** (brussels sprouts, broccoli, cabbage, cauliflower, kale) should be lightly cooked and thoroughly chewed when eaten in order to fully benefit from their anti-cancer potential. Chewing releases the active molecules.
- Freshly crushed garlic is by far the best source of anti-cancer compounds and should be preferred over supplements.
- The key to benefiting from the anti-cancer effects of soy lies in consuming about 50 grams per day of the whole food, such as raw (edamame) or dry roasted soybeans. Supplements containing isoflavones are not an acceptable alternative to the whole food and should be avoided.
- Colon cancer appears to be one of the cancers on which curcumin may have the greatest positive impact. The daily addition of a teaspoon of **turmeric** to soups, salad dressings, or pasta dishes is a simple way of providing curcumin intake sufficient to prevent the development of cancer.
- **Green tea** contains large amounts of catechins, compounds that boast many anti-cancer properties. To maximize the preventive effects afforded by tea, select Japanese green teas, allow for an 8-to-10-minute brewing period and always drink freshly brewed tea, avoiding Thermoses.
- Eating **cranberries** should be preferred over drinking cranberry juice.
- The best way to increase **omega-3** levels in diet is to eat fatty fish (wild salmon, sardines, and mackerel) once or twice a week or add one tablespoon of freshly milled flaxseeds to your breakfast cereal.
- Eating two **tomato** sauce-based meals per week may lower your risk of developing prostate cancer by up to 25 per cent.
- **Citrus** fruits are essential foods in cancer prevention: for their capacity to act directly on cancerous cells as well as their potential for enhancing the anti-cancer effects of other phytochemical compounds present in diet.

- The resveratrol present in red **wine** possesses powerful anti-cancer activity, which may be responsible for the beneficial effects of wine on the prevention of certain cancers. Grape juice and cranberry juice contain resveratrol but at levels 10 times less than red wine.
- The daily consumption of 40 grams of **dark chocolate** (chocolate containing 70 per cent cocoa mass) may have definite health benefits and should replace or reduce that of sugar- and fat-filled candies with no phytochemical content.
- Many herbs and spices used as seasonings, in particular ginger, contain large quantities of molecules that act as anti-inflammatory compounds, which also reduce the risks of developing certain chronic diseases.
- Instead of replacing butter with margarine, use **olive oil** as much as possible as a source of dietary fat; you will benefit from its healthful lipids knowing that it also possesses anti-cancer properties of its own.

CHAPTER 4

Fruits

When you see a piece of fruit hanging from a tree that tree is telling you something: "Eat my fruits and help me spread my seeds." Humans eat vegetables and fruits, consequently help the plants to spread. That's how nature works.

Talking about fruits; they are not mere sources of vitamins and minerals. They are rich source of, thousands of phytochemical compounds that play a key role in maintaining the good health of all of us.

Phytochemicals have powerful anti-cancer benefits. They target the very processes involved in the development of cancer.

A diet based on regular intake of wholesome fresh fruits, containing high levels of phytochemical compounds is the strongest weapon we have got as on today, in preventing and controlling cancer.

AMLA

(Indian Gooseberry)

"It is believed that what gold is to the minerals, amla is to the herbs"

Amla is a gift of nature to mankind. It is an indispensable part of the Ayurvedic and Unani systems of medicine. In Sanskrit, it is called amalaki. It belongs to the family Euphorbiecae and its scientific name is *Emblica officinalis*.

The Amla tree is a moderate-size deciduous tree with gray bark and reddish wood that grows in the tropical subcontinent of India. All parts of the plant are used in various ayurvedic herbal preparations, including the fruit, seed, leaves, root, bark and flowers.

This wonder herb 'Indian Gooseberry', that is amla, is cooling, diuretic, and a laxative. It has anti-bacterial, cardio-tonic, anti-viral and resistance building properties.

Its anti-bacterial and astringent properties help to prevent infection and help in the healing of ulcers and hyper acidity. It is anti-spasmodic, and has a mild stimulant action on the heart and helps in lowering cholesterol. The medicinal value of this fruit is endless...

Amla is a rare fruit which contains all tastes except salty flavor. With sourness as the foremost taste, it is at the same time sweet, astringent, bitter and pungent. It is light, dry and cold in effect. Its use in medicines is at least 2,300 years old.

Maharshi ("great sage") Chyavana is said to be the originator of this preparation and legend has it that he regained youth in his old age by the consumption of Chyavanaprasha. Amla has been revered in Ayurvedic medicine since the 7th century for its anti-aging and immune-enhancing benefits and as a general tonic for optimal health.

It is believed that "by consuming a rasayana made with amla as the main ingredient, one will live for a hundred years without any sign of decrepitude". -(*Charaka Samhita*, the main text of Ayurvedic herbal medicine).

There are two varieties of amla - cultivated (gramya) and wild (vanya). The wild amla is small, hard and has lots of fiber while the cultivated amla is big, smooth and juicy.

There also exists a quite distinct strain of amla, which grows wild in the mid-hill regions of the Western Himalayas, called "Wild Himalayan amla".

This amla bears smaller fruits and is a very heavy in cropper. A very good quality of this strain is that it can survive is much cold and is hardy in comparison to the commercial amla. The wild Himalayan amla can therefore be successfully used to extend amla cultivation to colder areas.

Amla fruits are graded into 3 categones. Large sized, sound fruits are mostly utilized for preservatives and candy; small sized for Chyavanaprasha and Trifala (powder of the three herbs) and blemished fruits for powder and shampoo making.

As per one research Amla fruit contains 30 times the amount of Vitamin C, than found in oranges making it useful for treating throat and respiratory tract infections.

RICH SOURCE

There is no better source of natural vitamin C, with its full spectrum of bioflavonoids and supporting nutrients than amla berry. It also has protein, carbohydrate, fiber, minerals and vitamins.

Mother Nature's very best source of vitamin C, amla berries are well documented as much easier to assimilate than synthetic vitamin C, which is known as ascorbic acid. Vitamins from an all-natural whole-food source like amla are also safer and more effective than laboratory-created synthetic or crystalline vitamins.

Amla fruits are reputed to contain high amounts of *ascorbic acid* (vitamin C), 445 mg/100g, the specific contents are disputed, and the overall *anti-oxidant* strength of amla may derive instead from its high density of *tannins*. The Purdue University Center (USA) for New Crops and Plant Products website notes that amla has the second highest content of vitamin C of all fruits. In addition, this small fruit contains calcium, phosphorus, iron, vitamin A, thiamin, riboflavin, niacin and a range of amino acids.

The fruit also contains polyphenols: flavonoids, kaempferol, ellagic acid and gallic acid. As a wonderful anti-oxidant, amla aids the body's natural defenses against bacteria and viruses, and even supports digestion.

ANTI-CANCER BENEFITS

Chinese researchers have discovered that amla fruit is a rich source of therapeutic chemicals, including quercetin (which is also found in apples) gallic, ellagic acids (found in green tea), and other less well-known ones such as chebulinic acid, chebulagic acid, corilagin, and isostrictiniin.

All of these chemicals are powerful anti-oxidants, which help protect you from harmful free radicals that increase the risk of a wide range of serious diseases including cancer.

Stomach, Skin and Womb Cancers: Studies done in Japan by scientists at the Faculty of Pharmaceutical Sciences at Nagasaki University discovered through preliminary research that amla fruit extracts prevent the growth of cancerous cells.

The cells that reacted best to the amla fruit extracts were the cells of the stomach, skin and womb. Along with these results and the powerful combination of anti-oxidant chemicals found in amla fruit, it is no wonder that this fruit is playing an important role in the fight against cancer.

Pancreatic Cancer: Amla may prove to have potential activity against some cancers, claims a recent research. In one animal study, it was discovered that treatment with amla reduced the severity of acute pancreatisis in rats. Not only that, amla also promoted the spontaneous repair and regeneration process of the pancreas occurring after an acute attack.

Cancer Chemotherapy Side Effects: Amla helps counteract the harmful side effects of anti-cancer drugs. Research is also revealing that amla fruit is effective when used alongside conventional cancer treatments such as the anti-cancer drug Doxorubicin.

This drug is able to kill a large number of cancerous cells, and can save cancer patients' lives even when the disease has progressed. However, one major drawback associated with the drug use is that it can damage the heart muscle.

Recently, Thai scientists from the Department of Pharmacology, Srinakharinwirot University, in Bangkok, tested various plant extracts to determine whether they could prevent Doxorubicin's detrimental effect on the heart. Other plants involved in the study included curcuma longa (curcumin), piper rostratum and morus alba, all of which are used by Ayurvedic practitioners to help fight against cancer.

The scientists found that all of the plants were successful when it came to protecting the heart from Doxorubicin. However, amla extract demonstrated the best heart-protective benefit and was in fact 12 times stronger than the rest. This finding is important because it shows that amla may counteract the dangerous side effects of conventional cancer treatments like chemotherapy.

SELECTION

Amla is a fleshy fruit with a sour, citrus flavor. It generally reaches the size of a golf ball when at its ripe stage. You generally will not find this exotic fruit in your local grocery store; look to specialty retailers to find it or herbal treatments made with its extracts. If buying fresh amla, look for fruits that are green and have a tight smooth skin.

STORING

Amla possesses the highest level of heat and storage stable vitamin C known to man. The fresh fruits need to be stored in the refrigerator and will keep up to 2 weeks. Store the dried pieces or powder in an airtight container for up to a year.

SERVING

Generally amla is used in pickles, preserves and jams. A very tasty and healthy recipe is made from amla called 'amla murabba'.

Amla Murabba Recipe

Ingredients: 1 cup of grated Amla (gooseberries)
2 tbsps. water
1 1/4 cups sugar
1 tsp. cardamom seeds (crushed)
2-inch piece of cinnamon stick

Preparation: Wash and grate the amla. Combine with sugar and water in a heavy saucepan and place over medium heat. Stir constantly till sugar melts. Reduce the heat to low and add remaining ingredients and simmer until the amla is clear and the juice gets thick, about 15 minutes and you get a semi-thick consistency. It would look like a spread.

Remove the cinnamon stick from the murabba and cool. Transfer it to a glass jar. Store, refrigerated, can be used up to a month. Use as a spread like a jam or have a tsp. of murabba every day as it is.

Coming to the culinary uses of amla, rural folk in India eat this highly acid, fresh, raw fruit, followed by water, producing a sweet and refreshing aftertaste. Amla juice can be mixed in smoothies or other fruit or vegetable juices.

The fruits can be used fresh or dried. Dried amla is sometimes ground into a powder and are also available stoned and chopped so they are easy to reconstitute.

Bottom Line

"Oh please God! Not another gooseberry bush!"

1. Amla is called sarvadosha hara – remover of all diseases.
2. Cancer to common cold-amla is useful in alleviating.
3. Chyavanaprasha - a paste of amla with other herbs is good way to include this life-saving berry on daily basis.

APPLE

"Even if I knew that tomorrow the world would go to pieces,
I would still plant my apple tree"
–Martin Luther

Delicious and crunchy apple fruit is one of the most popular fruits favored by health conscious, fitness freaks who believe in "health is wealth."

Who does not know the story of "The start of everything and the mistake of Adam and Eve with the apple in the Garden of Eden?"

Apple is a wonderful fruit packed with rich phytonutrients that in the true sense are indispensable for optimal health. The anti-oxidants in apple have many health-promoting and disease prevention properties; thus justifying the adage, "an apple a day keeps the doctor away."

Alexander the Great is credited with finding dwarfed apples in Kazakhstan in Asia in 328 BCE. Over the centuries, many hybrids and cultivars have been developed, giving us the 7,000 varieties in the market today.

Apples' most recent appearance in history occurred in the 1800s in the U.S., a person named John Chapman; walked barefoot across an area of 100,000 square miles, planting apple trees that provided food and a livelihood for generations of settlers.

China accounts for about 35% of the world production of apples. The USA is the second leading producer, with more than 7.5% of world production. Iran is third, followed by Turkey, Russia, Italy and India.

In Norse mythology, apples were given a more positive persona: a magic apple was said to keep people young forever. The pectin in apples lowers LDL ("bad") cholesterol. People who eat two apples per day may lower their cholesterol by as much as 16 per cent.

RICH SOURCE

Apple is a good source of fiber, including the soluble fiber pectin, and it's also a good source of vitamin C.

A study published in the journal Nature offers more evidence that the health benefits of fruits and vegetables are not easily packaged as supplements sold in pharmacies and health food stores.

It is despite the fact that the actual amount of vitamin C in apple is very small. (~ 8 milligrams of vitamin C). It is the synergy with other nutrients that makes Vitamin C much more effective.

"The pharmaceutical companies will not be happy with me, but I think the consumer gets more health benefits from eating whole fruits and vegetables," lead researcher Rui Hai Liu, MD, PhD, told WebMD.

"You get much more anti-oxidant activity, and you don't have to worry about toxicity."

Researchers from Cornell's Food Science and Toxicology Department in Ithaca, N.Y., found that the anti-oxidant properties of one fresh apple were equal to 1,500 milligrams of vitamin C despite...

ANTI-CANCER BENEFITS

After comparing seven commonly available varieties, Canadian researchers, found that Red Delicious apples had the highest amount of anti-oxidant polyphenols. This study also supports previous USDA research done in USA. Red Delicious had more than twice the anti-oxidant activity. While all apples are good for you, Red Delicious apples pack the biggest anti-oxidant punch Apple nutrients are disproportionately present in the skin, which is a particularly valuable part of the fruit with respect to its nutrient content. Put down that peeler because these protective polyphenols were five times higher in the apple skin than in the flesh. Apple peel is very commonly used in animal studies and is often called standardized apple peel polyphenol extract, or APPE.

Lab studies have shown that several compounds in this juicy fruit curb the growth of cancer cells — but they're most potent when the apple is eaten whole (minus the stem and seeds, of course).

People who munch more than one apple a day lower their risk for several cancers (oral, esophageal, colon, breast, ovarian, prostate, and others) by 9 to 42 per cent, Italian researchers found.

In terms of flavonols, quercetin is the primary phytonutrient found in apples, and it's far more concentrated in the skin than in the pulp. If apples are red, it's because of their anthocyanins, which are largely restricted to the skin. When an apple is more uniformly red in color, or when its red color is deeper in hue, it's because there are more anthocyanins.

Lung Cancer: Although some preliminary results show apple benefits for several different cancer types (especially colon cancer and breast cancer), it's the area of lung cancer benefits that stand out in the apple research.

There are numerous studies involving vegetable/fruit intake and risk of lung cancer. Except apples! It's really quite remarkable how apples have been one of the few fruits to demonstrate this unique relationship with lung cancer risk reduction.

Researchers aren't certain why apples are so closely associated with reduction of lung cancer risk. Their anti-oxidant and anti-inflammatory benefits are definitely involved here.

According to a study of 10,000 people, those who ate the most apples had a 50 per cent lower risk of developing lung cancer. Researchers believe this is due to the high levels of the flavonoids quercetin and naringin in apples.

Breast Cancer: A study done in Cornell University of USA found that rats who ate one apple per day reduced their risk of breast cancer by 17 per cent. Rats fed three apples per day reduced their risk by 39 per cent and those fed six apples per day reduced their risk by 44 per cent.

Colon Cancer: Research shows that the pectin in apples reduces the risk of colon cancer and helps maintain a healthy digestive tract.

Using colon cancer cells treated with apple extract, Liu and colleagues found that 50 milligrams of apple extracted from the skins decreased the cancer cell growth by 43%, while the same amount of extract from the flesh of the apple decreased cancer cell growth by 29% only.

Liver Cancer: Research found that rats fed an extract from apple skins had a 57 per cent lower risk of liver cancer. Likewise, 50 milligrams of extract from apples with the skin on decreased liver cancer cell growth by 57%, compared to 40% for samples extracted from apples without the skin.

SELECTION

Look for firm fruits with rich coloring. For maximum anti-cancer benefits –give me Red Delicious apple.

Whole apples are a much better nutritional choice than apple juice. Not only are whole apples richer in dietary fiber, but the current processes of juicing seems to drastically reduce the polyphenolic phytonutrient concentrations originally found in the whole fruit.

STORING

We can easily store apples for relatively long (3-4 months) periods of time. Cold storage at low refrigerator temperatures (35-40F/2-4C) is able to help minimize loss of nutrients.

In addition, it's helpful to maintain some moisture in the cold storage area, for example, by inclusion of damp cheesecloth in the crisper bin of a refrigerator.

Over a period of time involving months, there is loss of total polyphenols from apples, including both flavonoid and non-flavonoid polyphenols. However, valuable amounts of polyphenols (and all other nutrients) remain.

You've no doubt heard the saying, "one bad apple can spoil the whole bunch." Well, research studies agree. An apple that has been bruised from being dropped (or that has been damaged in some other way) will start to release unusual amounts of ethylene gas.

This ethylene gas can pose a risk to other apples that have not been damaged and greatly decrease their shelf life. For this reason, it's important to handle apples with tender loving care, and also to remove any damaged apples from groups of apples stored in bulk.

SERVING

The skin of the apple is unusually rich in nutrients, and even if the recipe you've chosen requires peeled apples, consider leaving the skins on to receive the unique benefits found in the skins. Ideally, of course, choose organic apples to avoid problems related to pesticide residues and other contaminants on the skins.

If you cannot obtain organic apples, and you are willing to accept some level of risk related to consumption of residues on the apple skins, we believe that it can still be a good trade-off between nutrients and contaminants if you leave the skin of the apple intact and eat the apple unpeeled.

Just be sure to thoroughly rinse the entire apple under a stream of pure water while gently scrubbing the skin with a natural bristle brush for 10-15 seconds.

To prevent browning when slicing apples for a recipe, simply put the slices in a bowl of cold water to which a spoonful of lemon juice has been added. For use in future recipes, sliced apples freeze well in plastic bags or containers.

There's an important loss of nutrients that usually occurs when apples are processed into applesauce, and an even greater loss when they are processed into juice.

Processing can take a special toll on polyphenols. We've seen recent studies where only 10% of the flavonols and 3% of the catechins from the original apples remained present in the processed apple juice; even chlorogenic acid (one of the more stable polyphenols in apples) tends to be decreased by at least 50% during the processing of whole apples into juice.

Obviously, there are exceptions to these generalized findings. For example, it is possible to put whole apples into a powerful blender and consume the resulting juice. In this case, very little of the nutrients are lost.

However, this type of blending is not used in the commercial production of apple juice. Commercial apple juices are typically either "clear" or "cloudy."

Cloudy apple juices typically retain some of these pulpy solids because even though the pulpy solids have been removed from the juice through pressing and filtering, they are added back in at some designated level. When purchasing apple juice, always choose cloudy juices if possible.

Add diced apples to fruit or green salads, Braise a chopped apple with red cabbage, looking for an alternative to sweet desserts? Sliced apples–either alone or with other fruits–is a good option.

Bottom Line

"IS IT ORGANIC"

1. Give me RED delicious apple which has given twice the amount of anti-cancer benefits.
2. Peel of the apple contain 5 times more nutrients than the flesh.
3. No match for freshly cut whole apple, convenient, clear, bottled juice is an apology only.

30/52

GRAPEVINE

"The Queen of fruits"

Few fruits have garnered as much attention in the health research literature as grapes. With the exception of Antarctica, grapes are cultivated on all of the earth's continents, and researchers from many different countries have been especially interested in this fruit.

Grapes, "queen of the fruits", are a storehouse of numerous health-promoting phytonutrients, vitamins and minerals. Every year, the list of health-supportive grape nutrients grows longer.

Areas of benefit in grape research include the cardiovascular system, respiratory system, immune system, inflammatory system, blood sugar regulating system, and nervous system.

Grapes are small round or oval berries that feature semi-translucent flesh encased by a smooth skin. Some contain edible seeds while others are seedless. Like blueberries, grapes are often covered by a protective, whitish bloom.

Grapes have a long and abundant history. While they've grown wild since prehistoric times, evidence suggests they were cultivated in Asia as early as 5000 BC.

In the United States, well over 90% of all commercially grown table grapes come from California, where over 700,000 acres of grapes (including table, wine, and raisin grapes) are in cultivation.

Worldwide, about 30,000 square miles of land are planted with grapes, resulting in the annual production of 150 trillion pounds of grapes. Grape production in five countries–Italy, China, Spain, and France–accounts for about half of all commercial production,

> *"Men are like a fine wine. They all start out like grapes, and it's our job to stomp on them and keep them in the dark until they mature into something you'd like to have dinner with."*
>
> –Kathleen Mifsud

RICH SOURCE

> *"It's important to note that the seed and the skin contain the richest concentration of antioxidants"*

In addition to providing us with conventional anti-oxidant nutrients like vitamin C and manganese, grapes are chock-full of anti-oxidants and phytonutrients.

It ranges from common carotenoids like beta-carotene to unusual stilbenes like resveratrol, and the total number of different anti-oxidant nutrients in grapes runs well into the hundreds. It's important to note that the seed and the skin contain the richest concentration of anti-oxidants.

For this reason, most of the health research on grape anti-oxidants has not been conducted on whole grapes. Instead, this research has been conducted on grape skin, grape skin extract, grape seed, grape seed extract, or on grape extracts that contain skin and seed and flesh.

As a general rule, the flesh of the grape contains only 1 -5% of the total anti-oxidant capacity of the seed or the skin. Grape seeds are highly valuable for their content of essential fatty acids and vitamin E, which protect your skin, blood vessel and nerve cells from free radical attacks.

Red and black colored grapes are especially acclaimed for their health values. The variations of color indicate different types and quantities of phyto-antioxidants on the grape skin.

Resveratrol, the Prize of Darker Grape Skin - All grapes are beneficial for your health, but what makes darker skinned grapes significantly more valuable is their content of resveratrol. Resveratrol is a natural anti-pathogenic compound found on the skin of dark skinned grapes and other fruits and vegetables with a reddish pigment.

Anti-aging: Studies have shown that resveratrol has certain life extension properties and has been incorporated into anti-aging cosmetic formulas; also resveratrol is a powerful bactericide and fungicide. Oral intake or topical application of resveratrol can lower your risk of pathogenic infections and inflammations.

> *"Moderate quantities of wine two small glasses of 120 ml for men and one small glass for women, per day; significantly decrease the risk of death from all causes of death. However if these amounts are exceeded the mortality risk increases very rapidly"...*
>
> Dr. Richard Beliveau, author of Foods to Fight Cancer

ANTI-CANCER BENEFITS

With their overwhelming number of health-supportive phytonutrients, it is not surprising that grapes have been shown to provide many of our body systems with predictable benefits.

Wine or Grape Juice: Eating red or black grapes is one great way of getting resveratrol, but you get the maximum concentration and benefit of this compound by drinking red wine. The fermentation process helps release resveratrol from the cell walls of the skin and seeds, multiplying its bioavailability by the hundreds.

Skin and seeds are rapidly removed from the fermentation process during making of white wine that, why it does not contain resveratrol.

Though not as high as in wine, red grape juice also contains much more resveratrol than fresh fruits. If you have impaired liver function or cannot drink alcohol, you can drink red grape juice instead.

Resveratrol has shown the greatest effectiveness in treatment of skin and gastrointestinal cancers. It has also shown tumor suppressive effects in lung, breast, prostate and pancreatic cancers as well as leukemia.

The anti-oxidant and anti-inflammatory properties of grapes make them a natural protection against cancer because chronic oxidative stress and chronic inflammation can be key factors in the development of cancer.

Mainly research on grapes, grape components and cancer has focused on three cancer types: breast cancer, colon cancer, and prostate cancer.

Breast Cancer: In the case of breast cancer, the grape phytonutrients receiving the most research attention have been the catechins, pro-anthocyanidins, and stilbenes (especially resveratrol).

Grape juice has been found to suppress breast cancer cell growth by preventing the synthesis of the female hormone estrogen, which plays a major role in the development of breast cancer. Approximately 60% of pre-menopausal and 75% of post-menopausal patients have estrogen-dependent tumors as per Researcher Dr. Shiuan Chen of USA.

Studies have also demonstrated that procyanidin B dimers in red wine and grape seeds could be used as chemo-preventive agents against breast cancer by suppressing in situ estrogen biosynthesis, as per research funded by California Breast Cancer Research Program, University of California.

Colon Cancer: More research attention has been focused on grape flavonoids and grape anthocyanins.

●●●

"Wine or Grape Juice: Eating red or black grapes is one great way of getting resveratrol, but you get the maximum concentration and benefit of this compound by drinking red wine. The fermentation process helps release resveratrol from the cell walls of the skin and seeds, multiplying its bioavailability by the hundreds".

●●●

One interesting development in the research on grapes and colon cancer prevention has involved studies on GADF, or grape anti-oxidant dietary fiber. GADF is a proprietary product that may eventually be sold in the marketplace as a dietary supplement.

The idea that grape fiber and grape anti-oxidants combine to provide our colon with special support makes perfect sense. Fiber is greatly needed for a healthy colon, and grapes provide us with approximately 1 gram of fiber in every 60 calories.

Anti-oxidants are also needed, and grapes come through strong in the anti-oxidant category. This anti-oxidant-plus-fiber combination may be one of the reasons that colon cancer prevention has jumped out in health research on grapes.

Drinking wine and eating grapes can fight colon cancer, say Colorado State University researchers. Their study looks at how two grape compounds work in conjunction to kill colon cancer cells while leaving healthy cells unharmed.

Although researchers have known that resveratrol, a compound in grape skin, and compounds in grape seed extract may prevent colon cancer cells from growing, scientists have not known how the two compounds work together. CSU's study shows that the compounds must work together — making the whole, seeded red or purple grape a perfect colon-cancer fighting food.

Prostate Cancer: In the area of prostate cancer, it is the stilbenes (including resveratrol) have been the major focus in research on the anti-cancer properties of grapes.

Men who take high doses of Grape Seed Extract over a longer period are 62 per cent less likely to develop prostate cancer than men who don't take the supplement. Researchers at the University of Washington discovered this when they tracked 35,000 men aged between 50 and 76 over a period of six years.

> *'A little wine is an antidote to death; in large amounts, it is the poison of life"...*
>
> Persian proverb

The study, the results of which were published in Nutrition and Cancer, is part of the Vital Study, an epidemiological research project to study the positive effects of long-term supplement use. This particular part of the project focused on prostate cancer.

In experiments with prostate cancer cells, Grape Seed Extract and its components inhibit the transcription factor nuclear factor kappa-B, the inflammatory protein interleukine-6 and the biosynthesis of inflammatory factors produced by cyclooxygenase enzymes, thereby blocking the growth of prostate cancer cells.

SELECTION

For the best tasting grapes with high concentrations of anti-oxidants select those which are fully ripe. Fully ripened grapes are plump and free from wrinkles. They should be intact, firmly attached to a healthy looking stem, and not leaking juice. The area around the attachment should have the same color as the rest of the grape.

Table grape varieties are most often larger in size, have been propagated to be seedless, and have relatively thin skins. Wine grapes are usually smaller in size, contain seeds, and have relatively thick skins.

You can also buy "MANUKA" throughout the year; it is available in practically all parts of India. Brown Manuka Raisins are grapes with edible seeds.

STORING

Since grapes tend to spoil and ferment at room temperature, they should always be stored in the refrigerator. Loosely wrap unwashed grapes in a paper towel and place them in an airtight container or plastic bag. This way, they'll keep fresh in the refrigerator for up to 5 days.

While freezing detracts from some of their flavor, frozen grapes are a wonderful snack and particularly intriguing to children. To freeze grapes, wash and pat them dry, then arrange in a single layer on a cookie sheet and place in freezer.

> *Wine, wrote Hippocrates, the founder of the modern medicine, "...is wonderful thing apt in health as well as in illness, if prescribed by the necessity and in certain amounts in compliance with individual build"*

Patting the grapes dry is important, because excess moisture can cause the grapes to stick together and become one large frozen fruit clump. Once frozen, transfer grapes to a heavy plastic bag and return them to the freezer.

SERVING

Grapes should be washed under cold running water right before consuming or using in a recipe. After washing, either drain the grapes in a colander or gently pat them dry.

If you are not going to consume the whole bunch at one time, use scissors to separate small clusters of grapes from the stem instead of removing individual grapes. This will help keep the remaining grapes fresher by preventing the stem from drying out.

While some recipes call for peeled grapes, evaluate the recipe to see whether including the skin would actually greatly change the taste and texture, since the grape skin contains many of the fruit's vital nutrients.

Grapes retain their maximum amount of nutrients and their maximum taste when they are enjoyed fresh and not prepared in a cooked recipe. Cooking temperatures used in baking of 350°F/175°C can damage some of the unique and delicate phytonutrients found in this amazing fruit.

Grapes are a wonderful addition to any fruit salad. For enhanced visual effects, consider using a few different varieties of grapes.

Give your curries a fruity punch by including fresh grapes in the recipe. Add grapes to mixed green salads. Grapes are great served with cheese as a snack or within a green salad. Grapes can be very conveniently added in the fresh mint and coriander chutney.

Bottom Line

"So, how do you like it? Crushed the grapes myself!"

1. Dark red grapes with seeds in any form are good for health. Chew the seeds also.
2. For ideal results consider taking a glass of red wine or Ayurveda's "Drakshasava" with food.
3. Red wine made with Pinot Noir grapes is considered to have maximum amount of resveratrol – the real health rejuvenator.

31/52

GUAVA

The fruits are not only relished by humans, but by many mammals and birds as well. The spread of introduced guavas owes much to this fact, as animals will eat the fruit and disperse the seeds in their droppings.

Guava is another tropical fruit rich in nutrition. With its unique flavor, taste, and health-promoting qualities, the fruit easily fits in new functional foods category, often called "super fruits." You can very easily find this fruit in countries like India, Thailand, Malaysia or Indonesia.

The fruit is soft when ripe with sweet musky aroma and creamy in texture. Internally, the flesh varies in color depending upon the cultivar and may be white, pink, yellow, or red. Ripe fruits have rich flavor with sweet-tart taste. Each fruit contains numerous tiny, semi-hard edible seeds.

Guava is an evergreen, tropical shrub or low-growing small tree probably originated in Middle Americas. Guavas actually thrive in both humid and dry climates and can tolerate brief periods of cold spells, but can survive only a few degrees of frost.

A few species – notably strawberry guavas – can survive temperatures several degrees below freezing for short periods of time.

Guavas are also of interest to home growers in temperate areas, being one of the few tropical fruits that can grow to fruiting size in pots indoors. When grown from seed, guavas can bloom and bear fruit as soon as two years, or as long as eight years.

Botanically, this wonderful fruit belongs to the family of Myrtaceae of the genus: psidium. Scientific name: *Psidium guajava*. Guava fruit, usually 4 to 12 cm long, are round or oval depending on the species.

Guava fruit generally has a pronounced and typical fragrance, similar to lemon rind but less sharp. Packaged guava juice, available in the market, contains lot of extra sugar and has doubtful nutritional benefits. Whole guava should be preferred over the juice.

If you take one guava during breakfast it will provide you much needed daily dose of folic acid, calcium, fiber, protein, iron, vitamins A, B and C.

Various researches have proved that guava prevents cancer, diabeties and heart diseases. It also prevents age-related diseases like cataract, alzheimer's and rheumatoid arthritis. As guava is rich in Vitamin C, it can effectively treat male infertility caused by sperm clumping. Even the leaves of guava have many health benefiting nutrients.

RICH SOURCE

Guavas are rich in dietary fiber, vitamins A and C, folic acid, and the minerals, potassium, copper and manganese. A single common guava fruit contains about four times the amount of vitamin C as an orange.

If you want to look stunning and improve the texture of your skin, you can start taking Guava. This fruit controls skin problems as well. Guava also treats bleeding in nose and gums. People suffering from constipation can get recovered as it contains dietary fiber in abundance.

Guavas contain both carotenoids and polyphenols like gallocatechin, guaijaverin, leucocyanidin and amritoside – giving them relatively high potential anti-oxidant value among plant foods.

As these pigments produce the fruit skin and flesh color, guavas that are red-orange have more pigment content as polyphenol, carotenoids and pro-vitamin A, retinoid sources than yellow-green ones.

Guava leaf extract was found to have anti-oxidant properties in a study published in May 2007 in "Wei Sheng Yan Jiu", Taiwan.

ANTI-CANCER BENEFITS

Guava is one of the super fruits. One of the amazing things about guava is that it contains lycopene, anti-oxidant to fight cancer.

Researchers working for the US Department of Agriculture (USDA) have found that guava may be among the fruits richest in anti-oxidants, suggesting that there may be significant health benefits for people who regularly include guava in their diets.

Lycopene can keep our body healthy and keep it away from free radicals that can cause all kinds of damage, including blocked arteries, joint degeneration, nervous system problems, or even cancer.

The chemical composition of lycopene, a carotenoid in guava, is highly reactive toward oxygen free radicals, according to an article in the October 2008 issue of "Cancer Letters." The researchers found that lycopene isolated from guava reduces cancer risk through its anti-oxidant activities and by inducing apoptosis, or genetically programmed cell death, in cancer cells.

Prostate Cancer: There is a relationship between dietary intake, physical activity and prostate cancer, according to an article in the March 2011 issue of the "Asian Pacific Journal of Cancer Prevention."

For this study, the researchers recruited 105 men, 35 diagnosed with prostate cancer and 70 without, who were used as a control group. Data on dietary intake, especially the consumption of lycopene, and physical activity were obtained using questionnaires.

The results showed that those with prostate cancer had a considerably higher fat intake in their diets, whereas the control group consumed more fruits and vegetables, including guava.

The authors found that consumption of lycopene from guava and other fruits reduced the incidence of prostate cancer by up to sevenfold. The study concluded that exercise, a diet high in lycopene and reducing fat intake reduced the risk of prostate cancer in men aged 45 years and older.

The male hormone androgen is required for the proliferation of prostate cancer cells by activating growth pathways. A study included in the February 2010 issue of "Nutrition and Cancer" investigated the effect of an aqueous extract of guava on the growth of prostate cancer by interfering with androgen receptors.

Mice treated with 1.5 mg of guava extract per day significantly reduced the incidence of prostate cancer and that the guava extract was an effective agent for reducing the size of tumors of the prostate.

The study comes out of Taiwan, a country which makes frequent use of guava leaves for a variety of ailments. Journal Nutrition and Cancer reported that an" "aqueous extract of *Psidium guajava* L budding leaves (PE) has been shown to possess anti-prostate cancer activity in a cell line model".

The researchers reported that they were drawn to study guava leaves' effect on prostate cancer cells after conducting a study which showed that guava leaves were "potent anti-glycative agents".

The effects of glycation are associated with many progressive diseases and can also trigger cancer formation. Since guava leaves showed strong anti-glycative properties, the scientists chose to study the leaves' action against an abundant form of prostate cancer.

Breast Cancer: An enzyme (known as NFkappaB) regulates the expression of several genes in an apoptotic pathway, which, in turn, regulates cell-proliferation of cellular death.

A study in the September 2007 issue of the "Journal of Ethno-pharmacology" tested the anti-inflammatory effects of guava extract through its ability to regulate the concentration of enzyme using an experimental breast cancer cell line.

The researchers found that an extract of guava containing 55 mcg per ml inhibited the growth of breast cancer cells and their ability to metastasize, or spread, to other parts of the body.

Gastric Cancer: There is some evidence that points to guava leaf extract as a potential treatment for gastric cancer, according to the findings of a study published in 2011 in "Food Chemistry." The researchers found that guava leaf extract resulted in apoptosis, or the death of gastric cancer cells.

SELECTION

In the store, buy fresh fruits featuring intact skin without any cuts, bruises, or patches. The outer skin may be rough, often with a bitter taste, or soft and sweet. Varying between species, the skin can be of any thickness, is usually green before maturity, but becomes yellow, maroon, or green when ripe.

Pick up the red-fleshed ones as they contains more nutrition and have more anti-oxidants.

STORING

Oftentimes the fruits are left to ripen in the tree to experience their natural flavor. They can also be picked green when mature and ripe at room temperature. Ripe guavas have a characteristic color and aroma.

Placing the fruit wrapped in a paper with a banana or apple will hasten ripening. Mature green fruit can be stored for two to five weeks at temperature. Over ripen fruits can keep well in the refrigerator for few days.

SERVING

Wash them in cold running water in order to remove any dust or insecticide residues. Fresh ripe guava is best eaten as they are along with skin. Remove any floral remnants (sepals) at the apex, and then cut tip ends with sharp knife. It can be then sliced as in apples.

Here are some serving tips: Eat fresh fruit as it is to enjoy its natural flavor and unique taste. Sliced guava-cubes are a great addition to fruit salads.

It is also often used in dessert preparations. The fruit is also extensively used to make candies, preserves, jellies, jams, marmalade etc. A kind of tea is made from the fruit and leaves in some Asian countries.

Bottom Line

1. Fresh guava has all the health benefits, juices generally are loaded with extra sugar have doubtful real value.
2. Red guava has more health benefiting lycopene.
3. Green young leaves of guava have also been found to have anti-cancer properties.

32/52

LEMON & LIME

Lemon

Lime

"When fate hands you a lemon, make lemonade" – Dale Carnegie

Citrus fruits are very well-known for their flavor, fragrance and juiciness. They have long been valued as part of a nutritious and tasty diet. The citrus flavors are among the most preferred in the world, and they not only taste good, but are also extremely beneficial for health.

Lemons, like other vitamin C rich fruits, were highly prized by the miners and developers during the California Gold Rush in the mid-19th century, since they were used to protect against the development of scurvy.

They were in such demand that people were willing to pay up to $1 per lemon (Rs.50), a price that would still be considered costly today and was extremely expensive back in 1849.

Lemons are oval in shape and feature a yellow, texturized outer peel. They were originally developed as a cross between the lime and the citron and are thought to have originated in China or India, having been cultivated in these regions for about 2,500 years.

Brought to America by Christopher Columbus in his second voyage to the New World in 1493, and have been grown in Florida since the 16th century. The major producers of lemons today are the United States, Italy, Spain, Greece, Israel and Turkey.

Limes are usually smaller than lemons, and are oval or round in shape having a diameter of one to two inches with green flesh and skin. They can be either sour or sweet depending on the variety.

Limes are grown on trees that flourish in tropical and subtropical climates. They were thought to originate in Southeast Asia. They also made their way to the New World with Columbus on his second voyage in 1493, and were subsequently planted in many Caribbean countries.

Citrus fruits have several medicinal and nutritive properties, which help in treating and preventing several diseases. Citrus fruits like lemons may help in reducing the pain caused due to bee stings. They may also help in reducing the risk of cancers and heart diseases.

Studies show that people, who eat fruit such as lemons, tangerines, oranges and other whole foods, tend to eat less at subsequent meals–great way to reduce weight.

RICH SOURCE

The nutritional benefits of limes do not differ very much from those of lemons. They are both excellent sources of vitamin C, B6, potassium, folic acid, and flavonoids.

The vitamin C found in citrus fruits can help your body absorb iron, according to the Food and Agriculture Organization of the United Nations. Consuming citrus with iron supplements can increase your body's iron absorption by two or four times.

Since limonene is collected and used for other products during extraction and processing of oranges or lemons or limes fruits, there isn't much of it left in packaged ready-made juices.

Vegetarians and vegans can especially benefit from consuming citrus fruits to increase their iron levels. Lime and lemon both taste acidic and sourish but when consumed, they are really alkaline-forming in the stomach.

Vitamin C is an important anti-oxidant, helps protect against cancers, heart disease, stress, it is part of the cellular chemistry that provides energy, it is essential for sperm production, and for making the collagen protein involved in the building and health of cartilage, joints, skin, and blood vessels.

Vitamin C helps in maintaining a healthy immune system, it aids in neutralizing pollutants, is needed for antibody production, and thins the blood. Incidentally lemons have 30% more vitamin C than limes.

Owing to the multitude of vitamin C's health benefits, it is not surprising that research has shown that consumption of vegetables and fruits high in this nutrient is associated with a reduced risk of death from all causes including heart disease, stroke and cancer.

ANTI-CANCER BENEFITS

Lemons and limes contain unique flavonoid compounds that have anti-oxidant and anti-cancer properties. They have flavonoids called flavonol glycosides and the outstanding phytochemicals like limonene.

These flavonoids have been shown to stop cell division in many cancer cell lines. Several other fascinating research studies on the healing properties of lemons and limes have also been published.

Limonene has anti-cancer effects and helps increase the level of enzymes that detoxify carcinogens. The highest content of limonene is found in the white spongy inner parts and peel of the lemon.

You can get limonene if you squeeze your own orange juice or make lemonade with fresh lemons. Even better is using grated peels, or zest in your recipes, or using whole preserved lemons. Limonene is present in a variety of citrus fruits such as oranges, grapefruits, lemons, limes and tangerines.

Make it a habit to put in cut limes/lemons (together with peel) into your drinking water or juices, to enjoy all its medicinal properties. With lemon juice in your drink, the absorbability of the other nutrients in your drink is increased up to five times!

Mouth, Skin, Lung, Stomach and Colon Cancer: Limonene, in laboratory studies, has been shown to induce apoptosis, which is the "death signal", kills a cancer cell, or prevents it from dividing. It also increases the levels of enzymes in the liver that can detoxify carcinogens.

In animal studies and laboratory tests with human cells, compounds in citrus fruits, including lemons and limes, called limonoids have been shown to help fight cancers of the mouth, skin, lung, breast, stomach and colon.

Now, scientists from the US Agricultural Research Service (ARS) have shown that our bodies can readily absorb and utilize a very long-acting limonoid called limonin that is present in citrus fruits in about the same amount as vitamin C.

In citrus fruits, limonin is present in the form of limonin glucoside. In the ARS study, 16 volunteers were given a dose of limonin glucoside in amounts ranging from those that would be found in from 1 to 7 glasses of orange juice.

Blood tests showed that limonin was present in the plasma of all except one of the subjects, with concentrations highest within 6 hours after consumption. Traces of limonin were still present in 5 of the volunteers 24 hours after consumption!

Limonin's bioavailability and persistence may help explain why citrus limonoids are potent anti-carcinogens that may prevent cancerous cells from proliferating. Other natural anti-carcinogens are available for much less time; for example, the phenols in green tea and chocolate remain active in the body for just 4 to 6 hours.

Breast Cancer: University of California, Davis College of Agriculture and Environmental Sciences explain that limonoids, or phytochemicals, found in citrus fruits, such as lemons and limes, may be of benefit in the prevention of cancer.

Limonoids can stimulate the production of glutathione-S-transferase, which is known to detoxify carcinogenic compounds responsible for cancer. These phytochemicals have also shown promise in inhibiting the proliferation of hormone-sensitive cancer cells, as is seen in the breast cancer.

SELECTION

When buying lemons, look at the stem end of the lemon. There should be about four or five little lines radiating out of the stem. The greater the number of these lines, the higher the mineral content of the lemon.

One of the tricks to finding a good quality lemon is to find one that is rather thin-skinned since those with thicker peels will have less flesh and therefore be less juicy. Therefore, choose lemons that are heavy for their size. They should be fully yellow in color.

Choose limes that are firm and heavy for their size, free of decay and mold. They should have a glossy skin that is deep green in color; although limes turn more yellow as they ripen, they are at the height of their lively, tart flavor when they are green in color.

Research conducted at the University of Innsbruck in Austria suggests that as fruits fully ripen, almost to the point of spoilage, their anti-oxidant levels actually increase. For the most anti-oxidants, choose fully ripened lemons and limes.

STORING

Lemons will stay fresh kept at room temperature, away from exposure to sunlight, for about one week. If you will not be using them within this time period, you can store the lemons in the refrigerator crisper where they will keep for about four weeks.

Lemon juice and zest can also be stored for later use. Place freshly squeezed lemon juice in ice cube trays until frozen, subsequently storing them in plastic bags in the freezer. Dried lemon zest should be stored in a cool and dry place in an airtight glass container.

Limes can be kept out at room temperature where they will stay fresh for up to one week. Make sure to keep them away from sunlight exposure since it will cause them to turn yellow and will alter their flavor.

Limes can be stored in the refrigerator crisper, wrapped in a loosely sealed plastic bag, where they will keep fresh for about 10-14 days.

Lime juice and zest can also be stored for later use. Place freshly squeezed lime juice in ice cube trays until frozen, then subsequently store in plastic bags in the freezer. Dried lime zest should be stored in a cool and dry place in an airtight glass container.

SERVING

Lemons and limes are often called for in recipes in the form of juice. As they will produce more juice when warmer, always juice them when they are at room temperature or place them in a bowl of warm water for several minutes. Rolling them under the palm of your hand on a flat surface will also help to extract more juice.

If your recipe calls for lemon or lime zest, make sure that you use fruit that is organically grown since most conventionally grown fruits will have pesticide residues on their skin.

After washing and drying the lemon or lime, use a zester, paring knife or vegetable peeler to remove the zest, which is the colored part of the peel. Make sure not to remove too much of the peel as the white pith underneath is bitter.

Juice a glass of either lime or lemon juice and make ice cubes out of it. When you have a drink, pop a few lime/lemon cubes into your drink for a refreshing taste while enjoying its immense health benefits.

Place thinly sliced lemons, peel and all, underneath and around fish before cooking. Baking or broiling will soften the slices so that they can be eaten along with the fish.

Combine lemon juice with olive or flax oil, freshly crushed garlic and pepper to make a light and refreshing salad dressing.

If you are watching your salt intake (and even if you are not), serve lemon wedges with meals as their tartness makes a great salt substitute.

Combine freshly squeezed lime juice, evaporated cane juice and either plain or sparkling water to make limeade.

Add an easy-to-prepare zing to dinner by tossing seasoned cooked brown rice with garden peas, chicken pieces or tofu, scallions, pumpkin seeds, lime juice and lime zest.

Squeeze some lime juice onto an avocado quarter and eat as it is.

Bottom Line

1. Lemons have got 30% more vitamin C as compared to limes.
2. The spongy inner part and the peel of lemons and limes has maximum health benefiting nutrients.
3. Freeze the lemon and lime juice, and make cubes for quick and convenient future use.

MANGO

"The King of Fruits"

Mango is one of the most popular, nutritionally rich fruit with unique flavor, fragrance, taste, and health promoting qualities making it a common ingredient in new functional foods often called "super fruits".

Mango is the delicious tropical seasonal fruit and believed to be originated in the sub-Himalayan plains of Indian subcontinent. It is a tropical tree cultivated in many regions of India and now distributed wide across the world in many continents.

It comes is various sizes and shapes. Its weight ranges from 150 gm. (5 ounces) to around 750 gm.(one and half pounds), Outer skin is smooth and is green in un-ripe mangoes but turns into golden yellow, bright yellow or orange-red when ripen depending on the cultivar.

Internally, juicy flesh has orange-yellow in color with numerous soft fibrils radiating from the husk (enveloping a single large kidney-shaped seed).

Flavor is pleasant and rich, and tastes sweet with mild tartness. A high quality mango fruit should feature no or very less fiber content and minimal sour taste.

While mangoes can add a tropical twist and a burst of flavor to any meal, this "king of fruits" can also greatly help improve your health—it can help fight off illness, improve cholesterol levels and can even help prevent certain cancers and heart diseases.

Having gained a better understanding of the phenolic compounds found in mangos, the National Mango Board of USA commissioned a cell culture study to determine whether mangos possess properties that might help to reduce the incidence of cancer and other diseases.

RICH SOURCE

Mango fruit is rich in pre-biotic dietary fiber, vitamins, minerals, and poly-phenolic flavonoid and other anti-oxidant compounds.

Mango fruit is an excellent source of vitamin A and flavonoids like beta-carotene, alpha-carotene, and beta-cryptoxanthin. 100 g of fresh fruit provides 765 mg or 25% of recommended daily levels of vitamin A. Together, these compounds are known to have anti-oxidant properties and are essential for vision.

Leslie Taylor, naturopath and author of "The Healing Power of Rainforest Herbs," writes that East Indian healers employ mangoes to combat viruses, support cardiac functioning, relieve constipation and lower blood pressure.

Vitamin A is also required for maintaining healthy mucus membranes and skin. Consumption of natural fruits rich in carotenes is known to protect body from lung and oral cavity cancers.

Fresh mango is a very rich source of potassium. Potassium is an important component of cell and body fluids that helps controlling heart rate and blood pressure.

It is also a very good source of vitamin-B6 (pyridoxine), vitamin C and vitamin E. Mango peels are also rich in phytonutrients, such as the pigment anti-oxidants like carotenoids and polyphenols.

ANTI-CANCER BENEFITS

According to new research study, mango fruit has been found to protect against colon, breast, leukemia and prostate cancers. Several trial studies suggest that polyphenolic anti-oxidant compounds in mango are known to offer protection against breast and colon cancers.

Breast and Colon Cancers: Drs. Stephen and Susanne Talcott of Texas A&M University, College Station, USA, studied the anti-oxidants in mangoes to help determine how bioactive compounds from mangoes are broken down and absorbed.

Dr. Susanne Talcott, tested mango polyphenol extracts *in vitro* on colon, breast, lung, leukemia and prostate cancers. Polyphenols are natural substances in plants and are associated with a variety of compounds known to promote good health.

Mango showed some impact on lung, leukemia and prostate cancers but was most effective on the most common breast and colon cancers.

"What we found is that not all cell lines are sensitive to the same extent to an anti-cancer agent," she said. "But the breast and colon cancer lines underwent apoptosis, or programmed cell death. Additionally, we found that when we tested normal colon cells side by side with the colon cancer cells, the mango polyphenols did not harm the normal cells."

Because the colon can absorb nutrients in two ways – from the bloodstream and from direct contact with the intestines – polyphenols are more likely to be absorbed in the colon than in other areas. (Cells in the lungs, breasts or prostate, for example, only have access to anti-oxidants through the bloodstream.

Based on these initial findings, the researchers opted to focus their research on mango and colon cancer.

Based on the promising findings of the cell study, the National Mango Board of USA is currently pursuing a human clinical trial in volunteers with inflammatory bowel disease and related conditions to study the possible beneficial effects of mango supplementation.

SELECTION

Mangoes are seasonal summer fruits; fresh mango fruit season begins in the month of May in India, when the rich fragrance of the fruit heralds its arrival.

Mangoes are usually harvested while they are green but perfectly mature. Unripe ones are extremely sour in taste. Organic mangoes are left to ripen on the tree but over-ripen fruits fall off from the tree and get spoiled.

In the store, mangoes come with various sizes and colors; therefore select the one based on the serving size and variety of fruit you love to devour. "*Alphanso*" variety from India (Maharashtra state) and "*sindhuri*" (kesar) varieties from Pakistan are known for their uniqueness. Choose the ones with intact skin without any bruises or cuts.

STORING

Unripe mangoes can be kept at room temperature for few days, and to ripen, keep them in paper covers. Ripen ones should be stored in the refrigerator. Bring back to normal temperature when the fruit is to be eaten to get the natural taste and flavor.

SERVING

To enjoy, wash mangoes in cold running water to remove dust and any pesticide residues. Mop dry outer surface using soft cloth. Mango fruit should be eaten all alone without any additions to experience its rich flavor.

Cut the fruit lengthwise into three pieces in such a way that the middle portion consists of husky seed. Slice underneath the skin to separate the skin from the pulp. Then, chop the pulp into small cubes.

Also, using a sharp knife, cut through the flesh down either side of the central seed. This way you get two big halves of a mango fruit. Then, take one half and score the flesh in a horizontal and vertical pattern taking care not to cut deep through skin. Invert the whole half to push out the cubes as shown in the photo:

Here are some of the popular serving tips:

Mango fruit can be enjoyed all alone without any additions.

Fresh mango cubes are a great addition to fruit salads.

Mango juice with ice cubes is a popular, delicious drink.

Mango fruit juice blended with milk as "mango-milk shake".

Mango fruit is also used to prepare jam, ice cream and in candy industries.

The unripe, raw, green mangoes are used in the preparation of pickles and chutney in the Asian countries.

Bottom Line

1. World is waking up to a new " Super –Food" called Mango.
2. Eat slightly unripe mango to keep your blood sugar under control. Most of the mango drinks contain less than 10% mango pulp and rest is sugar, artificial colors and preservative.
3. Mango "The King of Fruits" is under- researched, but exceptionally beneficial fruit as per ancient wisdom of India, bring home the KING.

ORANGE

"The Citrus king...accounting for over 70% of world citrus production"

Juicy and sweet and renowned for its concentration of vitamin C and many other health nutrients, oranges make the perfect snack and add a special tang to many recipes. It is no wonder that they are one of the most popular fruits in the world.

Oranges are round citrus fruits with finely-textured skins that are, of course, orange in color just like their pulpy flesh. Oranges originated around 3000 years ago in Asia, in the region from southern China to Indonesia from which they spread to India.

Before the 20th century, oranges were very expensive and therefore they were not regularly consumed, but rather eaten on special holidays such as Christmas.

After more efficient means of transportation were developed, and food processors invented methods for utilizing orange by-products such as citric acid and bioflavonoids, the price of oranges dropped, and they could be consumed on a wide scale.

Currently, the countries that are some of the largest commercial producers of oranges include the United States, Brazil, Mexico, Spain, China and Israel.

The abundance of anti-oxidants, vitamins, fiber and phytonutrients in orange foods are good for your skin, eyes and heart, and they may also decrease your risk of cancer.

Leave in the albedo (the white matter under the orange peel) as much as possible as the albedo contains the highest amount of valuable bioflavonoids and other anti-cancer agents.

RICH SOURCE

Oranges are an excellent source of vitamin C and flavonoids. One orange (130 grams) supplies nearly 100 per cent of the recommended daily dietary intake of vitamin C.

Vitamin C is the primary water-soluble anti-oxidant in the body, disarming free radicals and preventing damage in the aqueous environment both inside and outside cells.

Vitamin C supplements or Orange Juice: Seven healthy test subjects were given each of three drinks, two weeks apart: orange juice containing 150 milligrams of vitamin C, fortified water containing 150 milligrams of vitamin C, and a sugar and water solution containing no vitamin C.

Blood samples were collected immediately before the drink was consumed, then every hour for 8 hours, and finally 24 hours after consumption of each drink.

Blood samples were exposed to hydrogen peroxide, and free radical damage to DNA was evaluated at 3 and 24 hours. Only when orange juice was consumed was any protective effect seen.

After drinking orange juice, DNA damage was 18% less after 3 hours, and 16% less after 24 hours. No protection against DNA damage was seen after consumption of the vitamin C fortified drink or the sugar drink.

Italian researchers in the Division of Human Nutrition at the University of Milan, Italy, thus concluded that consuming vitamin C supplements does not provide the same protective benefits as drinking a glass of orange juice.

Lead researcher Serena Guarnieri stated that, "It appears that vitamin C is not the only chemical responsible for anti-oxidant protection." In oranges, vitamin C is part of a matrix involving many more beneficial phytochemicals."

"But how they are interacting is still anyone's guess," she added. Fortunately, we don't have to wait until scientists figure this out–the oranges' DNA-protective benefits.

Practical Tip: For the best DNA protection, skip the vitamin C-fortified bottled drinks and enjoy a glass of real (preferably organic as organic foods have been shown to contain higher amounts of phytonutrients), freshly squeezed orange juice with full fiber or the best is simply eat an orange!

Especially in areas of the body where cellular turnover is especially rapid, such as the digestive system, preventing DNA mutations translates into preventing cancer. This is why a good intake of vitamin C is associated with a reduced risk of colon cancer.

When you eat a whole orange, it provides good dietary fiber. In addition, oranges are a good source of vitamin A, the B vitamins, amino acids, beta-carotene, pectin, potassium, folic acid, calcium, iodine, phosphorus, sodium, zinc, manganese, chlorine and iron.

But it is yet another flavanone in oranges, the hesperidin molecule, which has been singled out in phytonutrient research on oranges. Arguably, the most important flavanone in oranges, hesperidin, has been shown to lower high blood pressure as well as cholesterol in animal studies, and to have strong anti-inflammatory properties.

Importantly, most of this phytonutrient is found in the peel and inner white pulp of the orange, rather than in its liquid orange center, so this beneficial compound is too often removed by the processing of oranges into juice.

ANTI-CANCER BENEFITS

An orange packs over 200 different phytonutrients, more than 60 flavonoids and several members of a very fragrant class of molecules, the terpenes.

Many of which have been shown to have anti-inflammatory, anti-tumor and blood clot inhibiting properties, as well as strong anti-oxidant effects.

The combination of the high amount of anti-oxidant (vitamin C) and flavonoids in oranges makes it one of the best fruits in helping to promote optimal health.

Leave in the albedo (the white matter under the orange peel) as much as possible as the albedo contains the highest amount of valuable bioflavonoids and other anti-cancer agents.

In recent findings, children who regularly consumed orange juice in the first two years of life had reduced risk of later developing leukemia. –Source Dr. Richard Beliveau's book "Foods to Fight Cancer".

Mouth, Larynx and Stomach Cancer: The government's key research group, the Commonwealth Scientific and Industrial Research Organization (CSIRO), Australia, found that consuming citrus fruits like orange could reduce the risk of mouth, larynx and stomach cancers by up to 50 per cent.

Breast Cancer: Orange juice may be a strong ally in the fight against breast cancer and high cholesterol, according to new research released at the International Congress of Nutrition.

Researchers from the Centre for Human Nutrition at the University of Western Ontario, Canada, announced results of two new studies that link orange and grapefruit juice to significantly delaying the growth of breast cancer cells and reducing LDL, or "bad" cholesterol.

"The implications are potentially enormous because a powerful weapon against breast cancer and high cholesterol may be as close as your kitchen," said Dr. Kenneth Carroll, director of the Centre for Human Nutrition.

In the breast cancer study, researchers tested the ability of orange juice, grapefruit juice and their constituent flavonoids (naturally-occurring, compounds found in many fruits and vegetables, including citrus fruits) to inhibit human breast cancer cells in mice.

"Mice that received orange juice or grapefruit juice in place of drinking water had 50 per cent fewer tumors and metastases," said Najla Guthrie, lead researcher on the Centre's cancer study.

The study groups receiving flavonoids also had a reduction in tumors, but not to the extent of the groups receiving juices. This leads us to believe that in the juice study groups, the flavonoids were working with other components in the juices to reduce the tumors.

Lung Cancer: A prospective study that followed 870 men over a period of 25 years found that those who consumed more than 83 mg of vitamin C daily had a striking 64% reduction in lung cancer compared with those who consumed less than 63 mg per day. That is about just taking one orange a day for extra vitamin C.

Stomach Cancer: A number of observational studies have found increased dietary vitamin C intake to be associated with decreased risk of stomach cancer, and laboratory experiments indicate that vitamin C inhibits the formation of carcinogenic compounds in the stomach.

Infection with the bacteria, *Helicobacter pylori* (*H. pylori*), is known to increase the risk of stomach cancer and also appears to lower the vitamin C content of stomach secretions.

SELECTION

Choose oranges that are firm and heavy for their size. This indicates that they are full of juice. Lighter fruit has more skin and drier pulp indicating less juice.

In general, oranges that are smaller will be juicier than those that are larger in size, as will those that feature thinner skins. For the most anti-oxidants, choose fully ripened oranges:

Research conducted at the University of Innsbruck in Austria suggests that as fruits fully ripen, almost to the point of spoilage, their anti-oxidant levels actually increase.

STORING

Vitamin C gets destroyed fast when exposed to the air, so eat up an orange quickly once cut up. Do not leave the juice exposed for too long to preserve optimal nutrients.

Oranges can be stored at room temperature for up to two weeks or stored loosely in the refrigerator. Do not store wrapped to prevent moisture and mold.

SERVING

Orange fruit can be carried to any place without much cumbersome. Fresh oranges can be eaten at anytime, anywhere; just wash them under running water to remove surface dirt and any pesticide residues, peel the skin, and enjoy!

Remove skin after scoring superficially on the skin with your fingers or using a knife. Remove rind and fibers and gently peel off membranes and seeds. They are usually eaten this way. They can also be eaten by slicing the fruit horizontally into two halves and scooping out sections of the halves with a spoon.

Orange fruit juice is also as much popular as raw ones; however, use raw fruits instead of juice for the maximum benefit of anti-oxidants. Fiber content in the fruit is also lessened to a great degree in the juice.

If you wish to go for fresh orange juice, then prepare it yourself at home instead of commercial drinks that may contain preservatives and artificial colorants. To extract most juice from oranges, always juice them when they are at room temperature. Rolling them under the palm of your hand on a flat surface will also help extract more juice.

The outermost part of the rind grate using zester to produce orange zest, which also have many culinary values for its flavor rich oil glands.

Here are some serving tips:

- Orange fruit sections are a great addition to green and fruit salads.
- Orange fruit juice can be a re-freshening intra-day drink.
- The fruit is also used in the preparation of desserts, jams and jellies.
- Orange zest (peel) is also used in preparation of popular dishes for its rich flavor.
- Dried orange blossoms and leaves are used as herbal tea.

Bottom Line

"What happened to my orange Easter dye that was here a minute ago?"

1. Heating and frying destroys the vitamin C we are always short of this vital vitamin. Popping a pill vitamin C has doubtful benefits.
2. Eating full or drinking a glass of freshly squeezed orange, with fiber is all it takes to ward off cancer, younger looking skin and keeping the heart young.
3. The white matter under the orange peel is called albedo; it contains the highest amount of valuable bioflavonoids and other anti-cancer agents. Put back albedo in your orange juice or make smoothie with full orange of course minus seeds.

35/52

PAPAYA

"Fruit of the Angels" –Christopher Columbus

Papaya is called fruit of the angels by Conquistadors because of its heavenly taste. In its prime, it is a cerise-orange colored, unbelievably juicy fruit with an aroma to match its heavenly taste. Not only is papaya beautiful, fragrant and luscious, it is amazingly healthful!

How fortunate that this glorious fruit is available year-round. Once considered an exotic fruit, papayas' rise in popularity has made them much more available.

In the 20th century, papayas were brought to the United States and have been cultivated in Hawaii, the major U.S. producer since the 1920s. Today, the largest commercial producers of papayas include the United States, Mexico and Puerto Rico.

A ripe papaya can be as long as twenty inches, but most commercially grown fruits are pear-shaped, about seven inches in length and about a pound in weight. The inner cavity contains black round seeds, encased in a gelatinous-like substance. The seeds are not to be consumed as it is known to contain a toxic substance called carpaine. Carpaine, when consumed in large quantities, may lower the pulse rate and depress the nervous system.

The fruit, as well as the other parts of the papaya tree, contain papain, an enzyme that helps digest proteins. This enzyme is especially concentrated in the fruit when it is unripe. It is noticed that the Caribbean natives ate the fruit after huge meals and never encountered any digestive distress. And they are very strong too.

The papaya has remarkable medicinal virtues recognized from ancient times. Being one of the most easily digested fruits, it is an excellent wholesome food for young to old, a rejuvenating choice.

RICH SOURCE

The nutritional highlight of papaya is a proteolytic enzyme called papain which is an excellent aid to digestion. This enzyme is so powerful that it is said to digest an amazing

200 times its own weight in protein. It assists our body's own enzymes in assimilating the maximum nutritional value from the food we eat.

Papaya is a wholesome fruit, it is a rich source of anti-oxidant nutrients such as beta-carotene (which is what gives it the orange color; green papaya does not contain this carotene), vitamin A and C and flavonoids, B vitamins, folate and pantothenic acid.

It also contains the minerals–calcium, chlorine, iron, phosphorus, potassium, silicon and sodium. The carbohydrate content in papaya is mainly of invert sugar which is a form of pre-digested food. The ripe papaya is endowed with an abundance of energy-boosting natural sugars.

ANTI-CANCER BENEFITS

Papaya has been declared a new super fruit after scientists found that it can prevent and may be able to treat a wide range of cancers.

Cervix, Breast, Liver, Lung and Pancreatic Cancer: In a very recent study researchers found that papaya was an effective anti-cancer agent against cervix, breast, liver, lung and pancreas cancers.

They tested their theories by using a tea made from the extracts of dried papaya leaves and put them in dishes which contain cancerous cells.

The team of researchers found that the papaya leaf extract boosted the production chemicals that regulate the immune system.

Scientists from the University of Florida, who were behind the study, say that papaya may be used as an alternative cancer treatment.

Dr. Nam Dang, of the University of Florida, said the findings published in the Journal of Ethno-pharmacology were groundbreaking.

Colon Cancer: A very special ability of the fiber contained in papaya is that it can bind cancer causing toxins to it, preventing them from binding to cells in the colon. For individuals with a family history of colon cancer, papaya may be an important dietary addition.

Lung Cancer: If you or someone you love is a smoker, or if you are frequently exposed to secondhand smoke, then making vitamin A-rich foods, such as papaya, part of your healthy way of eating may save your life, suggests research conducted at Kansas State University.

While studying the relationship between vitamin A, lung inflammation, and emphysema, Richard Baybutt, associate professor of nutrition at Kansas State University, made a surprising discovery: a common carcinogen in cigarette smoke, benzo (a) pyrene, induces vitamin A deficiency.

(*Emphysema* is a long-term, progressive disease of the lungs that causes shortness of breath)

His latest animal studies indicate that not only does the benzo(a)pyrene in cigarette smoke cause vitamin A deficiency, but that a diet rich in vitamin A can help counter this effect, thus greatly reducing emphysema.

Baybutt believes vitamin A's protective effects may help explain why some smokers do not develop emphysema. "There are a lot of people who live to be 90 years old and are smokers," he said. Why? Probably because of their diet.

The implications are that those who start smoking at an early age are more likely to become vitamin A deficient and develop complications associated with cancer and emphysema.

If you or someone you love smokes, or if your work necessitates exposure to second hand smoke, protect yourself by making sure that at least one of the World's Healthiest Foods that are rich in vitamin A, such as papaya, is a daily part of your healthy way of eating.

Prostate Cancer: Another promising finding is that men who ate lycopene-rich foods are less likely to develop prostate cancer. Papaya is one of the high lycopene fruits, easy to eat and easy to obtain in today's markets.

Choosing to regularly eat lycopene-rich fruits, such as papaya, and drink green tea may greatly reduce a man's risk of developing prostate cancer, suggests research published the Asia Pacific Journal of Clinical Nutrition.

In this case-control study involving 130 prostate cancer patients and 274 hospital controls, men drinking the most green tea were found to have an 86% reduced risk of prostate cancer compared to those drinking the least.

A similar inverse association was found between the men's consumption of lycopene-rich fruits and vegetables such as tomatoes, apricots, pink grapefruit, watermelon, papaya, and guava. Men who most frequently enjoyed these foods were 82% less likely to have prostate cancer compared to those consuming the least lycopene-rich foods.

Regular consumption of both green tea and foods rich in lycopene resulted in a synergistic protective effect, stronger than the protection afforded by either, the researchers also noted. Get in the habit of drinking green tea and eating lycopene-rich foods like papaya regularly.

SELECTION

Since it loses nutrient strength as it ripens, papaya is best if purchased mostly ripe and eaten by the next day. Purchase fruit that is orangey-red in color and just a little soft to touch. Fruits that have yellow patches are less ripe and will take a few days at home to become their best.

Papayas that are totally green or overly hard should not be purchased, unless you are planning on cooking them, or unless you want to use green papayas in a cold dish like an Asian salad, as their flesh will not develop its characteristic sweet juicy flavor.

While a few black spots on the surface will not affect the papaya's taste, avoid those that are bruised or overly soft.

STORING

Papayas that are partially yellow should be left at room temperature where they will ripen in a few days. If you want to speed this process, place them in a paper bag with a banana.

Ripe papayas should be stored in the refrigerator and consumed within one or two days, so you can enjoy their maximum flavor.

For the most anti-oxidants, eat papaya fully ripened. Research conducted at the University of Innsbruck in Austria suggests that as fruits fully ripen, almost to the point of spoilage, their anti-oxidant levels actually increase.

SERVING

Papayas can be used in many different ways. It can be eaten as it is, added to a fruit salad or to a host of different recipes.

One of the easiest (and most delightful) ways to eat papaya is to eat it just like a melon. After washing the fruit, cut it lengthwise, scoop out the seeds and then eat it with a spoon. For a little extra zest, you can squeeze lemon or lime juice on top.

To cut papaya into smaller pieces for fruit salad or recipes, first peel it with a paring knife and then cut into desired size and shape. You can also use a melon baller to scoop out the fruit of a halved papaya.

If you are adding it to a fruit salad, you should do so just before serving as it tends to cause the other fruits to become very soft.

Mix diced papaya, cilantro, jalapeno peppers and ginger together to make a unique salsa that goes great with shrimp, scallops and halibut.

Slice a small papaya lengthwise and fill with fruit salad. In a blender, combine papaya, strawberries and yogurt for a cold smoothie treat.

Bottom Line

1. Choose *papayas* that have *reddish*-orange skin and are slightly soft to the touch.
2. Fully ripe papayas are most beneficial.
3. For great digestion one can eat papaya as sweet dish after the food.

36/52

POMEGRANATE

"Jeweled fruit of winter"

Pomegranate is being touted as a miracle drug for aging, alzheimer, cancer, heart disease, arthritis and even protecting unborn babies from brain injuries. It cures about anything that can ail an aging senior citizen. It has become a popular ingredient for mixed drinks, ice cream and even bottled water.

It's now a popular decoration for table displays. President Bush even brought it up in his meeting with Afghanistan President Karzai, suggesting they grow pomegranate trees rather than poppies. The Center for Disease Control, USA, honored pomegranate by naming it the fruit of the month.

Pomegranate is among the most popular, nutritionally rich fruit with unique flavor, taste, and health promoting characteristics. Along with berries, and some tropical exotics such as mango, it too has novel qualities of functional foods often called as "super fruits."

The pomegranate fruit originally native to Iran and the Himalayas in northern India has become widely cultivated throughout India. The pomegranate tree was introduced into California by Spanish settlers in 1769. Often referred to as jeweled fruit of winter, pomegranate seeds provide vitamins, minerals and fiber.

Completely grown-up tree bears numerous spherical, bright red, purple, or orange-yellow colored fruits depending on the cultivar types. Each fruit measures about 6-10 cm in diameter and weighs is about 200 gm. Its outer skin or rind is tough and features leathery texture.

World's best pomegranates are grown in the southern states of Afghanistan in Kandahar, Balkh, Helmand, and Nimroz provinces. The pomegranate fruit is judged ripe when it develops distinctive color and sound metallic when tapped with the finger.

Fruits must be picked before over-maturity otherwise, the seeds become hard, inedible, and the whole fruit tends to crack open. Modern science has only recently realized the importance of this super anti-oxidant rich fruit, for its ability to fight most dreaded diseases like cancer and alzheimer. The fruit is also suggested in the diet for weight reduction and cholesterol controlling programs.

RICH SOURCE

Pomegranates are rich in vitamin C providing 48 per cent of the recommended daily intake in a one-cup serving. Vitamin C helps immune function, collagen formation and neurotransmitters and acts as an anti-oxidant in the body.

One-cup serving of pomegranates also provides 5 percent of the daily iron needs. This plant based source of iron helps red blood cell production, oxygen transport and cell growth.

There are several key mineral nutrients found in pomegranates. The highest mineral content is copper. One raw fruit contains 22 per cent of the daily recommended amount of copper, 19 per cent of potassium, 17 per cent of manganese and 10 per cent of phosphorus. It is also a good source of magnesium, iron, calcium, zinc and selenium.

Pomegranate is a rich source of soluble and insoluble dietary fibers, providing about 4 g per 100 g (about 12% of RDA), which aid in smooth digestive and bowel movements.

Pomegranate is also a good source of many vital B-complex group of vitamins such as vitamin B-5, folate, pyridoxine.

Pomegranates contain polyphenol phytochemicals known as tannins, anthocyanins, and ellagic acid. These powerful phytochemicals are responsible for reducing risk of chronic diseases such as cancer, arthritis and heart disease.

ANTI-CANCER BENEFITS

Every year researchers are adding to the list of cancer types, for which pomegranates seem to halt growth. Pomegranate fruits offer an array of phytochemicals. These include anthocyanins, cyanidin, ellagic acid, ellagitannins, pelargonidin, punicalagin and punicalin.

Anti-oxidants can protect us against the oxidative stress in our industrialized world, such as pollution, chemicals, viruses and bacteria, and consequently cardiovascular diseases and cancer.

Recent scientific research is demonstrating that pomegranate may be helpful in the prevention and treatment of various types of cancer such as breast cancer, skin cancer, prostate cancer and lung cancer.

Prostate Cancer: Pomegranate juice contains the highest concentration of ellagitannins as compared to any other widely

Scientists at the University of California, Berkeley, have independently confirmed that pomegranate juice contains at least three major phytochemicals. Pomegranate juice has three times the anti-oxidant power of red wine or green tea.

consumed fruit juice. The anti-oxidant and anti-inflammatory properties of ellagitannins have demonstrated efficacy in fighting prostate cancer, as reported by the National Institutes of Health.

A study led by Dr. Allan Pantuck of UCLA involving 48 men with recurrent prostate cancer showed that drinking 8 ounces of pomegranate juice daily significantly increased the time it took for PSA levels to rise. In addition, there was decreased cancer cell division, decreased proliferation of cancer cells and increased cancer cell death.

A longer PSA doubling time indicates that the cancer may be progressing less rapidly. Other studies have found that certain compounds in pomegranate juice inhibited growth of prostate cancer cells in the laboratory.

Skin Cancer: Pomegranates are the richest source of a natural substance called ellagic acid. Dr. Hasan Mukhtar and colleagues from the University of Wisconsin have shown that a topically-applied pomegranate fruit extract can block skin tumor formation in mice.

Pomegranate also contains the anthocyanidins and proanthocyanidins, which are substances that have been shown in animal and test tube experiments to reduce tumor angiogenesis (formation of new blood vessels necessary for the spread of tumor).

Lung Cancer: Lung cancer has increased at alarming rates in the last decade, particularly because of trends in smoking. Lung cancer is now the most common cause of cancer death in the world, representing 28 per cent of all cancer deaths.

Physicians have found this cancer difficult to control with conventional therapeutic and surgical approaches, and the prognosis is poor with an overall five-year survival rate of 10-14 per cent in the United States.

A study at the University of Wisconsin–Madison using a mouse model shows that consuming pomegranates could potentially help reduce the growth and spread of lung cancer cells or even prevent lung cancer from developing.

"Pomegranate fruit continues to show great promise," says Mukhtar, professor of dermatology. And further adds that "We have earlier shown that pomegranate fruit contains very powerful skin and prostate cancer-fighting agents. These recent findings expand the possible health benefits of the fruit to the leading cause of cancer death in the country and worldwide: lung cancer."

In the study, the research team examined the effect of oral consumption of a dose of pomegranate fruit extract on the growth, progression, blood-vessel development and signaling pathways in two mouse lung tumor protocols. The dosages tested were comparable to what humans could reasonably consume in a day.

Chemicals were used to induce lung tumors, and the mice received pomegranate extract in drinking water. Lung tumor yield was then examined at different times during several months.

Mice who were exposed to cancer-inducing chemicals and who were treated with pomegranate had significantly lower lung tumor growth than mice treated with carcinogens only. Tumor reduction was 53.9 per cent at 84 days and 61.6 percent at 140 days.

According to master herbalist and certified nutritionist Donald Yance (author of book Herbal Medicine, Healing & Cancer), ellagic acid "inhibits cancer formation and is believed to inhibit cancer mutation by latching onto DNA-masking sensitive sites on the genetic material that might otherwise be occupied by harmful chemicals. Ellagic acid is particularly effective in the inhibition of lung cancer caused by tobacco."

Breast Cancer: More than 400,000 women die from breast cancer globally every year. About 75 per cent of breast cancers are estrogen-receptor positive, meaning they are fed by estrogen.

Enzyme-blocking chemicals in pomegranates may reduce the risk of estrogen-fueled breast cancers, say U.S. researchers. An acid found in pomegranates appears to block aromatase, an enzyme that converts androgen to estrogen, a hormone that plays a role in the development of breast cancer, the researchers wrote in the journal Cancer Prevention Research.

"We identified some of these chemicals in pomegranates that actually have properties that can suppress aromatase," researcher Shiuan Chen, of the City of Hope Cancer Research and Treatment Center in Duarte, California, said in an interview.

Many women who have had breast cancer take medicines called aromatase inhibitors -- such as Pfizer's Aromasin, Novartis' Femara and AstraZeneca Plc's Arimidex -- to keep estrogen from feeding tumors.

Chen and colleagues studied whether compounds, or phytochemicals, in pomegranates can suppress aromatase and ultimately block cancer growth. They found that 10 natural compounds in the fruit may potentially prevent estrogen-related breast cancer. However Chen said the compounds would not be a replacement for aromatase inhibitors.

"We do not recommend people start taking this as a replacement for the AI's," Chen said. "They (pomegranate compounds) are not as potent as the real drugs so we think that the interest probably is more on the prevention end rather than in a therapeutic purpose."

Other researchers not associated with the study told the journal that the results are promising, and suggested more studies involving animals and humans were needed to confirm the findings.

Dr. Powel Brown, an oncologist at the University of Texas, said in a statement that future studies should focus on testing pomegranate juice for its effect on estrogen levels, menopausal symptoms, breast density or even as a cancer preventive agent.

Research using both mouse mammary organ culture and human breast cancer cells in test tube has demonstrated anti-cancer effects of pomegranate extracts.

SELECTION

The whole fruit is about the size of an orange. The rind color can range from yellow-orange to deep reddish-purple.

Fruits should be plump and round, heavy for their size, with a rich and fresh color. Larger fruits promise more juice. Choose pomegranates that have smooth skin, free from any bruises, cuts or mold.

STORING

Whole fruits can be stored for a month in a cool, dry area or refrigerated up to two months. The seed pips can be frozen in an airtight bag up to one year. Fresh juice should be refrigerated and used within two to three days.

SERVING

Wash pomegranate fruit in cold water or rinse in tepid water to bring to normal temperature if kept in the cold storage.

To experience its rich flavor, eat fresh fruit as it is without adding anything. Generally, the fruit is eaten out of hand by making superficial vertical incision on the tough skin and then breaking it apart.

Clusters of juice sacs are then lifted out and the white membranes and rinds are separated from the arils. Separating the red arils is simplified by performing this task in a bowl of cold water, whereby seeds sink and pulp floats, then remove water and gently pat dry seeds.

Arils also make an attractive garnish when sprinkled on salads and dishes.

Fresh fruits make fantastic refreshing juice. Pomegranate juice can be used in soups, jellies, sorbets, sauces as well as to flavor cakes, baked apples.

The juice can also be made into a wine. Pomegranate concentrate is a popular item used in the Middle Eastern and Mediterranean recipes. The juice is concentrated to about 250% stronger, and when added in cooking, gives unique flavor and intense sweet taste.

Bottom Line

1. Pomegranate juice has three times the anti-oxidant power of red wine or green tea.
2. Benefits of pomegranate in prostate cancer are well documented.
3. Eating one medium size pomegranate a day is an excellent way to a great health.

RASPBERRY

"There is something in the red of a raspberry pie that looks as good to a man as the red in a sheep looks to a wolf" – E. W. Howe

Fragrantly sweet with a subtly tart overtone and almost-melt-in-your-mouth texture, raspberries are wonderfully delicious and are usually in limited supply.

Raspberries are known as "aggregate fruits" since they are a compendium of smaller seed-containing fruits, called drupelets, which are arranged around a hollow central cavity. Their shape conveys to them a very delicate structure.

While the most common type of raspberry (*Rubus idaeus*) is red-pink in color, raspberries actually come in a range of colors including black, purple, orange, yellow and white.

RICH SOURCE

Raspberries are an excellent source of fiber, manganese and vitamin C. They are a very good source of vitamin K and a good source of magnesium, folate, omega-3 fatty acids, copper, vitamin E and potassium. In addition, they contain significant amounts of the anti-cancer phytochemical ellagic acid.

One cup of Raspberries supplies about eight grams of fiber, roughly 40% of your manganese needs, and nearly that same amount of your vitamin C needs for the day.

Red raspberry is most often the source of a dietary supplement sold in many health food stores called ellagic acid. This substance found naturally in raspberries belongs to the family of phytochemicals called tannins, and it is viewed as being responsible for a good portion of the anti-oxidant activity of this (and other) berries.

ANTI-CANCER BENEFITS

Raspberries are chock full of compounds with potentially anti-carcinogenic effects, including vitamins, minerals and plant nutrients such as anthocyanins strong anti-oxidants that give berries their color.

Ellagic acid is the phytonutrient in the Raspberries, which has shown maximum promise for the fight against various cancers. Hollings Cancer Institute at the University of South Carolina recently finished a study showing that ellagic acid:

- Stops cancer cells from dividing in 48 hours.
- Causes normal cell death (apoptosis) within 72 hours in cases of breast, pancreas, esophageal, skin, colon and prostate cancers.
- Prevents the destruction of the p53 gene that leads to cancer caused apoptosis (normal cell death) in HPV (human papilloma virus) exposed to it.

One cup (150 grams) per day of red raspberries is good enough to prevent development of cancer cells.

Raspberries contain the most ellagic acid when compared to other foods, reports Florida State University. They contain 3.39 mg of ellagic acid per 1 g. Raspberry leaves contain the highest concentration of ellagic acid, but the fruit and seeds also contain a healthy concentration.

> *Raspberries possess almost 50% higher antioxidant activity than strawberries, three times that of kiwis, and ten times the antioxidant activity of tomatoes, shows research conducted in the Netherlands and published in the journal "Bio Factors".*

Esophagus Cancer: Esophageal cancer is the sixth leading cause of cancer-related deaths worldwide. The outlook is bleak for those diagnosed with the disease – five-year survival rates range from 8 to 12 per cent.

In a recent Ohio State University study, rats who feasted on black raspberries, a variety of the common red raspberry, were 50% less prone to developing cancerous esophageal tumors. Also, if tumors did develop, they were only half the control size!

Black raspberries beat back cancer on various fronts: suppressing growth of cancer cells, reducing inflammation, inhibiting capillary networks that support tumors and triggering cancer cell death.

"Black raspberries are loaded with nutrients and phytochemicals that may prevent the development of cancer," said Gary Stoner, a study co-author and a professor of public health at Ohio State University.

In another study, the researchers looked at black raspberries' ability to halt the onset of cancer, as well as the fruit's ability to inhibit the progression of precancerous cells to cancer.

They conducted experiments on two groups of rats. Some of the rats from each group were injected with NMBA, a chemical carcinogen that induces esophageal cancer. NMBA is one of a group of chemicals called nitrosamines, compounds that have been linked to cancer. Nitrosamines are found in fried bacon, cured meats, tobacco products, beer and certain industrial products.

Feeding the rats 5 and 10 per cent black raspberries before and after NMBA treatment reduced the number of tumors per rat by 39 and 49 per cent, respectively, when compared to animals not fed black raspberries.

The fruit also hindered the development of esophageal cancer in individual rats fed black raspberries after NMBA treatment. By week 35 of the study, a diet of 5 per cent black raspberries had reduced the number of tumors per animal by 66.5 per cent, compared with NMBA-treated control mice fed a regular diet.

Skin, Colon, Stomach and Breast Cancer: Raspberry extract has been found to kill stomach and colon cancer cells. Researchers from Clemson University in the US said that 90 per cent of these cells were destroyed when exposed to an extract of red raspberries, a popular variety in the US.

Anti-oxidants in the fruit were also shown to kill breast cancer cells, the Daily Mail reports.

It is also found that freeze-dried berries were highly protective in the esophagus and colon. The study was funded by a grant from the Ohio Department of Agriculture and the National Cancer Institute.

Tests conducted at the Hollings Cancer Center at the Medical University of South Carolina have revealed that the ellagic acid from red raspberries is readily absorbed by the human body. This ellagic acid has been clinically shown to cause apoptosis (cell death) in cancer cells.

Ellagic acid is active in anti-mutagenesis assays, and has been shown to inhibit chemically induced cancer in the lung, liver, skin and esophagus of rodents, and TPA-induced tumor promotion in mouse skin.

Additional tests have revealed that the ellagic acid in red raspberries retains its potency after heating, freezing and concentration processing. So whether consumed fresh, in juices, fruit spreads, preserves or sorbets, the red raspberry should become a part of any healthy diet.

Additionally, research is suggesting that raspberries may have cancer protective properties. Research with animals has suggested that raspberries have the potential to inhibit cancer cell proliferation and tumor formation in various parts of the body, including the colon.

Throat Cancer: In another study scientists concluded that Raspberries reduced throat tumors by 50%.

SELECTION

As raspberries are highly perishable, they should only be purchased one or two days prior to use. Choose berries that are firm, plump and deep in color, while avoiding those that are soft, mushy or moldy.

If you are buying berries prepackaged in a container, make sure that they are not packed too tightly, since this may cause them to become crushed and damaged, and that the container has no signs of stains or moisture, indication of possible spoilage.

STORING

Raspberries are one of the most perishable fruits, so extreme care should be taken in their storage. Before storing in the refrigerator, remove any berries that are molded or spoiled so that they will not contaminate the others.

Place the unwashed berries back in their original container or spread them out on a plate lined with a paper towel, and then cover the plate with plastic wrap. Raspberries will keep fresh in the refrigerator for one or two days.

Make sure not to leave raspberries at room temperature or exposed to sunlight for too long, as this will cause them to spoil.

Raspberries freeze very well. Wash them gently using the low pressure of the sink sprayer so that they will maintain their delicate shape and then pat dry with a paper towel. Arrange them in a single layer on a flat pan or cookie sheet and place them in the freezer.

Once frozen, transfer the berries to a heavy plastic bag and return them to the freezer where they will keep for up to one year. Adding a bit of lemon juice to the raspberries will help to preserve their color.

Baby foods containing berries do not contain any anthocyanins, the water-soluble plant pigments responsible not only for the blue, purple, and red color of berries, but also for many of their health benefits.

Anthocyanins, the health benefiting nutrients, are found in fresh and frozen berries, but not in processed foods. A study published in the Journal of Agricultural and Food Chemistry found anthocyanins were almost undetectable in canned foods, bread, cereals, and baby foods containing berries.

To get the full health benefits of berries, purchase fresh or frozen berries and purée them.

SERVING

Raspberries are very delicate and should be washed very gently and then patting them dry. They should be washed right before eating.

Raspberries contain the highest amounts of ellagic acid, and it doesn't matter if the fruit is boiled, baked, canned, sugared, dehydrated, or fresh, the ellagic acid is still potent.

Mix fresh raspberries with creamy millet porridge for a sweet morning breakfast treat.

Plain yogurt mixed with raspberries, honey and freshly ground mint is delicious eaten as it is or used as a topping for waffles or pancakes.

They are also a good addition to fruit salads, bread, muffins, pancakes and waffles. You can top raspberries with whipped cream for an indulgent dessert or puree with bananas or strawberries for a morning smoothie.

Bottom Line

1. Raspberry flavored foods do not have any health benefits.
2. One cup of fresh or frozen is all you need for day.
3. Supplements of Raspberry have very doubtful anti-cancer benefits.

37A/52

STRAWBERRIES

"We do not rejoice in victories. We rejoice when a new kind of cotton is grown and when strawberries bloom in Israel" – Golda Meir

Strawberry is the most popular type of berry anywhere in the world. There are hundreds of varieties of strawberries that vary in size, color, taste and texture. But they all basically have the same characteristic heart shape and red flesh with seeds on the surface.

When farmers grow strawberries they will often cover the soil with straw to protect the fruits from rot. Maybe this is how the strawberry got its name.

Ripe, fresh strawberries are sweet and juicy. They can be eaten as they are, used to garnish a variety of sweets and desserts, or enjoyed as delicious refreshing juice and smoothies.

Strawberry is a highly nutrient dense fruit, with such huge amount of healthy substances that they are included in the list of so-called "super foods", tasty and packed full of nutrients.

Eating strawberries and drinking strawberry juice stimulate the release of serotonin, which improves mood and is responsible for a feeling of relaxation and a general sense of well-being.

It has been shown that, besides having an anti-anemic effect, folic acid found in strawberries can help improve memory, concentration and the brain's ability to process information. It is also essential for preventing brain defects in babies during pregnancy.

In terms of U.S. fruit consumption, blueberries rank only second to strawberries in popularity of berries.

Blueberries are not only popular, but also repeatedly ranked in the U.S. diet as having one of the highest anti-oxidant capacities among all fruits, vegetables, spices and seasonings. They have similar health benefits as strawberries.

RICH SOURCE

Strawberries are packed with a variety of anti-oxidant substances, including the flavonoid anthocyanidins (which gives the fruit its characteristic red color), vitamins C, E and beta-carotene.

They are also rich in dietary fiber, flavonoids, potassium, folic acid, vitamins of the B complex (B2, B5, B6), biotin, manganese, iodine and zinc; and very low in protein, sugar and calories, and virtually devoid of fat and cholesterol.

Many foods commonly consumed in the U.S. are valuable sources of anti-oxidants. But researchers have recently ranked the 50 best anti-oxidant sources among commonly eaten foods and found strawberries to be quite exceptional. In this evaluation based on common serving sizes, strawberries came out 3rd among all U.S. foods including spices, seasonings, fruits, and vegetables!

ANTI-CANCER BENEFITS

Strawberry is included in the list of top "super foods" that help lower cancer death rates. This is because of the very high content of various anti-oxidants with flavonoids that work synergistically and more powerfully against oxidation and preventing damages caused by free radicals in our body.

Strawberries have amazing combination of phytonutrients - including anthocyanins, ellagitannins, flavonols, terpenoids, and phenolic acids. It's not surprising to find increasing research interest in the anti-inflammatory properties of strawberries.

Breast, Cervical and Colon Cancer: Since chronic, excessive inflammation and chronic, excessive oxidative stress are often primary factors in the development of cancer, strawberries would definitely be expected to have cancer risk-lowering properties given their outstanding anti-oxidant and anti-inflammatory nutrient content.

Anti-cancer benefits from strawberries are best documented in the case of breast, cervical, colon, and esophageal cancer. Most of the tumor-inhibiting studies on animals have focused on the phytonutrient content of strawberries.

Among the strawberry phytonutrients, ellagic acid and ellagitannins in strawberry have emerged as anti-cancer substances of special interest. While the anti-cancer (chemo-preventive) properties of these phytonutrients have yet to be fully understood, their ability to lower risk for some forms of cancers have been accepted.

It may be related to their ability to boost the activity of anti-oxidant enzymes. Whatever the mechanism or combination of mechanisms, strawberries are likely to bring anti-cancer health benefits to your diet.

The French philosopher Bernard de Fontenelle, who died at the age of 100 (1657-1757), attributed the secret of his longevity to annual strawberry cures

Esophageal Cancer: Both Strawberry and Raspberry extracts are able to counter the growth of tumor cells, these effects being directly related to the quantity of polyphenols contained in these berries and not to their anti-oxidant potential.

In animals, studies showed that a diet containing 5% of total diet led to significant decrease in the numbers of esophageal tumors, triggered by powerful carcinogen– Source book "Foods to Fight Cancer" by Dr. Richard Beliveau.

SELECTION

Medium-sized strawberries are often more flavorful than those that are excessively large. If you are buying strawberries prepackaged in a container, make sure that they are not packed too tightly (which may cause them to become crushed and damaged) and that the container has no signs of stains or moisture, indication of possible spoilage.

As strawberries are very perishable, they should only be purchased a few days prior to use. Choose berries that are firm, plump, free of mold, and which have a shiny, deep red color and attached green caps.

Since strawberries, once picked, do not ripen further, avoid those that are dull in color or have green or yellow patches since they are likely to be sour and of inferior quality.

Strawberries are very delicate so are being sprayed with pesticides to prevent them being destroyed by pests. Choose organic if possible.

> *"The seductive Madame Tallien, an ambassador of Parisian fashion, regularly crushed 20 pounds of Strawberry in the lukewarm water for bath to preserve her skin's legendary freshness and firmness"*

If non-organic, you can soak them in clean water and a cupful of apple cider vinegar and a pinch of sea salt for 10 minutes; then rinse to remove the pesticide residues wherever possible.

STORING

The very fragile nature of strawberries means that great care should be taken in their handling and storage. Before storing in the refrigerator, remove any strawberries that are molded or damaged so that they will not contaminate others.

Place the unwashed and un-hulled berries in a sealed container to prevent unnecessary loss of humidity. Strawberries will maintain excellent nutrient content if properly stored in a refrigerator for two days. Make sure not to leave strawberries at room temperature or exposed to sunlight for too long, as this will cause them to spoil.

On average, studies show 2 days as the maximal time for strawberry storage without major loss of vitamin C and polyphenol anti-oxidants. It's not that strawberries become dangerous to eat or invaluable after 2 days. It is just that more storage time brings along with it substantially more nutrient loss.

To freeze strawberries, first gently wash them and pat them dry. You can either remove the cap and stem or leave them intact; depending upon what you will do with them once they are thawed.

Arrange them in a single layer on a flat pan or cookie sheet and place them in the freezer. Once frozen, transfer the berries to a heavy plastic bag and return them to the freezer where they will keep for up to one year.

Adding a bit of lemon juice to the berries will help to preserve their color. While strawberries can be frozen whole, cut or crushed, they will retain a higher level of their vitamin C content if left whole.

SERVING

Commercial food processing can dramatically lower the nutrient content of strawberries, especially their phytonutrient content. For example, we've seen several studies showing very little retention of certain anthocyanin phytonutrients in baby foods made from strawberries or other brightly-colored berries.

In any case, a much safer bet in terms of strawberries and nourishment is to stick with fresh berries or carefully frozen berries, and in the case of baby food or the feeding of young children, to puree the berries in a blender so that overall processing is kept to a minimum.

Despite their perishable nature, strawberries do appear to hold up well for a day or two in fruit salad if properly stored and chilled. This is good news for those of us who are pressed for time but love fresh fruit salad. And who doesn't since it's a perfect addition to any meal and makes a great snack or dessert?

Strawberries retain their maximum amount of nutrients and their maximum taste when they are enjoyed fresh and not prepared in a cooked recipe. That is because their nutrients—including vitamins, anti-oxidants, and enzymes—are unable to withstand the temperature (350°F/175°C) used in baking.

Add sliced strawberries to mixed green salad. Layer sliced strawberries, whole blueberries and plain yogurt in a wine glass to make a parfait dessert.

Blend strawberries with a little bit of orange juice and use as a refreshing coulis sauce. Add strawberries to breakfast shakes, smoothies and cereals to give them a more vibrant taste and texture.

Bottom Line

1. Heating, processing and long storage can rob strawberries of practically all the health benefits.
2. Eating fresh or using them in smoothies is the ideal way to eat.
3. Firm and pink glowing skin to long life strawberries are super stars.

CHAPTER **5**

Grains & Beans

Beans, lentils and whole grains are commonly ignored foods that have a lot of health benefits. All are bursting with nutrition and always ready to fill your life with impressive list of disease prevention powers.

Beans are one of the most common protein-rich foods for vegetarians. One cup of canned kidney beans contains about 13.4 grams of protein. They are also a great source host of cancer fighting nutrients, including fiber.

A whole grain contains all edible parts of the grain, including the bran, germ, and endosperm. Eating more whole grains is an easy way to make your diet healthier. Whole grains are packed with nutrients including protein, fiber, B vitamins, anti-oxidants, and trace minerals like iron, zinc, copper, and magnesium.

A diet rich in whole grains and beans has been shown to reduce the risk of heart disease, type 2 diabetes, obesity, and some forms of cancer. Whole-grain diets can also improve bowel health by helping to maintain regular bowel movements and promote growth of healthy bacteria in the colon.

The combination of beans and whole grains is very low in fat, have zero cholesterol and "SUPER SUPER" source of soluble and insoluble fiber, unlike meat. Combine beans or lentils with whole grain foods like whole wheat bread or brown rice, and your journey to a good health and long life starts.

Weight watcher should pay special attention; the combination has the amazing power of effortless weight-loss, and that too without dieting. If you are wondering what you should eat to have a healthy diet, the answer is surprisingly simple, beans with brown rice.

KIDNEY BEANS

True to their name, these popular beans are kidney shaped. Certain fruits and vegetables get plenty of recognition for being good sources of anti-oxidants, but beans often are unfairly left out of the picture.

Kidney beans are one of them, chockfull of anti-oxidants and other healthy nutrients. With their deep red color, cooked red kidney beans can liven up a wide range of meals including salads, soups and stews. They are very widely used in India and are known as "Rajma".

Packed with protein, soluble and insoluble fiber, folate, magnesium, potassium and a number of other health promoting nutrients, red kidney beans are a true "Super Food".

If you're wondering how to replace meat in your menus, become a fan of kidney beans. Beans provide protein comparable to that of meat or dairy foods without the high calories, cholesterol and saturated fat found in these foods.

Generally, proteins derived from animal foods (meats, poultry, seafood, dairy) are complete. However, also beans such as red kidney beans can provide a complete protein — when combined with rice or grains. As beans are a very inexpensive form of good protein, they have become popular in many cultures throughout the world.

Kidney beans were first cultivated by humans in South America over 7,000 years ago. Kidney beans, pinto beans, navy beans and black beans are known scientifically as *Phaseolus vulgaris*. They are all derived from a common bean ancestor that originated in Peru.

They spread throughout South and Central America as a result of migrating Indian traders who brought kidney beans with them from Peru. Portuguese traders introduced kidney beans into Africa and Asia.

Today, the largest commercial producers of dried common beans are India, China, Indonesia, Brazil and the United States.

Kidney beans have a higher anti-oxidant capacity than blueberries with their ORAC score of 6,552.

RICH SOURCE

Legumes — a class of vegetables that includes beans, peas and lentils — are among the most versatile and nutritious foods available in the world.

Legumes are typically low in fat, contain no cholesterol, and are high in folate, potassium, iron and magnesium. They also contain beneficial fats and soluble and insoluble fiber.

Seven countries (US, Finland, Italy, former Yugoslavia, Greece, Japan, and Netherlands), researchers have concluded in a study, that higher legume consumption could reduce the risk of heart attack by more than 80%.

They are a very good source of folate and dietary fiber. Kidney beans are a good source of protein, vitamin B1, phosphorus, iron, copper, magnesium, manganese, potassium, and vitamin K.

In addition to lowering cholesterol, kidney beans' high fiber content prevents blood sugar levels from rising too rapidly after a meal, making these beans an especially good choice for individuals with diabetes, insulin resistance or hypoglycemia or overweight problems.

Kidney beans are an excellent source of the trace mineral, molybdenum, which is responsible for detoxifying. Just one cup of cooked kidney beans supplies 177.0% of the daily value for molybdenum.

ANTI-CANCER BENEFITS

Some beans, particularly pinto and red kidney beans, are outstanding sources of anti-oxidants and should be included in your anti-cancer diet. Beans also contain fiber, and eating a high-fiber diet may also help reduce your risk of cancer, according to the American Cancer Society.

Red kidney beans are exceptionally rich in anti-oxidants type called flavonoids, particularly in proanthocyanidins. According to an analysis conducted by USDA researcher Ronald Prior, they contain more proanthocyanidins than blueberries, cranberries, and small red beans.

The Oxygen Radical Absorbance Capacity (ORAC) score for a particular food is a way to measure the effectiveness of that food as an anti-oxidant. This method of evaluating anti-oxidant capacity was developed by the National Institutes of Health, USA.

Kidney beans receive an ORAC score of 8,459 which means that they have a very high capacity to absorb free radicals and therefore may be of value in preventing certain diseases.

The June 21, 2004, edition of the "Los Angeles Times" described the results of research on the anti-oxidant content of more than 100 different foods including fruits, vegetables, nuts, spices, breads, cereals and beans.

The research was carried out by Dr. Ronald L. Prior and his colleagues at the U.S. Department of Agriculture's Arkansas Children's Nutrition Center in Little Rock and published in the "Journal of Agricultural and Food Chemistry."

The results indicated that small red beans ranked first, containing the highest concentration of anti-oxidants per serving of all the foods tested. The method used prior to assay anti-oxidant capacity placed red kidney beans third and pinto beans fourth in anti-oxidant concentration. It is noteworthy that three of the top 10 anti-oxidant foods were beans.

Mammary Cancer: To address whether dry bean consumption is associated with a reduction in mammary cancer, scientists at Colorado State University studied the anti-cancer activity of six market classes of beans including; small red, great northern, navy, black, dark red and white kidney bean in the diet of laboratory animals. They also evaluated whether the level of anti-oxidants or seed coat pigments in the bean were related to mammary cancer.

Cooked dry bean powder from the six market classes and a control group without beans in the diet were fed to laboratory rats in a standard preclinical model for breast cancer. The dry bean powders were also evaluated for anti-oxidant capacity, phenolic and flavonoid content; all factors thought to be associated with anti-cancer activity.

Chemical analysis of the beans revealed that total phenolic and flavonoid content varied widely among market classes and the differences were strongly associated with seed coat color, where colored beans had ten times or greater phenolic and flavonoid content compared to white beans.

Anti-oxidant capacity of the beans also varied widely among dry bean market classes and was highly related to seed coat color, where colored beans had approximately two to three times greater anti-oxidant capacity than white beans.

Dry bean consumption from every market class reduced cancer incidence (number of animals with one tumor) and tumor number per animal compared to the control group. Cancer incidence was reduced from 95% in the control group to 67% in animals fed beans.

The average number of malignant tumors was also reduced from 3.2 in the control group to 1.4 tumors per animal in the group fed beans.

Research is ongoing at Colorado State University to investigate the mechanisms and molecules that contribute to the anti-cancer properties of dry beans. Clinical trials are also underway to determine if beans in the diet of humans are associated with biomarkers for cancer incidence.

Breast Cancer: The study was funded by a grant from the Beans for Health Alliance, and the Colorado Agricultural Experiment Station with assistance from Archer Daniels Midland Co. and Bush Brothers Inc.

Research carried out by the U.S. Department of Agriculture states that dark colored beans offer an extremely high grade of anti-oxidant protection.

Kidneys beans check the development of breast cancer. In an analysis of data collected in 1991 and 1995, researchers identified a substantially reduced frequency and occurrence of breast cancer in girls who had a larger intake of kidney beans.

The beans exerted maximum protection, greater than that offered by apples, broccoli and blueberries. Eating kidney beans and lentils two times or more per week was connected with a 24 % decreased danger of developing breast cancer.

SELECTION

Dried kidney beans are generally available in prepackaged containers as well as bulk bins. Whether purchasing kidney beans in bulk or in a packaged container, make sure there is no evidence of moisture or insect damage and that the beans are whole and not cracked.

Canned kidney beans can be found in most markets. Unlike canned vegetables, which have lost much of their nutritional value, there is little difference in the nutritional value of canned kidney beans and those you cook yourself.

Canning lowers vegetables' nutritional value since they are best lightly cooked for a short period of time, while their canning process requires a long cooking time at high temperatures. On the other hand, beans require a long time to cook whether they are canned or you cook them yourself.

Therefore, if enjoying canned beans is more convenient for you, by all means go ahead and enjoy them. We would suggest look for those that do not contain extra salt or additives.

If you're wondering how to replace meat in your menus, become a fan of kidney beans. Beans provide protein comparable to that of meat or dairy foods without the high calories, cholesterol and saturated fat found in these foods. On the other hand beans lower cholesterol

STORING

Store dried kidney beans in an airtight container in a cool, dry and dark place where they will keep for up to 12 months.

Cooked kidney beans will keep fresh in the refrigerator for about three days if placed in a covered container.

SERVING

There is nothing wrong with pre-cooked kidney beans in a can. First rinse them under cold water, and then blanch them (1 min. in boiling water) and drain them. They are just like the dry ones, without the work and ready to be transformed into whatever wonderful dish you want. Please, don't shoot the cook!

The long process of cooking the kidney beans from the dried stage is: Spread them out on a light colored plate or cooking surface to check for and remove stones and damaged beans. After this process, place the beans in a strainer and rinse them thoroughly under cool running water.

To shorten their cooking time and make them easier to digest, kidney beans should be presoaked (presoaking has been found to reduce the raffinose-type oligosaccharides, sugars associated with causing flatulence.) There are two basic methods for presoaking. For each, start by placing the beans in a saucepan with two to three cups of water per cup of beans.

The first method is to boil the beans for two minutes, take pan off the heat, cover and allow to stand for two hours. The alternative method is to simply soak the beans in water for eight hours or overnight, placing the pan in the refrigerator, so the beans will not ferment.

Before cooking the beans, regardless of pre-soaking method, drain the soaking liquid and rinse the beans with clean water.

The best way to cook the soaked beans is to cook them in a pressure cooker. The liquid should be about one to two inches above the top of the beans. Kidney beans generally will be cooked in a pressure cooker in about half an hour.

Regardless of cooking method, do not add any seasonings that are salty or acidic until after the beans have been cooked. Adding them earlier will make the beans tough and greatly increase the cooking time.

Quick Serving Ideas: Combine cooked kidney beans with black beans and white beans to make a colorful three bean salad. Mix with tomatoes and scallions and dress with olive oil, lemon juice, salt and black pepper.

In a food processor or blender, combine cooked kidney beans with garlic, cumin and chili peppers for a delicious spread that can be used as a crudité dip or sandwich filling.

Make a pot of chili, the hearty Mexican soup that traditionally features kidney beans. Make tacos with a vegetarian twist by using kidney beans in place of ground meat.

Kidney beans and brown rice are made for each other. Add caned or boiled beans, in a puree made of tomatoes, ginger, and garlic. You can add your roasted cumin seeds for enhancing the flavor. Heat them all together for 10 minutes. Serve them with boiled brown rice. You will be amazed at the taste and pairing of the two.

Bottom Line

1. Kidney beans can fulfil our complete protein requirements, by combining them with brown rice or whole wheat bread or Roti.
2. Wash the beans after soaking overnight in tap water; this will considerably decrease the stomach bloating and formation of intestinal gas after having a meal.
3. Control heart disease to cancer, diabetes to cholesterol by playing the Bean of Kidney Beans.

39/52

CHICKPEAS

"Chickpeas are beans with complexion problem !" –Jonny Bowden, author

Chickpeas are also known as Garbanzos, Bengal grams, and Egyptian peas. They have a delicious nutlike taste and buttery texture.

A very versatile legume, they are integral part of ingredients in many Middle Eastern and Indian dishes, such as hummus, falafels and curries.

Many public health organizations—including the American Diabetes Association, the American Heart Association, and the American Cancer Society—recommend legumes as a key food group for preventing disease and optimizing health.

Chickpeas are concentrated source of protein that can be enjoyed year-round and are available either dried or canned.

There are two basic types of garbanzo beans. Most commonly seen at salad bars and in canned products are the "kabuli-type." These beans are cream-colored or sometimes whitish in color, fairly uniform and rounded in shape, and about twice as large as the second "desi-type."

In addition to being much smaller, desi-type beans are darker (light tan to black in color) and more irregular in shape. From a botanical standpoint, the desi-type beans also have a thicker seed coat also called protective outermost layer of the bean.

While "kabuli-type" beans are the ones we are accustomed to finding in U.S., they actually represent only 10-20% of the garbanzo beans consumed worldwide, where the vast majority of garbanzos are desi-type beans.

There are great health benefits from both types of garbanzos. However, in the case of some nutrients – including some anti-oxidants – desi-type beans provide more concentrated amounts since these nutrients are found in the seed coat and this seed coat is thicker in desi-type beans.

Legumes or beans are a miracle food. They lower cholesterol, regulate blood sugar and insulin production, promote digestive health, and protect against cancer.

If you think of fiber, protein, and anti-oxidants and immediately think whole grains, meat, and fruit, thinks again -- beans offer all three in a single package.

Chickpeas beans originated in the Middle East, the region of the world whose varied food cultures still heavily rely upon this high protein legume. Their cultivation subsequently spread to India and Ethiopia.

Unlike canned vegetables, which have lost much of their nutritional value, there is little difference in the nutritional value between canned chickpeas and those you cook yourself.

Today, the main commercial producers of chickpeas are India, Pakistan, Turkey, Ethiopia and Mexico.

RICH SOURCE

In fact, just one cup of chickpeas can provide you with nearly 85% of the Daily Value (DV) for this key anti-oxidant. An increasing number of animal and human studies clearly show the ability of chickpeas to reduce our risk of heart disease.

They are also a very good source of heart-healthy folate and a good source of muscle-building protein, digestive-supportive dietary fiber, antioxidant-promoting copper, and energy-producing phosphorus and iron.

The fiber in chickpeas beans is mostly insoluble, and it has been shown to undergo conversion into short chain fatty acids (SCFAs) in the large intestine and provide support for our digestive tract.

Both the seed coat (outer layer) and cotyledon (large main inner portion) of chickpeas contain a wealth of phytonutrients.

The outer seed coat is concentrated in flavonoids, including quercetin, kaempferol, and myricetin. The interior of the beans is typically rich in ferulic acid, chlorogenic acid, caffeic acid, and vanillic acid.

All of these phytonutrients function as anti-oxidants, and many also function as anti-inflammatory nutrients. Chickpeas beans are an excellent source of detoxifying molybdenum and energy-producing manganese.

The 2005 Dietary Guidelines for Americans developed by the U.S. Department of Health and Human Services (USDHHS) and the U.S. Department of Agriculture (USDA) recommends 3 cups of legumes per week.

ANTI-CANCER BENEFITS

Many of our body systems are susceptible to oxidative stress and damage from reactive oxygen molecules. Plentiful amounts of anti-oxidant nutrients are critical for the support of these body systems, and chickpeas are a remarkable food in terms of their anti-oxidant composition.

Depending on the type of bean and color/thickness of the outer layer, chickpeas can also contain significant amounts of the anti-oxidant anthocyanins – delphinidin, cyanidin, and petunidin.

Colon Cancer: Chickpeas is a food you definitely want to keep on your "digestive support" list – especially if you are focusing on the colon. Between 65-75% of the fiber found in them is insoluble fiber, and this type of fiber remains undigested all the way down to the final segment of your large intestine – colon.

Recent studies have shown that chickpeas fiber can be metabolized by bacteria in the colon to produce relatively large amounts of short chain fatty acids (SCFAs), including acetic, propionic, and butyric acid. These SCFAs provide fuel to the cells that line your intestinal wall.

By supporting the energy needs of our intestinal cells, the SCFAs made from chickpeas fibers can help lower your risk of colon problems, including your risk of colon cancer.

Breast Cancer: Cancer rates in India are lower than those seen in Western countries. Large epidemiological studies have identified a possible association between increased dietary fiber and a decreased risk for cancers of the colon and breast.

The Indian diet, which generally includes adequate levels of vegetables, fruits, fiber-rich grains and beans, may be the reason for the low risk for these cancers.

An assortment of phytochemicals found in beans has been shown to protect cells from cancerous activity by inhibiting cancer cells from reproducing, slowing tumor growth.

Researchers at the Harvard School of Public Health reported that women who consumed beans at least twice a week were 24 per cent less likely to develop breast cancer.

Multiple studies have tied beans to a reduced risk of heart disease, type 2 diabetes, high blood pressure, and breast and colon cancers.

SELECTION

You will find many recipes containing beans giving you the choice between using home cooked beans and canned beans. If you are in a hurry canned beans can be a healthy option.

Unlike canned vegetables, which have lost much of their nutritional value, there is little difference in the nutritional value between canned chickpeas and those you cook yourself.

Select the canned chickpeas; look for those that do not contain extra salt or additives. Once you remove the beans from the can, place them in a strainer and rinse them thoroughly for one minute.

Enjoy a wide variety of beans, making selections for each dish based on color, texture and flavor. Black beans are earthy and flavorful, kidney beans are mild and absorb flavor from seasonings, and garbanzo beans add a nutty taste.

Most garbanzo or chickpeas found in the grocery (especially canned garbanzos) are cream-colored and relatively round. This type of chickpeas is called the "kabuli-type." Worldwide, there's a far more common type of garbanzo bean called the "desi-type."

Darker-colored "desi-type" garbanzo beans have greater concentrations of anti-oxidants than the larger and more regularly shaped cream-colored garbanzos.

But if you have previously shied away from darker-colored or irregularly-shaped garbanzo beans, we want to encourage you to reconsider and to enjoy all types of garbanzo beans, including the darker-colored and irregularly-shaped ones.

Dried garbanzos are generally available in prepackaged containers as well as bulk bins. Whether purchasing garbanzo beans in bulk or in a packaged container, make sure that there is no evidence of moisture or insect damage and that they are whole and not cracked.

STORING

Store dried chickpeas in an airtight container in a cool, dry and dark place where they will keep for up to 12 months. If you purchase chickpeas beans at different times, store them separately since they may feature varying stages of dryness and therefore will require different cooking times.

Cooked chickpeas will keep fresh in the refrigerator for about three days if placed in a covered container.

SERVING

Before washing chickpeas, you should spread them out on a light colored plate or cooking surface to check for, and remove, small stones, debris or damaged beans. After this process, place them in a strainer, and rinse them thoroughly under cool running water.

To shorten their cooking time and make them easier to digest, chickpeas should be presoaked. There are two basic methods for presoaking. For each you should start by placing the beans in a saucepan and adding two to three cups of water per cup of beans.

The first method is to boil the beans for two minutes, take pan off the heat, cover and allow it to stand for two hours. The alternative method is to simply soak them in water overnight or minimum of 4 hrs.

Several potentially desirable chemical changes can take place during the soaking period. There is a reduction in the beans' raffinose-type oligosaccharides, and this reduction may result in fewer problems with flatulence when the beans are eventually consumed.

Adding a pinch of Hing (asafoetida) or a teaspoon of fresh ginger paste can further reduce the flatulency experienced by some people after eating beans.

Finally, presoaking of the beans will reduce the time required for cooking. Before cooking, regardless of method, skim off any skins that floated to the surface, drain the soaking liquid, and then rinse them with clean water.

To cook the chickpeas, you can either cook them on the gas top or use a pressure cooker. For the gas top method, add three cups of fresh water or broth for each cup of dried beans.

The liquid should be about one to two inches above the top of the legumes. Bring them to a boil, and then reduce the heat to simmer, partially covering the pot. If any foam develops, skim it off during the simmering process.

Chickpeas generally take about one to one and a half hours to become tender using this method. You can alternatively pressure cook them in half an hour.

Quick Serving Ideas: Puree chickpeas, olive oil, fresh garlic, tahini (roasted sesame seeds) and lemon juice to make a quick and easy hummus spread.

Sprinkle chickpeas with your favorite spices and herbs and eat as a snack. Add chickpeas to your green salads.

Simmer cooked chickpeas in a sauce of tomato paste, curry spices and chopped walnuts and serve this Dahl-type dish with brown rice. Adding chickpeas to your vegetable soup will enhance its taste, texture and nutritional content.

Enjoy a wide variety of beans, making selections for each dish based on color, texture and flavor. Black beans are earthy and flavorful, kidney beans are mild and absorb flavor from seasonings, and chickpeas add a nutty taste.

Bottom Line

1. Bengal gram or "Desi-Chickpeas" have much more cancer fighting nutrients as compared to white Kabuli types.
2. Canned chickpeas are nearly as good as the home presoaked and boiled ones. Target eating at least twice a week.
3. Chickpeas and beans can be called vegetarian meat, without the ill effects of high fat, cholesterol and zero fiber, which is generally part of all meats.

BROWN RICE

"Almost all rice are born brown, than processed to death, for converting them to white variety"

Rice is one of the most important foods in the world, supplying more than half of the daily calories to half of the world's population. For centuries, brown rice has been a staple grain in the daily diets of millions of people.

In Asian countries, such as Thailand, rice is so highly valued that the translation of the word "to eat" literally means "to eat rice." Today, it is widely valued as a healthy food, and for good reason: In addition to its utility as a culinary dish, there are a number of nutritional benefits that this grain provides.

Brown rice is a type of whole, natural grain that has a mild nutty flavor and is characteristically brown in color. It is also called "hulled rice," brown rice is produced by removing the hull of each grain of rice, retaining its outer, brown-colored bran layer.

The scientific name for rice is *Oryza sativa*. There are over 8,000 varieties of rice in the world. Oftentimes, rice is categorized by its size as being short grain, medium grain or long grain.

Another way that rice is classified is according to the degree of milling that it undergoes. This is what makes a brown rice different than white rice. Brown rice is the least milled or processed rice.

Brown rice, often referred to as whole rice or cargo rice, is the whole grain with only its inedible outer hull removed. Brown rice still retains its nutrient-rich bran and germ.

White rice, on the other hand, is both milled and polished, which removes the bran and germ along with all the nutrients that reside within these important layers.

Rice was believed to have been first cultivated in China around 6,000 years ago,

Short grain, which has the highest starch content, makes the stickiest rice, while long grain is lighter and tends to remain separate when cooked. The qualities of medium grain fall between the other two types.

but recent archaeological discoveries have found primitive rice seeds and ancient farm tools dating back about 9,000 years.

For the majority of its long history, rice was a staple only in Asia. Alexander the Great brought it to India. Rice was introduced into South America in the 17th century by the Spanish during their colonization of this continent.

Rice cultivation is well-suited to countries and regions with low labor costs and high rainfall, as it is labor-intensive to cultivate and requires ample water.

The 92% of the world's rice is grown in Asia, where it plays an incredibly important role in their food culture. Thailand, Vietnam and China are the three largest exporters of rice.

RICH SOURCE

Brown rice is a good source of proteins, selenium, phosphorus, magnesium, manganese, iron and dietary fiber. It contains some amounts of calcium and B vitamins niacin, thiamine and riboflavin.

Brown rice also contains vitamin E. Most of the nutrients and minerals in rice are concentrated in the outer brown layers known as husk and germs.

Powerful anti-oxidant actions of selenium is helpful in the prevention not only of cancer, but also of heart disease, and for decreasing the symptoms of asthma and the pain and inflammation of rheumatoid arthritis.

Just one cup of brown rice will provide you with 88% of the daily value for manganese. This trace mineral helps produce energy and helps in the production of cholesterol, which is used by the body to produce sex hormones.

Manganese is also a critical component of a very important anti-oxidant enzyme called superoxide dismutase. Superoxide dismutase (SOD) provides protection against damage from the free radicals produced during energy production.

The complete milling and polishing that converts brown rice into white rice destroys 67% of vitamin B3, 80% of vitamin B1, 90% of vitamin B6, half of the manganese, half of the phosphorus, 60% of the iron, and all of the dietary fiber and essential fatty acids.

Fully milled and polished white rice is so nutritionally poor that it is artificially required to be "enriched" with vitamins B1, B3 and iron, as per law in some countries.

Parboiled rice, also known as converted rice, is treated at the harvesting stage while still in the hulls. It is soaked and steamed, before being dried. Nutritionally Parboiled rice is in between brown and white polished rice.

ANTI-CANCER BENEFITS

Research reported at the American Institute for Cancer Research (AICR) International Conference on Food, Nutrition and Cancer, by Rui Hai Liu, M.D., Ph.D., and his colleagues at Cornell University clearly indicates that:

"Whole grains, such as rice, contain many powerful phytonutrients whose activity has gone unrecognized because research methods have overlooked them".

Phenolics are powerful anti-oxidants that work in multiple ways to prevent diseases. Included in this broad category are such compounds as quercetin, curcumin, ellagic acid, and catechins.

Despite the differences in fruits', vegetables' and whole grains' content of "free" and "bound" phenolics, the total anti-oxidant activity in all three types of whole foods is similar, according to Dr. Liu's research.

Dr. Liu's findings may help explain why studies have shown that populations eating diets high in fiber-rich whole grains consistently have lower risk for colon cancer, yet short-term clinical trials that have focused on fiber alone in lowering colon cancer risk, by giving subjects isolated fiber supplements, yield inconsistent results.

As far as whole grains are concerned, Dr. Liu believes that the key to their powerful cancer-fighting potential is precisely their wholeness. A grain of whole wheat consists of three parts—its endosperm (starch), bran and germ. When wheat—or any whole grain—is refined, its bran and germ are removed.

Although these two parts make up only 15-17% of the grain's weight, they contain 83% of its phenolics. Dr. Liu says his recent findings on the anti-oxidant content of whole grains reinforce the message that a variety of whole foods should be eaten for good health.

"Different plant foods have different phytochemicals, "he said. "These substances go to different organs, tissues and cells, where they perform different functions. What your body needs to ward off disease is this synergistic effect—this teamwork—that is produced by eating a wide variety of plant foods, including whole grains."

Colon Cancer: For people worried about colon cancer risk, brown rice packs a double punch by being a concentrated source of the fiber needed to minimize the amount of time cancer-causing substances spend in contact with colon cells, and being a very good source of selenium.

Fiber in brown rice helps to protect you against colon cancer since fiber binds to cancer-causing chemicals, keeping them away from the cells lining the colon, plus it can help normalize bowel function, reducing constipation.

Trace mineral selenium has been shown to substantially reduce the risk of colon cancer. Accumulated evidence from prospective studies, intervention trials and studies on animal models of cancer have suggested a strong inverse correlation between selenium intake and cancer incidence.

Several mechanisms have been suggested to explain the cancer-preventive activities of selenium- from DNA repair to synthesis in damaged cells, to stop the multiplications of the cancer cells.

Selenium plays a critical role in cancer prevention as a cofactor of glutathione peroxidase, selenium also works with vitamin E in numerous other vital anti-oxidant systems throughout the body.

Long-grain brown basmati rice has the most amylose and least amylopectin, so it tends to be the fluffiest and least sticky. It also has a lower Glycemic Index number (rate at which the sugar is released in the body) and thus healthier, and even suitable for people with diabetes.

Breast Cancer: When researchers looked at how much fiber 35,972 participants in the UK Women's Cohort Study ate, they found a diet rich in fiber from whole grains, such as brown rice, and fruit offered significant protection against breast cancer for pre-menopausal women.

Pre-menopausal women eating the most fiber (>30 grams daily) more than halved their risk of developing breast cancer, enjoying a 52% lower risk of breast cancer compared to women whose diets supplied the least fiber (<20 grams/day).

Fiber supplied by whole grains offered the most protection. Pre-menopausal women eating the most whole grain fiber (at least 13 g/day) had a 41% reduced risk of breast cancer, compared to those with the lowest whole grain fiber intake (4 g or less per day).

Fiber from fruit was also protective. Pre-menopausal women whose diets supplied the most fiber from fruit (at least 6 g/day) had a 29% reduced risk of breast cancer, compared to those with the lowest fruit fiber intake (2 g or less per day).

So whole fruit with whole wheat bread or brown rice will save you from breast cancer, and fruit juice with white bread, will kill you.

Prostate Cancer: Excluding skin cancer, prostate is the leading form of cancer that afflicts men, and more than 35,000 men die annually as a direct result of it, the Ohio State University Medical Center, USA, reports.

As with all types of cancer, a number of lifestyle interventions can be taken to reduce your risk. Consuming whole grain foods -- including whole grain brown rice -- can keep prostate cancer at bay.

SELECTION

There are two types of starch in rice: amylose and amylopectin. Amylose is a long, straight starch molecule that does not gelatinize during cooking, so rice which contains more of this starch tends to cook fluffy, with separate grains.

Long-grain brown basmati rice has the most amylose and least amylopectin, so it tends to be the fluffiest and least sticky. It also has a lower Glycemic Index number (rate at which the sugar is released in the body) and thus healthier, and even suitable for people with diabetes.

Rice is available prepackaged as well as in bulk containers. If purchasing brown rice in a packaged container, check to see if there is a "use-by" date on the package since brown rice, owing to its natural oils, has the potential to become rancid if kept too long.

So for best heath benefits and great flavor choose long-grain brown basmati rice. While purchasing rice in bulk or in a packaged container, make sure that there is no evidence of moisture.

STORING

Since brown rice has an oil-rich germ, it is more susceptible to becoming rancid than white rice and therefore should be stored in the refrigerator. Stored in an airtight container, brown rice will keep fresh for about six months.

The storage of cooked rice is controversial. We believe it's best to cook only the amount of rice you can consume during the day it is cooked, or at most, the following day. Be sure to keep your cooked rice in a tightly sealed container when stored in your refrigerator.

SERVING

Brown rice has an aromatic nutlike fragrance, delicate flavor and light texture. The manner in which brown rice is prepared affects the nutritional value of the cooked dish, according to the book "Nutritional Properties of Rice."

A large proportion of the B vitamin content in brown rice, including thiamine, niacin and riboflavin, is discarded in recipes that require thorough pre-rinsing before cooking.

Cooking the brown rice in excess water that is then discarded also depletes the content of these vital nutrients. Using clean, well-packaged rice forgoes the need to pre-rinse the rice.

If you do not have pre-rinse and cleaned brown rice, then first remove any dirt or debris that you may find by hand, after that you can gently rinse the rice in running cold water.

Brown rice takes longer to cook than white rice because the outer layer which is full of nutrient is harder. A very simple method to soften this layer is to soak the rice for a minimum period of 4 hours before cooking. You can even leave brown rice overnight in the cold water for soaking.

Brown rice is best cooked in more liquid. You can try cooking brown rice by adding one part presoaked rice with two parts cold water. When the rice starts boiling reduce the heat and simmer for 35-40 minutes or until rice is tender when you bite into it.

Fluffing occasionally with a fork will keep the grains separate. You can also pressure cook the rice and may need to keep the cooker on the gas for about 5-7 minutes, after the whistle.

These days many rice cookers are coming with brown rice options. Then you do not have to do much, put the cleaned brown rice, water and press the brown rice option and watch your favorite TV show. Generally it would take between one hour and one and a half hours for the brown rice to be fully cooked. Even husbands can make great brown rice, by this method.

Whatever method you choose kindly Ladies do not throw out the rice water, since all the nutrients and health benefits will also be gone.

Quick Serving Ideas:

Heat up cooked rice with milk or soymilk. Add in cinnamon, nutmeg, raisins and honey for a delicious rice pudding.

Make homemade vegetable sushi rolls by wrapping brown rice and your favorite vegetables in sheets of well-moistened nori.

Use rice leftovers for cold rice salads that are great for on-the-go lunches. Be creative and add chicken or tofu plus your favorite vegetables, nuts, herbs and spices.

For a simple yet delicious lunch or dinner entrée, serve beans and rice accompanied by the vegetables of your choice.

Bottom Line

1. Long-grain brown basmati rice has the least starch, maximum nutrients and hence more health benefits.
2. Draining rice is like throwing the child with the bath water –don't do it!
3. You can add tones of vegetables, nuts, seeds, broths and spices to make the combination exceptionally healthy and potent cancer fighter.

WHOLE WHEAT

"The whiter the bread the sooner you are dead"

- Book Healthy at 100 by John Robbins

Wheat is one of the first cereals known to have been domesticated, a type of grass grown all over the world, known for its highly nutritious and useful grain. It is one of the top three most produced crops in the world, along with corn and rice.

As rice has been the dietary staple of Asia, wheat has served this role for many of other regions of the world. It is estimated that approximately one-third of the world's people depend upon wheat for their nourishment.

Grains, especially whole grains, are an essential part of a healthy diet. All types of grains are good sources of complex carbohydrates and some key vitamins and minerals. They have been linked to lower the risk of heart disease, diabetes, certain cancers and other health problems.

Therefore, to receive benefit from the wholesomeness of wheat it is important to choose wheat products made from whole wheat flour rather than those that are refined and stripped of their natural goodness.

Even the 2010 Dietary Guidelines for Americans recommends that at least half of all the grains you eat should be whole grains. In ancient times, wheat grains were eaten raw, later they were fried or boiled in water to make flat cakes.

Wheat is an ancient grain. Thought to have originated in southwestern Asia, it has been consumed as a food for more than 12,000 years. This exceptionally nutritious grain is still considered to be sacred in some areas of China and India.

Wheat was not native to the Western Hemisphere and was only introduced here in the late 15th century when Columbus came to the New World.

Today, the largest commercial producers of wheat include the Russian Federation, the United States, China, India, France and Canada.

Wheat is a major ingredient in wide range of foods including bread, nan, rotis, porridge, crackers, biscuits, muesli, pancakes, pies, pastries, cakes, cookies, muffins, rolls, doughnuts.

RICH SOURCE

Wheat is inexpensive and easy to prepare raw or cooked food.

100 grams (3/4 cup) of whole wheat contain about 12.6 grams of protein, 1.5 grams of total fat, 71 grams of carbohydrate, 12.2 grams of dietary fiber (50% of the daily requirement) and 3.2 mg of iron (17% of the daily requirement).

Whole wheat is a very good source of minerals viz. manganese, selenium, potassium, and magnesium along with host of other health promoting nutrients.

Whole grains: These are unrefined grains that haven't had their bran and germ removed by milling. Whole wheat flour thus made is healthiest and chockfull of nutrients.

Refined grains: Refined grains are milled, a process that strips out both the bran and germ to give them a finer texture and extend their shelf life. The flour thus obtained is bleached to make it whiter and flavorful.

In the process of extraction, over half of vitamins B1, B2, B3, E, folic acid, calcium, phosphorus, zinc, copper, iron, and fiber are lost, making it the poorest option, deprived of all the health benefits. The white refined flour is as bad as white sugar. Most of the standard breads, cereals, crackers, desserts and pastries are made with this white flour.

Enriched grains: Enriched means that some of the nutrients lost during processing and stripping are added back. Due to very poor nutritional value, some countries have enacted laws to enrich the white flour. Enriched flour is a poor cousin of wholesome whole wheat flour.

ANTI-CANCER BENEFITS

Whole wheat supplies multiple anti-cancer anti-oxidants including IP-6, orthophenols, phenolics, flavonoids, abscisic acid, ferulic acid, vanillic acid, carotenoids-lutein, zeaxanthin, beta-cryptoxanthin, selenium, zinc, and vitamin E.

Breast Cancer: When researchers looked at how much fiber 35,972 participants in the UK Women's Cohort Study ate, they found a diet rich in fiber from whole grains, such as whole wheat, and fruit offered significant protection against breast cancer for pre-menopausal women.

Pre-menopausal women eating the most fiber (>30 grams daily) more than halved their risk of developing breast cancer, enjoying a 52% lower risk of breast cancer compared to women whose diets supplied the least fiber (<20 grams/day).

Fiber supplied by whole grains offered the most protection. Pre-menopausal women eating the most whole grain fiber (at least 13 g/day) had a 41% reduced risk of breast cancer, compared to those with the lowest whole grain fiber intake (4 g or less per day).

In addition, in the subgroup of women who had ever used hormone replacement, those consuming the most fiber, especially cereal fiber, had a 50% reduction in their risk of breast cancer compared to those consuming the least.

Colon Cancer: Research reported at U.S., International Conference on Food, Nutrition and Cancer, by Rui Hai Liu, M.D., Ph.D. and team, of Cornell University, shows that whole grains, such as whole wheat, contain many powerful phytonutrients whose activity has gone unrecognized because research methods have overlooked them.

Despite the fact that for years researchers have been measuring the anti-oxidant power of a wide array of phytonutrients, they have typically measured only the "free" forms of these substances, which dissolve quickly and are immediately absorbed into the bloodstream.

They have not looked at the "bound" forms, which are attached to the walls of plant cells and must be released by intestinal bacteria during digestion before they can be absorbed.

When Dr. Liu and his colleagues measured the relative amounts of phenolics, and whether they were present in bound or free form, in common fruits and vegetables like apples, red grapes, broccoli and spinach, they found that phenolics in the "free" form averaged 76% of the total number of phenolics in these foods. In whole grains, however, "free" phenolics accounted for less than 1% of the total, while the remaining 99% were in "bound" form.

Despite the differences in fruits', vegetables' and whole grains' content of "free" and "bound" phenolics, the total anti-oxidant activity in all three types of whole foods is similar, according to Dr. Liu's research.

The health benefits of wheat depend entirely on the form in which you eat it. These benefits will be few if you select wheat that has been processed, extracted, bleached, grounded very fine and converted to white flour.

Dr. Liu's findings may help explain why studies have shown that populations eating diets high in fiber-rich whole grains consistently have lower risk for colon cancer, yet short-term clinical trials that have focused only on fiber supplements alone in lowering colon cancer risk, have shown inconsistent results.

The explanation is most likely that these studies have not taken into account the interactive effects of all the nutrients in whole grains--not just their fiber, but also their many phytonutrients.

As far as whole grains are concerned, Dr. Liu believes that the key to their powerful cancer-fighting potential is precisely their wholeness. A grain of whole wheat consists of three parts--its endosperm (starch), bran and germ.

When wheat--or any whole grain--is refined, its bran and germs are removed. Although these two parts make up only 15-17% of the grain's weight, they contain 83% of its phenolics.

Dr. Liu says his recent findings on the anti-oxidant content of whole grains reinforce the message that a variety of foods should be eaten for good health. "Different plant foods have different phytochemicals," he said.

"These substances go to different organs, tissues and cells, where they perform different functions. What your body needs to ward off disease is this synergistic effect--this teamwork–that is produced by eating a wide variety of plant foods, including whole grains."

Stomach, Colon, Breast and Prostate Cancer: Whole grains can protect against stomach and colon cancer as well as hormone-dependent cancers including breast and prostate. Evidence shows that they do this by way of four mechanisms.

According to Cornell University, the cancer protection of whole grains comes from their richness in anti-oxidants and plant estrogens.

Whole grains have the ability to mediate glucose response and create short chain fatty acids that lower the pH of the colon. The last two involve making the body less acidic. Cancer needs an acidic environment to flourish.

Mammary Cancers: Numerous studies done on animals, mice and rats in particular, had favorable results. In one study, mammary tumors decreased 27 per cent.

The animals fed diets that combined high soluble and insoluble fibers. Fiber has the capability of preventing tumor formation in humans making it a positive step for women.

Regardless of whether or not eating whole grains prevents cancer, you should integrate them into your diet because of their overall nutritive value. Eat whole wheat or whole grain bread, pasta, cereals, flour and switch to brown rice.

Increase your intake of fruits, vegetables and beans. Their vitamins, minerals, fiber and disease-fighting anti-oxidants will strengthen your immune system, your defense against cancer and other illnesses.

SELECTION

Whole wheat and whole wheat flour. Nothing less than this will work. Don't get enticed by beautiful packaging, big brand names, sale offers, words like enriched, fortified, easy to digest, super fine, made from whole wheat flour ... the list goes on.

Even words like multigrain tell you nothing about whether the grains are whole or refined. Even if you're getting 38 different grains, that isn't much good if they are all refined. Do not get faked out.

If the label doesn't say "100 per cent whole grain," or "100 per cent whole wheat" do not buy it. It is only when you select 100% whole wheat products, the bran and the germ of the wheat will remain in your meals, and the health benefits will be impressive!

STORING

Whole wheat should be stored in an airtight container in a cool, dry and dark place. The optimal way to store wheat products such as flour, bulgur, bran and germ is in an airtight container in the refrigerator as the cooler temperature will help to prevent them from becoming rancid.

SERVING

Make or buy whole wheat rotis, burritos, tortillas, chips etc
Use whole wheat bread when you make sandwiches, look for fiber content per slice–it should be more than 2 gm. Some of the whole wheat cereals have got 10 gm. fiber per serving.

Use sprouted wheat in vegetable and grain salads.

Make individual pizzas using whole wheat pita breads as the crust.

Whole wheat pasta has become very popular and is available in many different types (e.g., spaghetti, spirals, penne, etc.) to suit your recipe needs.

Bottom Line

1. Whole wheat breads or rotis can supply all the 26gm fiber recommended for the day.
2. From weight loss to cancer control whole wheat or whole grains can only give you wholesome gains, day after day.
3. All white things are not good, and so is the case with white flour.

CORN

A light wind swept over the corn, and all nature laughed in the sunshine

- Anne Bronte

What food is more synonymous with summer than the freshly picked corn on the cob? Corn is also known by the name of 'Maize' in many countries. In India, it is known as 'Bhutta' in Hindi.

Sweet corn has become a staple food and sweet corn soup is also very popular the world over. Native American tribes cultivate sweet corn and it contains plenty of nutrition and healthy calories.

Corn has gathered a diverse reputation in the U.S. For some people, corn is a "staple" food that provides the foundation for tortillas, burritos, or polenta. For others, corn is a "snack" food that comes in the form of popcorn, morning cereals and corn chips.

For still others, corn is a "special summertime food" that is essential at barbecues and cookouts. But regardless of its reputation, corn is seldom considered in the U.S. as a unique source of health benefits. Yet that's exactly what research results are telling us about this amazing grain.

Although corn is now available in markets year-round, it is the locally grown varieties that you can purchase during the summer months that not only taste the best but are usually the least expensive.

Although we often associate corn with the color yellow, it actually comes in host of different varieties featuring an array of different colors, including red, pink, black, purple, and blue.

Health benefits of corn include controlling diabetes, prevention of heart ailments, lowering hypertension, prevention of neural-tube defects at birth and stopping many types of cancers.

Perhaps no other food has been more closely identified with the Americas than corn. A large portion of maize crops are grown for purposes other than human consumption. Maize, wheat and rice together account for 87% of all grain production worldwide,

An increasing trend in U.S. production of corn has been cultivation for non-food purposes. Addition of ethanol to gasoline and biofuel production has been two important factors in the shift away from food-based cultivation of corn.

Along with the United States, other important commercial producers of corn currently include China, Brazil, Mexico, Russia, Ukraine, Romania, and South Africa.

RICH SOURCE

Corn in their natural form, as a whole grain, is a rich source of vitamins, minerals, carbohydrates, fats, oils, and protein.

It contains good amount of vitamin B1, vitamin B5, Folate, vitamin C, dietary fibers, etc. Vitamin B1 in maize helps in keeping the memory power intact, thereby preventing the dreaded "Alzheimer's" disease.

Folate helps in preventing birth defects and also in lowering the level of Homocysteine that has the potential of damaging the blood vessels.

However, when corn is refined by the removal of the bran and germ, the remaining endosperm is mostly carbohydrate and lacks the majority of the other nutrients.

Corn is a rich source of calories and forms a part of the staple diet among many populations. The calorific content of corn is 342 calories per 100 grams, among the highest in cereals.

Negative Health Effects: All products made from corn are not healthy and may even promote cancers instead of stopping them.

High Fructose Corn Syrup or HFCS: A sugar or sweetener made from corn is believed to promote pancreatic tumor cells as per latest research, done at the University of California, Los Angeles, USA.

Dr Anthony Heaney of UCLA's Jonson Cancer Center and colleagues wrote, "They have major significance for cancer patients given dietary refined fructose consumption, and indicate that efforts to reduce refined fructose intake or inhibit fructose-mediated actions may disrupt cancer growth."

As per one estimate over 70% of all corn produced in USA has been genetically modified in the form of herbicide-tolerant, or HT corn, or the form of insect-resistant, or BT corn. The only way to avoid this is to buy certified organic corn or locally grown NON –GM, traditional varieties.

Americans take in large amounts of fructose, mainly in high fructose corn syrup, a mix of fructose and glucose that is used in soft drinks, bread and a range of other foods.

Several states, including New York and California, have weighed a tax on sweetened soft drinks to defray the cost of treating obesity-related diseases such as heart disease, diabetes and cancer.

The industry always argues that sugar is sugar, which know is not correct. U.S. consumption of high fructose corn syrup went up 1,000 per cent between 1970 and 1990, researchers reported in 2004 in the American Journal of Clinical Nutrition.

Corn Oil: A high intake of omega-6 fatty acids may increase the likelihood that postmenopausal women will develop breast cancer. Similar effects were observed on prostate cancer. Unfortunately corn oil is very high in omega-6 fatty acid.

ANTI-CANCER BENEFITS

While it might sound surprising to some people who are used to thinking about corn as a plain, staple food, or a snack food, or a summertime party food, corn is actually a unique phytonutrient-rich food that provides us with well-documented anti-oxidant benefits.

Cooking sweet corn at high temperature for a long time unleashes beneficial nutrients that can substantially reduce the chance of heart disease and cancer, according to Cornell University food scientists.

In terms of conventional anti-oxidant nutrients, corn is a good source of vitamin C as well as the mineral manganese. Anti-oxidant phytonutrients in corn include anthocyanins, beta-carotene, caffeic acid, coumaric acid, ferulic acid, lutein, syringic acid, vanillic acid, protocatechuic acid, and zeaxanthin.

One great piece of news about corn's anti-oxidants involves the practice of drying corn while still on the cob or separated corn kernels. Research studies have shown that the drying of corn in temperature ranges as high as 150°-200°F (65°-93°C) does not significantly lower corn's anti-oxidant capacity.

This research confirms the wisdom of many North American and Mesoamerican cultures which relied on naturally-dried corn in the preparation of meal foods, especially during the winter months.

Sweet corn contains plenty of ferulic acid, which is a phenolic flavonoid anti-oxidant. Research reveals that ferulic acid prevents inflammation, aging and some types of cancer.

Breast and Liver Cancers: According to studies carried out at Cornell University, corn is a rich source of anti-oxidants which fight the cancer causing free radicals. In fact, cooking increases the anti-oxidants in sweet corn.

Corn is a rich source of a phenolic compound ferulic acid, an anti-cancer agent which has been shown to be effective in fighting tumors in breast cancer and liver cancer. Anthocyanins, found in purple corn, also act as scavengers of cancer-causing free radicals.

Colorectal Cancer: The fiber content of one cup of corn amounts to 18.4% of the daily recommended amount. This aids in alleviating digestive problems such as constipation and hemorrhoids, as well as lowering the risk of colon cancer.

Cooking sweet corn at high temperature for a long time unleashes beneficial nutrients that can substantially reduce the chance of heart disease and cancer, according to Cornell University USA's food scientists.

Cooking sweet corn for close to an hour significantly boosts the grain's health-giving anti-oxidant activity.

"There is a notion that processed fruits and vegetables have a lower nutritional value than fresh produce. Those original notions seem to be false, as cooked sweet corn retains its anti-oxidant activity, despite the loss of vitamin C," says Rui Hai Liu, Cornell assistant professor of food science.

Liu and his student cooked batches of sweet corn kernels at 115 degrees Celsius (239° F). The kernels produced more anti-oxidants the longer they cooked. After 10, 25 and 50 minutes the anti-oxidant content was boosted by 22, 44 and 53 per cent, respectively.

In addition to its anti-oxidant benefits, cooked sweet corn unleashes a phenolic compound called ferulic acid, which provides health benefits, such as battling cancer. "It's not a free acid," says Liu.

In the corn cooked at 115 degrees Celsius (239° F) for 10, 25 and 50 minutes, ferulic acid increased by 240 per cent, 550 per cent and 900 per cent, respectively.

Other plant foods that contain high levels of ferulic acid include rice bran, which may lower blood pressure, and blueberries and blackberries.

Lung Cancer: Another health benefit of sweet corn is that it prevents lung cancer. This is because sweet corn contains a chemical called beta cryptoxanthin, an orange-red carotenoid.

Beta cryptoxanthin reduces the risk of contracting lung cancer. Smokers can benefit by eating sweet corn regularly as it lowers the risk of lung cancer by 37%.

SELECTION

As per one estimate over 70% of all corn produced in USA has been genetically modified in the form of herbicide-tolerant, or HT corn, or the form of insect-resistant, or BT corn. The only way to avoid this is to buy certified organic corn or locally grown NON –GM, traditional varieties.

Look for corn whose husks are fresh and green and not dried out. They should envelope the ear and not fit too loosely around it. To examine the kernels, gently pull back on part of the husk. The kernels should be plump and tightly arranged in rows.

Select whole corn flour in recipes, wherever possible, instead of refined corn flour, also known as corn starch.

STORING

Traditionally to enjoy the optimal sweetness of fresh corn, it was recommended to eat it on the day of purchase. New varieties allow you 3 days to still enjoy its full flavor.

Store corn in an airtight container or tightly wrapped plastic bag in the refrigerator if you do not intend to cook it on the day of purchase.

Do not remove its husk since this will protect its flavor. Fresh corn freezes well if placed in heavy-duty freezer bags. To prepare whole ears for freezing, blanch them first for seven to eleven minutes depending upon their size.

If you just want to freeze the kernels, first blanch the ears for about five minutes and then cut the kernels off the cob at about three-quarters of their depths. Frozen whole corn on the cob will keep for up to one year, while the kernels can be frozen for two to three months.

SERVING

Corn can be cooked either with or without its husk in a variety of different ways. If using the wet heat methods of boiling or steaming, make sure not to add salt or overcook as the corn will tend to become hard and lose its flavor.

Many people do enjoy popcorn as a snack. Scientists discovered the snack food contains 'surprisingly large' levels of health-boosting anti-oxidants called polyphenols.

The U.S. study was led by the chemist Dr Vinson from the University of Scranton in Pennsylvania. It is the first to establish that snack foods and some wholegrain breakfast cereals are a good source of polyphenols.

He said: 'We really were surprised by the levels of polyphenols we found in popcorn. I guess it is because pop corns are not processed. You get all the wonderful ingredients of the corn undiluted and protected by the skin. In my opinion it's a good health food.'

The study measured polyphenol concentration in breakfast cereals and snacks, showing there are more anti-oxidants in less processed wholegrain cereals, while popcorn has the most among the snack foods tested.

Organic sweet corn soup is a good option.

One of the healthy ways to cook corn is by steaming it for about 5 minutes. For extra flavor, dress with extra virgin olive oil, sea salt, fresh lime and pepper.

Eat corn on the cob either just as it is or seasoned with a little organic butter, olive oil or flaxseed oil, salt and pepper, nutritional yeast or any other herbs or spices you enjoy.

Healthy sauté cooked corn with green chilies and onions. Served hot, this makes a wonderful side dish.

Enjoy a cold salad with an ancient Incan influence by combining cooked corn kernels, quinoa, tomatoes, green peppers and red kidney beans.

Use polenta (a type of cornmeal) as a pizza crust for a healthy pizza.

Add corn kernels and diced tomatoes to guacamole to give it extra zing.

Adding corn to soup, whether it chili or chowder, enhances the soup's hardiness, let alone its nutritional profile.

Eating rotis or tortillas made with whole corn flour is also very healthy.

Bottom Line

1. Say BIG NO to High Fructose Corn syrup and corn oil.
2. Eat only whole organic corn.
3. Organic sweet corn soup or popcorns are healthy options.

CHAPTER 6

Time to Change Oil

We know why we love fat: because it tastes good. But the lure of lard is stronger than we thought. According to one scientist, we're hardwired to hanker for it.

Dietary fats are essential to give your body energy and to support cell growth. They also help protect your organs and help keep your body warm.

Fats help your body absorb vital nutrients and produce important hormones, too. Your body definitely needs fat – but not as much fat as most people eat. Eating foods with a moderate amount of RIGHT fat is definitely part of a healthy diet.

There are nine calories in every gram of fat, regardless of what type of fat it is, from animal fat to extra virgin olive oil. Whatever source or type of fat you eat, the quantity has to be restricted.

Some fats can kill cancer cells and some will promote cancer growth, so quality also plays a very important role in turning off cancer.

AVOCADO

"Avocado is known as Mother Nature's butter"

How about a buttery green fruit that you can spread on a sandwich, dice into a salad, or mash into favorite dip? If avocados were only delicious and versatile, they would still be a treat worth serving frequently but they are much more than that.

Meat proteins, fat oil, vitamins and minerals from vegetables, they all are found in a single fruit: avocado. Eating this, it is like having a whole meal, with different types of food, and this is only one of the countless benefits of avocados.

Avocados are green, pear-shaped fruits that grow on subtropical trees. Unlike most other fruits, which tend to be juicy and sweet, avocados have a creamy texture, a high fat content, and a mild, buttery flavor. They are usually used as a fresh vegetable.

The delicious healthy monounsaturated fat in the avocado is one of its biggest Super Food health claims. The only other fruit with a comparable amount of monounsaturated fat is the olive. The monounsaturated fat in avocados is oleic acid, which may help lower cholesterol and does not make you fat.

Avocados have been cultivated for thousands of years. A favorite of the Aztecs, they were native to Central America.

Avocados are native to Central and South America and have been cultivated in these regions since 8,000 B.C. While avocados are now grown in most tropical and subtropical countries, the major commercial producers include the United States (Florida and California), Mexico, the Dominican Republic, Brazil and Colombia.

Even though avocado is found more and more in our shops, there are very few people that eat avocado routinely. This is probably because not many ones know the facts about avocado and about its health benefits.

RICH SOURCE

Avocados provide nearly 20 essential nutrients. They also act as a "nutrient booster" by enabling the body to absorb more fat-soluble nutrients, such as alpha and beta-carotene and lutein, in foods that are eaten with the fruit.

Avocados are a good source of bone supportive vitamin K as well as heart-healthy dietary fiber, vitamin B6, vitamin C, and folate. Avocados are also a good source of energy-producing vitamin B5 and muscle-healthy potassium; in fact, they are higher in potassium than a medium banana.

Avocados are Mother Nature's skin moisturizer too. With their healthy fats and phytonutrients, they offer remarkable benefits to human skin -- both when eaten and when used topically.

Avocados contain an amazing array of phytonutrients. Included are phytosterols; carotenoids (beta-carotene, alpha-carotene, and lutein); flavonoids; and poly-hydroxylated fatty alcohols.

Although they are fruits, avocados have a high fat content of between 71 and 88% of their total calories—about 20 times the average for other fruits. A typical avocado contains 30 grams of fat, but 20 of these fat grams are health-promoting monounsaturated fats, especially heart-friendly and health-promoting omega-3.

Research has shown that the greatest concentration of carotenoids in avocado occurs in the dark green flesh that lies just beneath the skin. You don't want to slice into that dark green portion any more than necessary when you are peeling an avocado.

ANTI-CANCER BENEFITS

Researchers believe that avocado's amazing carotenoid diversity is a key factor in the anti-inflammatory properties of this vegetable.

The ability of avocado to help prevent unwanted inflammation is absolutely unquestionable in the world of health research. The term "anti-inflammatory" is a term that truly applies to this delicious food. No single category of nutrients in avocado is more impressive than carotenoids.

One cup of fresh avocado (150 grams) added to a salad of romaine lettuce, spinach, and carrots increased absorption of carotenoids from this salad between 200-400%. This research result makes perfect sense because carotenoids are fat-soluble and would be provided with the fat they need for absorption from the addition of avocado.

Research has shown that the greatest concentration of carotenoids in avocado occurs in the dark green flesh that lies just beneath the skin.

Mouth, Skin, and Prostate Cancer: The ability of avocado to help prevent the occurrence of cancers in the mouth, skin, and prostate gland has been studied in a preliminary way by health researchers, mostly through the use of lab studies on cancer cells or lab studies involving animals and their consumption of avocado extracts.

But even though this anti-cancer research has been limited with respect to humans and diet, still the preliminary results are very impressive. The anti-cancer properties of avocado are definitely related to its unusual mix of anti-inflammatory and anti-oxidant nutrients.

That relationship is to be expected since cancer risk factors almost always include excessive inflammation (related to lack of anti-inflammatory nutrients) and oxidative stress (related to lack of anti-oxidants). But here is where the avocado story gets especially interesting.

In healthy cells, avocado works to improve inflammatory and oxidative stress levels. But in cancer cells, avocado works to increase oxidative stress and shift the cancer cells over into a programmed cell death cycle (apoptosis), lessening the cancer cell numbers.

In other words, avocado appears to selectively push cancer cells "over the brink" in terms of oxidative stress and increase their likelihood of dying, while at the same time actively supporting the health of non-cancerous cells by increasing their supply of anti-oxidant and anti-inflammatory nutrients.

Oral Cancer: Nutrients taken from avocados are able to thwart oral cancer cells, killing some and preventing pre-cancerous cells from developing into actual cancers, according to researchers at Ohio State University.

Researchers found that extracts from Hass avocados kill or stop the growth of pre-cancerous cells that lead to oral cancer. Hass avocados are year-round fruits known for their distinctive bumpy skin that turns from green to purplish-black as they ripen.

While there are more than 500 varieties of avocados grown worldwide, Hass avocados are the most readily available.

D'Ambrosio, who collaborated with researchers in Ohio State's College of Pharmacy, found that phytochemicals extracted from avocados target multiple signaling pathways and increase the amount of reactive oxygen within the cells, leading to cell death in pre-cancerous cell lines. But the phytochemicals did not harm normal cells.

"These studies suggest that individual and a combination of phytochemicals from the avocado fruit may offer an advantageous dietary strategy in cancer prevention," says Ding, who is a member of the division of radiobiology.

Avocados are chock-full of beneficial anti-oxidants and phytonutrients, including vitamin C, folate, vitamin E, fiber and unsaturated fats. They are naturally sodium-free, contain no trans fats and are low in saturated fat, making them a healthy addition to any diet, D'Ambrosio says.

Prostate Cancer: A very interesting recent research shows that avocado seems to be a potent warrior in the fight against prostate cancer. Avocados contain the highest amount of the carotenoid lutein of all commonly eaten fruits. In addition, they contain related carotenoids, including zeaxanthin, alpha-carotene, beta-carotene, as well as significant amounts of vitamin E.

Recent study showed that an extract of avocado containing these carotenoids and tocopherols inhibited the growth of prostate cancer cells. Interestingly, when

researchers used lutein alone, the cancer cells were unaffected, thus demonstrating once again that it's the synergy of health-promoting nutrients in whole foods that makes the difference.

SELECTION

A ripe, ready-to-eat avocado is slightly soft but should have no dark sunken spots or cracks. If the avocado has a slight neck, rather than being rounded on top, it was probably tree ripened and will have better flavor.

A firmer, less mature fruit can be ripened at home and will be less likely to have bruises. The average California Has avocado weighs between 165-170 grams (about 6 ounces) and has a pebbled dark green or black skin. Hass is the year-round avocado.

Fuerte avocado has smoother, brighter green skin and is also grown in California. Florida avocados, which can be as large as 3 pounds, have less fat and calories, but their taste is not as rich as California varieties.

STORING

A firm avocado will ripen in a paper bag or in a fruit basket at room temperature within a few days. As the fruit ripens, the skin will turn darker. Avocados should not be refrigerated until they are ripe.

Once ripe, they can be kept refrigerated for up to a week. If you are refrigerating a whole avocado, it is best to keep it whole and not slice it in order to avoid browning that occurs when the flesh is exposed to air.

If you have used a portion of a ripe avocado, it is best to store the remainder in the refrigerator. Store in a plastic bag or wrap with plastic wrap, or place on a plate and cover with plastic wrap.

You can sprinkle the exposed surface(s) with lemon juice or vinegar, to prevent the browning that occurs when the avocado flesh comes in contact with oxygen in the air.

SERVING

Use a stainless steel knife to cut the avocado in half lengthwise. Gently twist the two halves in opposite direction if you find the flesh clinging to the pit. Remove the pit, either with a spoon or by spearing with the tip of a knife.

Next, take each of the avocado halves and slice lengthwise to produce four avocado quarters. Just take your thumb and index finger to grip an edge of the avocado skin and peel it away from the flesh, in exactly the same way that you would peel a banana.

The final result will be a peeled avocado that contains most of that dark green outermost flesh that is richest in carotenoid anti-oxidants.

Use minimum possible heat for cooking avocado in case the recipe demands, but it is best to add it in the last. This is a similar approach to some traditional Mexican recipes. In Mexico they add sliced avocado to chicken soup after it is cooked. The avocado warms and mingles well with the soup but retains its nutritional concentration since it is not cooked.

Use chopped avocados as a garnish for black bean soup.

Add avocado to your favorite creamy tofu-based dressing recipe to give it extra richness and a beautiful green color.

Mix chopped avocados, onions, tomatoes, cilantro, lime juice and seasonings for a rich-tasting twist on traditional guacamole.

Spread ripe avocados on bread as a healthy replacement for mayonnaise when making a sandwich.

For an exceptional salad, combine sliced avocado with fennel, oranges and fresh mint.

For a beautiful accompaniment to your favorite Mexican dish, top quartered avocado slices with corn relish and serve with a wedge of lime.

In a perfect world, an Avocado-Mango (Avoango?) would exist but in the meantime, let's create it ourselves by making this delicious Mango Avocado Salsa!

Ingredients

4 medium avocados, chopped

1 mango, chopped

1 tomato, chopped (optional)

1 white onion, finely diced

¼ cup chopped cilantro

1 lime, juice and zest

Method

- Carefully place avocados in a medium bowl, and season with salt, pepper and lime juice and zest.
- Fold in mango chunks, onion, cilantro and lime zest. Taste test with a chip and re-season with salt and pepper.
- Serve as a dip at your next summer party or as a side dish to grilled fish. Not only is it healthy but it's a refreshing side dish that involves no heat preparations !

Bottom Line

1. Avocado is the perfect food to replace the normal butter from our life.
2. Should be eaten raw or with minimum amount of heating. Can be added in the dishes in the last like dairy cream.
3. From face to human race all can be immensely benefited by eating avocados regularly.

44/52

BRAZIL NUT

Parrots seem to know by instinct what we are only now discovering--that is nuts are one of the most nutritious gifts of nature.

Most nuts are seeds or the dried fruit from trees and natural to the diet of wild parrots. Nuts are so high in protein content that they have been listed as an alternative to meat in the USDA Food Guide Pyramid. Like all the other types of nuts, Brazil nuts are also known for their great taste and amazing health benefits.

The Brazil nut tree (*Bertholettia excelsa*) is a magnificent jungle tree of the steamy Amazon Rain Forest. The extremely hard-shelled seeds are dark brown and wedge shaped. The kernel is white, oily, and rich tasting.

They are large, in comparison to other nuts, and are often included in nut mixes. Just six nuts comprise a 1 oz. (30 gm) of serving. Nuts are considered a healthy snack, may help you feel fuller and longer, according to the University of Nebraska.

Brazil nuts are particularly good for health because of their high selenium content, which makes their protein content "complete". This means that, unlike the proteins in most plant products, Brazil nuts' protein contain all the necessary amino acids to foster optimal growth in humans (in the same way as proteins from animal products do).

Selenium is considered to be part of the group of heart-healthy compounds called anti-oxidants. It works with proteins in the body to make anti-oxidant enzymes. Anti-oxidants are known for their ability to prevent cellular damage.

Brazil nut's high selenium content also discourages the ageing process and stimulates the immune system. In a study of patients with early alzheimer's disease, anti-oxidants - including selenium – boosted mood and mental performance.

The trace mineral selenium is essential for proper functioning of the immune system and thyroid gland. Low selenium levels contribute to pain, infection, and disease.

RICH SOURCE

Brazil nuts are excellent source of selenium. They are also a good source of protein, fiber (one ounce of nuts has as much fiber as two slices of whole wheat bread), vitamin

E, Magnesium, calcium, zinc, copper, potassium, phosphorus, biotin, riboflavin, niacin, and phytochemicals.

Brazil nuts have about 2,500 times as much selenium as any other nut. Selenium is a powerful anti-oxidant which has been proven to protect against heart disease and many types of cancer.

This has led some health commentators and nutritionists to recommend the consumption of Brazil nuts as a protective measure.

The fat content of Brazil nuts is slightly high as compared with other nuts, but the fat is monounsaturated, which is considered healthy. Brazil nuts contain 184 calories and four grams of protein per ounce.

ANTI-CANCER BENEFITS

Cancer and the side effects of invasive treatments can take a toll on your body. A high-quality, nutritious diet can help promote healthy tissue and potentially contribute toward your recovery. Brazil nuts contain the essential mineral selenium, which may support cancer treatment.

Your body uses selenium to carry out a number of biological processes. This mineral makes up a portion of several proteins, called selenoproteins, which carry out a range of chemical reactions, and help guide cellular maturation, hormone production, muscle metabolism and energy production.

It also activates anti-oxidant enzymes, a class of proteins that protect your cells from oxidative damage that can cause genetic mutations and aging. The activity of certain selenoproteins is linked to cancer prevention.

Selenium can play a role in controlling cancer development by helping to regulate cell proliferation. Tumors develop due to abnormal and uncontrolled cell division, leading to aggregations of rapidly dividing cells that become cancerous.

As per one study, a handful of Brazil nuts a day can reduce the risk of eight types of cancer by up to 76 per cent. They are cancer of the liver, lung, stomach, prostate, pancreas, brain, kidney and esophagus, by blocking the formation of tumors.

Selenium also fights tumors once they appear, improving the chances of survival. Dr David Servan-Schreiber MD has written in his very famous book 'Anti-Cancer A New Way of Life', selenium stimulates and increases body's immune cells and particularly NK (natural killer cells) by whopping 80%.

Cervical Cancer: A study published in "Cell Biology and Toxicology" in 2008 found that selenium can activate signaling pathways to promote apoptosis in cervical cancer cells, allowing the damaged cells to die instead of contributing to tumor progression.

Research suggests that selenium might affect cancer risk in two ways. As an anti-oxidant, selenium can help protect the body from damaging effects of free radicals and also prevent or slow tumor growth.

Brazil nuts have about 2,500 times as much selenium as any other nut. Selenium is a powerful anti-oxidant which has been proven to protect against heart disease and many types of canceres.

Breast Cancer: The mineral selenium may help protect some women from developing breast cancer, research has suggested. The element selenium, which can be found easily in Brazil nuts, animal organ meat like liver and kidneys, may help the body defend itself.

Scientists from the University of Illinois believe they may have worked out how selenium interacts with a natural body chemical to offer protection.

The latest study looked at tissue samples from more than 500 women who did not have breast cancer, and compared their genetic makeup with those in 79 breast cancer tissue samples.

They found that different versions of genes were more common in the breast cancer tissue samples. Their conclusion was that certain women – with a certain genetic makeup – might benefit from extra selenium in their diet.

Professor Alan Diamond said: "For over 20 years, animal studies have shown that tiny amounts of selenium in the diet can suppress cancer in several types of organs. The animal data is very strong, but human data is just emerging.

"There's obviously no harm in women eating Brazil nuts, but people should consult their Doctor before taking selenium supplements as selenium itself has toxic effects if too much of it is taken." The study was published in the journal 'Cancer Research'.

Lung and Prostate Cancer: Dr Margaret Rayman of the University of Surrey told the British Association Festival of Science in Exeter that people should aim for a daily intake of around 200 micrograms (mcg) of the mineral selenium.

Studies have found that this cuts risk by 46 per cent in the case of lung cancer and 76 per cent for prostate cancer.

A study published in "Cancer Research" in 2002 reported that treating laboratory-cultured prostate cancer cells with selenium was able to slow cell proliferation, highlighting selenium's potential importance in fighting prostate cancer.

Selenium may also have an effect on cancer growth by controlling cell death, or apoptosis. Apoptosis proves essential for healthy tissue function, because your body kills off very damaged or mutated cells to help prevent disease.

Cancerous cells evade cellular apoptosis, so the cells continue to grow despite accumulating numerous genetic mutations.

A recent study in the Journal of Medicinal Food suggests that the selenium found in Brazil nuts, along with soy, may help fight prostate cancer by inhibiting the growth of cancerous cells.

Skin Cancer: Basal cell carcinoma, a type of skin cancer, is among the most common forms of cancer; with more than half a million new cases reported each year.

By taking 150 to 200 micrograms of selenium daily one greatly lowers the risk that existing basal cell carcinomas will spread to the colon, prostate, or lungs. You can get this much amount of selenium by simply eating one or two Brazil nuts a day. Each nut contains approximately 120 micrograms of selenium.

SELECTION

Sodium is always a concern when it comes to packaged or processed foods. Brazil nuts fall into this category when they are salted and packaged for purchase. Salted nuts can greatly increase your daily sodium intake and excess sodium is associated with high blood pressure, or hypertension.

Lightly salted nuts can be a good choice, just check the nutrition label to know how much sodium you are consuming in a serving. Adults should consume less than 2,300 mg/day of sodium. Best is to choose unsalted raw nuts for a lower sodium and optimum nutrition.

STORING

The nuts should be stored in the shell and refrigerated until ready to eat, according to the University of Nebraska. Keeping the nuts cool will make it easier to remove the shell.

SERVING

The best benefits come from eating raw nuts. The nuts can also be heated up in the microwave or in a pan with a small amount of butter to make for a richer taste. Otherwise, adding the nuts to breads, cakes or entrees is a great way to spice up a recipe.

While Brazil nuts are full of nutrients, consuming too many can have a negative effect on your health. These nuts are incredibly high in selenium and while it is a necessary nutrient, too much selenium can cause stomach upset, hair and nail loss, irritability and fatigue.

While the specific amount of selenium in each nut can vary, it is estimated that ONE Brazil nut provides 160% of an adult's daily need for selenium. One or maximum Two Brazil nuts a day, is all you need to fulfill the body's selenium requirement.

Bottom Line

NUTS ARE PROTEIN-RICH FOODS

1. Some of us are not getting enough selenium due to multi-cropping and depleted soils; Brazil nut is good plant-based option.
2. Eating one or two nuts a day is sufficient for all your selenium needs.
3. Raw and unsalted Brazil nut is the best option.

FLAXSEEDS

"Wherever flaxseed becomes a regular food item among the people, there will be better health" – Mahatma Gandhi

The warm, earthy and subtly nutty flavor of flaxseeds with an abundance of omega-3 fatty acids, are increasingly popular addition to the diets of many a health-conscious consumer.

Flaxseeds are slightly larger than sesame seeds and have a hard shell that is smooth and shiny. Their color ranges from deep amber to reddish brown depending upon whether the flax is of the golden or brown variety. While whole flaxseeds feature a soft crunch, the nutrients in ground seeds are more easily absorbed.

The true nature of flaxseed as a health food has been known for centuries. In the eighth century, Charlemagne, also known as Charles the Great, Emperor of the Romans, considered flaxseed so essential for health that he actually passed laws requiring its use.

Flaxseed was one of the original medicines used by father of medicine, Hippocrates himself. They add years to your life expectancy.

The benefits of omega-3s present in plenty in flaxseeds include reducing the risk of heart disease and stroke while helping to reduce symptoms of hypertension, depression, attention deficit hyperactivity disorder (ADHD), joint pain and other rheumatoid problems.

Recent research also indicates that omega-3s can boost the immune system and help protect us from an array of illnesses including Alzheimer's disease and Cancer.

Just how do omega-3s perform so many health "miracles" in people? One way, experts say, is by encouraging the production of body chemicals that help control inflammation -- in the joints, the bloodstream, and the tissues.

Other sources of omega-3s include broccoli, cantaloupe, kidney beans, spinach, grape leaves, Chinese cabbage, cauliflower, algae, cold water oily fish and walnuts or products fortified with omega-3s.

How to get the nutrients from fish without eating them? The answer is very simple, by just adding flaxseeds to our daily diets.

Many food products now boast that they have added omega-3 to support various aspects of your health. But be aware that the amount of omega-3 they contain may be very small.

RICH SOURCE

Flaxseeds contain a high quality protein, vitamins B-1, B-2, C, E, and carotene. These seeds also contain iron, zinc, and trace amounts of potassium, phosphorus, calcium, vitamin E and carotene.

Flaxseeds are rich in ALA (alpha linolenic acid), an omega-3 fat that is a precursor to the form of omega-3 found in fish oils called EPA (eicosapentaenoic acid).

ALA, in addition to providing several beneficial effects of its own, can be converted in the body to EPA, thus providing EPA's beneficial effects. Another advantage of getting one's omega-3s from the ALA in flax oil is that the body does not create more EPA and DHA than it needs.

In addition to nutritious fats, flaxseed meal or flour contain other nutrients which make eating the whole seed superior to consuming just the extracted flax oil.

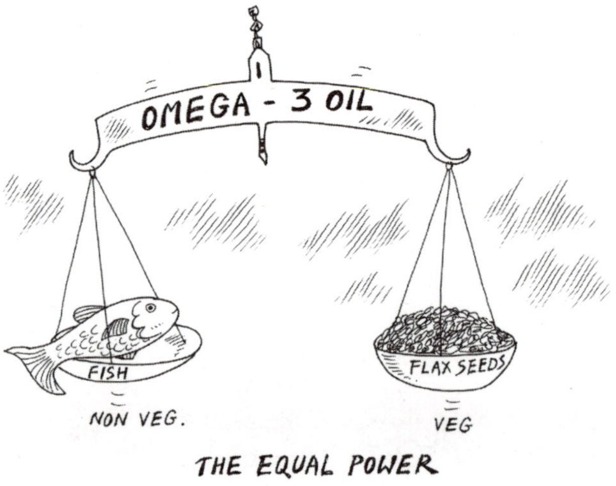

Flaxseed meal and flour provides a very good source of fiber that can lower cholesterol levels in people with atherosclerosis and diabetic heart disease, reduce the exposure of colon cells to cancer-causing chemicals, help relieve constipation and stabilize blood sugar levels in diabetic patients.

Flaxseeds are also a good source of magnesium, which helps to reduce the severity of asthma by keeping airways relaxed and open, lowers high blood pressure and reduces the risk of heart attack and stroke.

Omega-3 fats are also needed to produce flexible cell membranes. Cell membranes are the cell's gatekeepers, allowing in needed nutrients while promoting the elimination of wastes. While important for everyone, flexible cell membranes are critical for persons with diabetes.

ANTI-CANCER BENEFITS

Lignins have received a lot of attention lately because of possible anti-cancer properties, especially in relation to breast and colon cancer.

Lignins seem to flush excess estrogen out of the body, thereby reducing the incidence of estrogen-linked cancers, such as breast cancer. Besides anti-tumor properties, lignins also have antibacterial, antifungal, and anti-viral properties.

Colon Cancer: In the colon, omega-3 fats help protects colon cells from cancer-causing toxins and free radicals, leading to a reduced risk for colon cancer.

Laboratory experiments and animal studies have also been conducted that indicate that Omega-3 can also lessen the symptoms of colon cancer, as well as slow down this disease, at the very least for those who are at the early stages of this illness.

Researchers tested blood samples from about 450 men, some of whom had cancer of the colon and rectum. The results were very specific. The presence of omega-3 fats in the blood was associated with a decreased risk of colon cancer.

But even as important is Omega-3s ability to reduce the negative impact from excess amount of yet another essential type of fattyacid known as omega-6s, found in foods such as eggs, poultry, cereals, vegetable oils, baked goods, and margarine.

Flaxseeds contain over a hundred times more of phytochemicals, known as lignin, than any of its closest competitors, such as wheat bran, buckwheat, rye, millet, oats, and soybeans.

Breast Cancer: Women who follow a diet that has a lot of Omega-3 fatty acids are at less risk of developing breast cancer. As per one study' eating flaxseeds could 'reduce risk of dying from breast cancer by 40 per cent'.

Phytoestrogens are estrogen-like chemicals found in plant foods such as beans, seeds, and grains. Flaxseeds were found to be particularly high in phytoestrogen lignans type. Once in the body, these phytoestrogens attach to oestrogen, the female sex hormone, and are thought to help protect against cancer.

German researchers analyzed blood samples of over 1,000 women diagnosed with pre-menopausal breast cancer over a three-year period. They analyzed levels of enterolactone, which is what phytoestrogens become when they enter the bowel.

Results showed that women with the highest levels of enterolactone had their mortality rate reduced by two-fifths compared to women with the lowest levels of the same substance.

They also showed that having a high level of enterolactone also afforded similar levels of protection against the spread of cancer and the formation of secondary tumors.

The study authors, whose findings are published in the Journal of Clinical Oncology, claim that phytoestrogens helped curtail cancer both because of its hormonal properties, as well as by killing off cancer cells and preventing the growth of new blood vessels.

Study author Professor Jenny Chang-Claude, from the German Cancer Research Centre in Heidelberg said: 'We now have first clear evidence showing that lignans lower not only the risk of developing post-menopausal breast cancer, but also the mortality risk.

Prostate Cancer – Population studies that have been conducted showed that men, who follow a low-fat diet that's rich in Omega-3, can help prevent prostate cancer.

As per American Cancer Society website, there have been some small studies of the effects of flaxseed in humans. A small study of 15 men found that a low-fat diet supplemented with flaxseed lowered their blood prostate-specific antigen (PSA) levels and slowed the growth of benign prostate cells.

Another study of 25 men with prostate cancer found that a low-fat diet along with ground flaxseed reduced serum testosterone, slowed the growth rate of cancer cells, and increased the death rate of cancer cells.

A 2008 study looked at men with prostate cancer who were scheduled for surgery. Researchers gave some men flaxseed while others ate their usual diets; some were put on low fat diets. The men who got the flaxseed had slower cancer growth than those who did not, regardless of total fat intake.

SELECTION

Flaxseed is available in health food stores and many supermarkets, sold as whole seeds, ground seeds, or oil. When buying seeds, be sure they are whole, not split; splitting exposes the inner seed to light and heat and decreases the nutritional value.

If you're thinking that maybe the easiest and most low-cal way to get omega-3s is with flaxseeds oil capsules, not so fast. Many nutritionists say it's a bad idea.

"There is something about whole food that when it goes into the body it's more than 90% absorbed, while [with] a supplement you absorb only about 50%," says nutritionist Lona Sandon, RD, assistant professor of clinical nutrition at the University of Texas.

Moreover, says Sandon, because the components of different foods work together, they may offer a more complete and balanced source of nutrients.

As per recent research most consumers prefer simply using the oil for its omega-3 fatty acids and not having to bother with grinding the seeds. But nutritionally speaking, it's worth the trouble to grind fresh flaxseeds (say, in a coffee grinder).

Freshly ground flaxseeds are a much better choice because it also contains 3 grams of fiber per tablespoon, as well as healthy chock-full of phytoestrogens.

STORING

If you purchase whole flaxseeds, store them in an airtight container in a dark, dry and cool place where they will keep fresh for several months.

Ground flaxseeds are usually available both refrigerated and non-refrigerated. It is highly recommended to purchase ground flaxseed that is in a vacuum-sealed package or has been refrigerated since once flaxseeds are ground; they are much more prone to oxidation and spoilage.

Likewise, if you either purchase ground flaxseeds or you grind them at home, it is important to keep them in a tightly sealed container in the refrigerator or freezer to prevent them from becoming rancid.

Flaxseed oil is especially perishable and should be purchased in opaque bottles that have been kept refrigerated. Flaxseed oil should have a sweet nutty flavor. Never use flaxseed oil in cooking; add it to foods after they have been heated.

SERVING

Grind flaxseeds in a coffee or seed grinder in order to enhance their digestibility and therefore their nutritional value. If adding ground flaxseeds to a cooked cereal or grain dish, do so at the end of cooking since the soluble fiber in the flaxseeds can thicken liquids if left too long.

Sprinkle ground flaxseeds onto your hot or cold cereal.

Add flaxseed powder in the wheat flour before making chapattis or bread etc.

Add flaxseeds to your homemade muffin, cookie or bread recipe.

To pump up the nutritional volume of your breakfast shake, add ground flaxseeds.

To give cooked vegetables a nuttier flavor, sprinkle some ground flaxseeds on top.

Bottom Line

1. Flaxseed is the fish for the vegetarians, since it contains same healthy omega-3 oil and without the dangers of mercury very commonly found in fish.
2. Freshly ground flaxseeds powder is much better option than flaxseed oil capsules.
3. Simple way to eat daily and each meal is mix it in your daily wheat flour.

OILY FISH

"One-fifth of human kind depends on fish to live. Today now 70 per cent of the fish stocks are over-exploited. According to FAO if we don't change our system of fishing the main sea resources will be gone in 2050. We don't want to believe what we know.

–Yann Arthus-Bertrand

Healthy diets almost always contain fish, a protein food with fewer calories than other meat sources. It's also one of nature's most versatile foods. As well as different species of fish, you can steam, bake, fry or poach.

Harvard School of Public Health of USA reviewed existing studies that looked at the health effects of eating fish -- and the jury's come back in favor of... eating fish!

The Harvard study recommended eating up to two servings of fish a week and that eating fish could cut the risk of death from heart disease by a third.

The oils in some fish appear to reduce the blood from clotting by reducing the stickiness of the blood. The most beneficial fish in this context is oily fish such as salmon or mackerel or Sardine or Herring etc.

Fish intake has also been linked to a lower risk of stroke, depression, and mental decline with age. Studies have also shown that fish alleviates a range of ailments including cancer, arthritis, prostatitis and cystitis.

In fish long regarded as low in fat and high in "good fats," the health benefits have been overwhelmed by concerns about the environmental problems caused by over-fishing and health risks caused by pollutants the world over.

RICH SOURCE

If you ask folks what food group they should avoid, most will probably answer "fats." While it's true that, in large amounts, some types of fat are bad for your health, there are some which simply can't live without.

Among them are the omega-3 fatty acids, found in foods including flaxseeds, walnuts, and cold water fish. Omega-3 is very important for its ability to reduce the negative impact of yet another essential type of fatty acid known as omega-6.

Omega -3 Fatty Acid	
Animal Sources	EPA & DHA*
Sardine	2.0
Herring	2.0
Mackerel	1.8
Atlantic Salmon	1.6
Rainbow trout	1.0
* From 100 gm serving	
Adopted from USDA Nutrient Data Lab.	

Earlier in good old times, the ratio of omega-3 vs. omega-6, in our daily diets, used to be 1:1 and now it is more than 1:20. We are flooded with Omega-6 oils and omega-3 is very scarce and hardly part of our daily diet.

Commercial meats, eggs, poultry, dairy products like milk, cheeses, and yoghurts (curds), are produced by raising the animals on grains and seeds, instead of grass as in past good old days, thus topping them with omega-6 fats.

Our cereals, vegetable oils, bakery items like cakes, pastries, patties, biscuits, french fries, potato wafers, packaged items, and margarines are other daily sources of, unlimited and uninterrupted amount of omega-6 fat supplies.

Oil-rich fish or oily fish are those that have oil distributed throughout their body. Oily fish are a very rich source of omega-3 fatty acids. They also contain large amount of vitamins A and D. Sardines, herring, mackerel, salmon, and trout are all examples of oily fish.

Whitefish on the other hand are called non-oily fish. They hardly have any trace of omega-3. Their oil is only located in the liver. Cod, haddock and flatfish are examples of whitefish.

For this reason the consumption of oily fish can be more beneficial to humans, but the problem is oily fish are known to carry higher levels of contaminants, such as mercury or dioxin, than whitefish.

A very judicious choice should be made, after understanding the type of fish, source and the amount to be included in our daily diets. The idea is to minimize the dangers and maximize the health benefits.

ANTI-CANCER BENEFITS

"Omega -3 not only plays a vital role in the health of the membrane of every cell in our body, it also helps protect us from a number of key health threats," says Laurie Tansman, MS, RD, CDN, a nutritionist at Mount Sinai Medical Center in New York.

The benefits of omega-3s include reducing the risk of heart disease and stroke while helping to reduce symptoms of hypertension, depression, attention deficit hyperactivity disorder (ADHD), joint pain and other rheumatoid problems, as well as certain skin ailments.

Some research has even shown that omega-3s can boost the immune system and help protect us from an array of illnesses including Alzheimer's disease.

Just how do omega-3s perform so many health "miracles" in people? One way, experts say, is by encouraging the production of body chemicals that help control inflammation – in the joints, the bloodstream, and the tissues.

Oil-rich fish or oily fish are those that have oil distributed through their body, as opposed to whitefish, whose main concentration of oils is located in the liver.

Breast Cancer: Researchers at the Fred Hutchinson Cancer Research Center in Seattle USA, led by Emily White, Ph.D., asked 35,016 post-menopausal women who did not have a history of breast cancer to complete a 24-page questionnaire about their use of non-vitamin, non-mineral "specialty" supplements in the Vitamins and Lifestyle (VITAL) cohort study.

After six years of follow-up, 880 cases of breast cancer were identified using the Surveillance, Epidemiology and End Results registry.

Regular use of fish oil supplements, which contain high levels of the omega-3 fatty acids, EPA and DHA, was linked with a 32 per cent reduced risk of breast cancer.

Kidney Cancer: Renal cell carcinoma (RCC) involving the renal parenchyma (the functional tissue of the kidney) accounts for more than 80 per cent of all kidney cancers.

Alicja Wolk, D.M.Sc., of the Karolinska Institutet, Stockholm, Sweden and colleagues investigated the association between oily fish and lean fish consumption and the risk for development of RCC in a population with a relatively high consumption of fatty fish.

The participants, from the Swedish Mammography Cohort, included 61,433 women aged 40 to 76 years without previous diagnosis of cancer. During an average of 15.3 years of follow-up, 150 RCC cases were diagnosed.

After adjustment for potential confounders, an inverse association of oily fish consumption with the risk of RCC was found, while no association was found with the consumption of lean fish or other seafood.

"In this large population-based cohort with data on long-term diet, we found that women who consumed one or more servings of fatty fish per week had a statistically significant 44 per cent decreased risk of RCC compared with women who did not consume any fish. Women who reported consistent long-term consumption of fatty fish at baseline and 10 years later had a statistically significant 74 per cent lower risk," the authors write.

If you're thinking that maybe the easiest and most low-cal way to get omega-3s is with fish oil capsules, not so fast. Many nutritionists say it's a bad idea. There is something about whole food that when it goes into the body it's more than 90% absorbed, while a supplement you absorb only about 50%.

It could be something more than just the omega-3s in fish that make it so healthy. Some leading nutritionists believe that it could be the amino acids that provide benefits, which we are not going to see in fish-oil supplements alone.

And if you're thinking fish-oil capsules will help you avoid the contamination risks of fresh fish, think again, because supplements are not regulated even in the USA. Some may contain concentrated amounts of the same toxins found in fresh fish.

More important, experts say, there is a danger of overdosing on fish-oil supplements, particularly if you take more than the recommended amount. Doing so can increase your risk of bleeding or bruising. This isn't likely to happen when you get your intake from foods.

Colon, Breast, and advanced Prostate Cancer: Omega-3s may help reduce the risk of colon cancer, breast cancer, and advanced prostate cancer, but more research is needed. The American Cancer Society recommends a diet that includes fish, but the organization stops short of endorsing omega-3 supplements for cancer prevention.

Colon Cancer: Certain studies have been conducted that indicate that having an Omega-3 rich diet can also protect you from having colorectal cancer. For example, the Inuit are shown to be at less risk of colorectal cancer even if they have a fatty diet, simply because of the large quantity of fish they eat.

Laboratory experiments and animal studies have also been conducted that indicate that Omega-3 can also lessen the symptoms of colon cancer, as well as slow down this disease, at the very least for those who are at the early stages of this illness.

In the colon, omega-3 fats help protect colon cells from cancer-causing toxins and free radicals, leading to a reduced risk for colon cancer.

Prostate Cancer: Population studies that have been conducted showed that men who follow a low-fat diet that's rich in Omega-3, primarily those taken from fish and fish oil, can help prevent prostate cancer.

Researchers tested blood samples from about 450 men, some of whom had cancer of the colon and rectum. The results were very specific. The presence of omega-3 fats in the blood was associated with a decreased risk of colorectal cancer, but only in men who weren't taking aspirin. (Taking aspirin seemed to have a similar effect as ingesting large amounts of omega-3 fatty acids.)

> *If you're thinking that maybe the easiest and most low-cal way to get omega-3s is with fish-oil capsules, not so fast. Many nutritionists say it's a bad idea. There is something about whole food that when it goes into the body it's more than 90% absorbed, while a supplement you absorb only about 50%.*

Omega-3 for Vegetarians: If you don't eat fish or fish oil, you can get a dose of DHA from algae supplements. Algae that is commercially grown is generally considered safe.

Vegetarians also can get the ALA version of omega-3 from foods such as flaxseed, walnuts, broccoli, and spinach -- or products fortified with omega-3s. Many food products now boast that they have added omega-3 to support various aspects of your health. But be aware that the amount of omega-3 they contain may be minimal.

> *The color of farmed salmon would be a dusty grey were it not for the addition of the petrochemical-derived coloring agent's canthaxanthin and astaxanthin.*

Risks of Eating Fish: Concerns have grown during the past several decades about toxic contaminants in fish. Recommendations from experts vary about how much fish to eat. Some claim that the benefits outweigh the risks.

However, the FDA's official advice is to eat fish twice a week, but not more often. This limit is especially important for young children and women who are pregnant or may become pregnant, because these toxins can impair neurological development.

Contaminants in fish can include mercury, other heavy metals including arsenic, industrial byproducts such as dioxins, industrial compounds such as PCBs, and pesticides such as DDT. Levels of various contaminants vary by species, by locale, and whether the fish are wild or farmed.

The human body can and does rid itself of contaminants. However, the process is slow for fat-soluble pollutants—which most of these are. It takes more than one year for mercury levels to drop significantly.

For some pollutants, it can take as much as ten years to reduce the load by half. Typically, our intake rates of these substances are higher than our ability to get rid of them, so levels build up.

Although there are numerous health benefits to be gained from consuming oily fish, there are still limitations on the amount of fish that we should consume per week. This is because some types of oily fish are prone to absorbing metals and toxins that have been pumped into our rivers and seas.

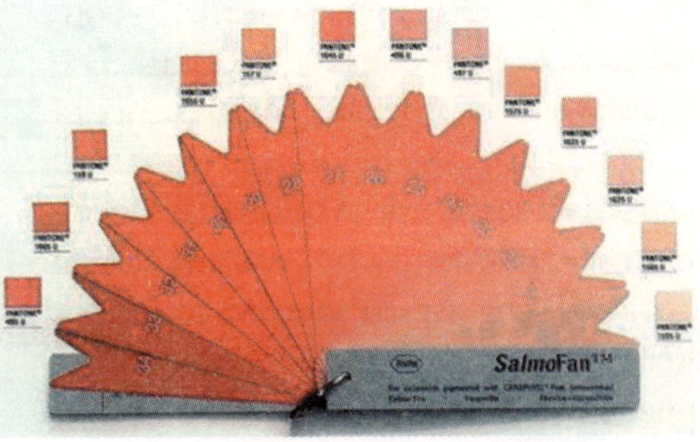

Unhealthy Practices: How about some antibiotics, pesticides, PCB's, and artificial color with that salmon?

The color fan is used by some salmon farmers to guide the shade of flesh they'd like to see in their salmon, post-slaughter. Consumers, you see, like their salmon pink.

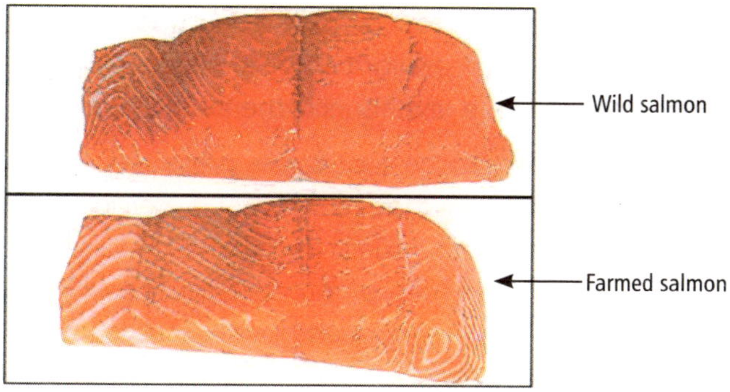

The bright pink color of wild salmon comes from naturally occurring pigments in the krill and shrimp that constitute a wild salmon's diet.

Yes, farmed salmon. And in case you're wondering about the history of the pink one you just ate, up to 90% of the fresh salmon in the US is farmed.

The salmon farming industry intentionally fattens its fish to maximize market weight, a process similar to fattening cows or hogs in a feed lot. As a result, an ounce of farmed salmon contains 52 per cent more fat than an ounce of wild salmon, according to the U.S. Department of Agriculture.

Cancer causing PCBs (polychlorinated biphenyls) collect in fat, as opposed to muscle or other organs. Farmed salmon, because they are intentionally fattened, are efficient collectors of PCBs. PCBs build up in salmon at 20 to 30 times the levels in their environment.

Your heart and gastrointestinal track should now and forever belong to the wild. The image above is the wild salmon; with the lower image is the farmed

SELECTION

In most cases, fresh is best when it comes to choosing oil-rich fish species because the natural fats occurring in these fish deteriorate and they lose their quality quickly. Oily fish tend to be landed and sold un-gutted to maintain their quality.

They're generally also good value for money. Look for fish that are still stiff and rigid and in 'rigor mortis' – this will indicate that the fish has been out of the water for no more than a day or so.

At this stage the fish will have bright, clear eyes, the gills will be a vibrant, red color and it will hardly have any smell at all. As the fish loses condition it will become softer and its smell will become stronger.

STORING

Oily fish must be stored in as cool a place as possible and eaten quickly, ideally on the day of purchase. Arrange it in a single layer on a tray and keep cool by covering the fish with ice.

Oil-rich species freeze well for a short period of time: gut or fillet them, pack into freezer bags as whole fish or two portions at a time, extract the air and secure the bag. Defrost the fish for a few hours in the fridge before use.

Oily fish can also be successfully preserved – smoking, brining and salting are all popular preserving methods. Mackerel is available both hot-smoked and salted; tuna and mackerel are both sold canned too.

SERVING

"The recommendation is two servings of fish a week," Tansman says. "At 3 to 4 ounces per serving, that's well below the FDA's safe limit of 12 ounces per week."

As oily fish contain a certain amount of fat in their flesh, it is best to use cooking methods where additional oil is not needed. Therefore, grilling, baking, steaming and pan-frying are ideal for oily fish but shallow frying and deep-fat frying aren't.

Oily fish are versatile. They suit grilling, barbecuing, roasting and baking and, in some cases, pan-frying. The natural oils give these fish an intense flavor that pairs well with other strong flavors.

Bottom Line

1. Only oily fish have health benefiting Omega-3 fat.
2. Farm fish are artificially colored, intentionally fattened and generally have doubtful health benefits.
3. One of the best options for healthy fish is eating wild salmon twice a week- eat less - eat right.

VIRGIN OLIVE

"Extra virgin olive oil is liquid Gold"

Olives are small fruits, packed with big health benefits. Even though more attention has sometimes been given to their delicious oil than their whole food delights, olives are one of the world's most widely enjoyed foods.

Botanically olives belong to a very special group of fruits called drupes. Drupes are fruits that have a pit or stone at their core. Other drupes commonly found in diets worldwide include mango, cherry, peach, plum, apricot, nectarine, almond, and pistachio.

While some olives can be eaten right off the tree, most olives sold commercially have been processed to reduce their intrinsic bitterness. Unripe olives, which are pear-shaped and green, will change to a dark purple and then black as they ripen and "fill" with oil. Olives can be processed for oil at any time.

When freshly picked from the tree, olives often have a bitter flavor. This bitterness is related to their extremely rich phytonutrient content. In order to help offset their bitter taste, olives are typically cured, also known as pickling.

Ripe olives will yield more oil and it will be less bitter. Like wine, the conditions and treatment of the olive tree throughout the year will have an effect on the yield and quality of the oil. In Spain, olives designated for "virgin" oil must, by law, be pressed within 72 hours of harvesting.

Olive oil is an ancient food that has been used by humans for thousands of years. Olive oil residue has been found in jugs that are over 4,000 years old! It has been called "liquid gold," and prized for its flavors in addition to being a valuable cooking and salad oil.

Olive oil provides a number of health benefits when selected right, cooked right and eaten right. Hippocrates, the father of medicine, was the first to recognize these health and therapeutic advantages.

"Drink wine old and oil young." Unlike wine, olive oil does not improve with age.

Recent research has shown that the Mediterranean diet, which includes olive oil, is not only generally healthy, but can actually help lower ones risk many diseases including heart disease and cancer.

Olive oil is easy to digest, helps assimilate vitamins and minerals, and has a positive effect on the digestive system by stimulating the gall bladder. It also contains Chlorophyll, giving the oil its color, which works on the metabolism, stimulating cellular growth and speeding the process of healing over wounds.

There are literally hundreds of varieties of olive trees, but all of them belong to the same scientific category of Olea europea. "Olea" is the Latin word for "oil," and reflects the high oil content of this food. Olive trees are native to the Mediterranean, as well as different parts of Asia and Africa.

Olives constitute one of the world's largest fruit crops, with more than 25 million acres of olive trees planted worldwide. On a worldwide basis, olives are produced in greater amounts than grapes, apples, or oranges.

Spain is the largest single producer of olives at approximately 6 million tons per year. Italy is second at approximately 3.5 million tons, followed by Greece at 2.5 million. Turkey and Syria are the next major olive producers.

RICH SOURCE

Olives have plenty of valuable vitamins and minerals to contribute to one's diet. The list of minerals includes calcium, iron, magnesium, potassium, zinc, copper, phosphorus, natrium, and selenium.

There are also many vitamins in olives, such as B1 – 6, vitamin A, vitamin E, and vitamin K. Olives can also contribute small amounts of sugar, carbs, and fiber to one's diet. One can get a good portion of daily healthy monosaturated fats by eating just a few olives each day.

Olives are unusual in their fat quality, because they provide almost three-quarters of their fat as oleic acid, a monounsaturated fatty acid. The high monounsaturated fat content of olives has been associated with reduced risk of cardiovascular disease.

Unlike a lot of other vegetable oils, olive oil is at its essence a fruit juice. Other vegetable oils must be extracted from their plant matter by solvents and heat treatment. On the other hand, olives are cold pressed and the olive oil is squeezed out of them.

Olive oil provides a number of health benefits when selected right, cooked right and eaten right. Hippocrates, the father of medicine, was the first to recognize these health and therapeutic advantages.

During the process of pressing the oil is separated from the rest of the olive solids and non-oil liquids, other microscopic "plant bits" get suspended in the olive oil.

This is one of the things that researchers think contribute heavily to the health benefits of olive oil. All of the things that were there to keep the olive oil fresh for use by the olives help preserve our bodies when we ingest it.

Olive oil is cholesterol free and is made up of 70% monounsaturated fatty acid which reduces bad blood-cholesterol (LDL) while boosting the good blood-cholesterol (HDL).

Greek-style black olives, Spanish-style green olives, Kalamata-style olives, and many different methods of olive preparation, all provide us with valuable amounts of many different anti-oxidant and anti-inflammatory nutrients.

ANTI-CANCER BENEFITS

Phytonutrient content of olives is nothing short of astounding. Few high-fat foods offer such a diverse range of anti-oxidant and anti-inflammatory nutrients – some of which are unique to olives themselves.

Some key phytonutrients in olives include 2 types of simple phenols, 7 types of terpenes, 2 types of flavones, 4 types of hydroxycinnamic acids, 2 types of anthocyanidins, 2 types of flavonols, 4 types of hydroxybenzoic acids, and 2 types of hydroxyphenylacetic acids.

Given this phytonutrient richness, it's not surprising that olives have documented

Like wine, the conditions and treatment of the olive tree throughout the year will have an effect on the yield and quality of the oil. In Spain, olives designated for "virgin" oil must, by law, be pressed within 72 hours of harvesting.

health benefits that extend to most of our body systems. Olive benefits have been demonstrated for the cardiovascular system, respiratory system, nervous system, musculoskeletal system, immune system, inflammatory system, and digestive system.

Virginity Test: There are varying degrees of "virginity" and it's measured by the percentage of oleic acid that the oil contains. To qualify as an extra virgin olive oil, the oil must contain between 1% and 4% oleic acid. If the percentage is above 4, the oil must be corrected or adjusted to retain the label "virgin olive oil". or become a lower grade olive oil.

Breast and Stomach Cancer: Researchers at the University of Jaén have become the first to win Castillo de Canena's Luis Vaño Olive Oil Research Prize awarded to the best olive or olive oil-related research study in Spain.

The study, titled "'The Influence of Minor Components Present in Virgin Olive Oils in the Prevention of Breast Cancer: In Vitro Study of 'Hydroxytyrosol and Tyrosol,' was conducted by José Juan Gaforio, Fernando Warleta and Cristina Sánchez of the University's Department of Immunology.

"We have studied the effects of four compounds present in the olive skin; erythrodiol, ovaol, maslinic acid and oleanolic acidon with human breast cancer cells and the results show that the compounds have the potential to provide a natural defense against breast cancer," researchers noted.

"The results of this research have an important social and economic impact on Spanish society. Highlighting the healthy properties of olive oil is an element of the first order to encourage their use in other countries," Gaforio told Science Watch.

Research on whole olives and cancer has often focused on two cancer types: breast cancer and stomach cancer. Olive phytonutrients have been shown to help interrupt the life cycle of breast and gastric cancer cells.

A study published in the January 2005 issue of Annals of Oncology has identified oleic acid, a monounsaturated fatty acid found in olive oil, as having the ability to reduce the effect of an oncogene (a gene that will turn a host cell into a cancer cell).

> *Unlike a lot of other vegetable oils, olive oil is at its essence a fruit juice.*

This particular oncogene is associated with the rapid growth of breast cancer tumors. The conclusion of the researchers was that oleic acid when combined with drug therapy encouraged the self-destruction of aggressive, treatment-resistant cancer cells thus destroying the cancer.

Prostate, Endometrial and Colon Cancer: Olive oil has been positively indicated in studies on prostate and endometrial cancers. Unlike other fats, which are associated with a higher risk of colon cancer, olive oil helps protect the cells of the colon from carcinogens.

A study published in the November 2003 issue of Food Chemistry Toxicology suggests that the anti-oxidants present in olives reduce the amount of carcinogens formed when meat is cooked in olive oil.

SELECTION

Many believe that the color will give an indication of the olive oil's quality, but this is not so. The color will depend on the ripeness of the olives upon harvesting, and the type of olives used.

When tasting olive oil, the first thing one must do is to smell the oil. Next, one should taste the olive oil with some bread, or preferably with a spoon so as to swill the oil around the mouth before swallowing.

The saying goes "Never use a wine or olive oil that does not taste good to you. An inferior one will leave an aftertaste. If you do the taste test and compare the 'pure' to the 'extra-virgin' and then you'll understand the difference".

Olive oil extraction is the process of extracting the oil present in the olive drupes for food use and separating the other fruit contents like vegetable extract and other solid residues etc.

It is possible to attain this separation by physical means alone, i.e., oil and water do not mix, so they are relatively easy to separate. This contrasts with other oils that are extracted with chemical solvents like hexane and heat.

This process of olive oil extraction is called the 'first cold pressing", in which the oil is obtained without heat or chemicals. A batch of ten pounds of olives will produce about one quart of oil. With this process, 90% of the oil is extracted with the first press and it is of the highest quality full of phytonutrients.

The residual paste is sent to the refinery to remove the remaining 10%, or pomace oil. There are actually four kinds of olive oils available in the market.

Extra-virgin: The best of the virgin oil is classified as "extra-virgin," which has superior characteristics, including very low rancidity and the best flavor. It also has the highest level of polyphenols and other phytonutrients.

Olive oil is typically produced from the first pressing of olives -- making it the most pure and least acidic (less than 0.8 per cent), and the best tasting. It's expensive, heavier, flavorful, but chockfull of health-benefiting phytonutrients.

Look for bottles that say "cold press" on the label. If it's not cold-pressed, the heat from the extraction process changes the chemistry and quality of the olive oil.

Virgin olive oil isn't blended with other oils but has a higher acidity -- up to 2 per cent. It's perfect for garnishing.

Pure olive oil or olive oil is a blend of refined pomace oil and virgin olive oil. Pomace is produced by processing the leftovers of the virgin olive oil extraction. The blend, which usually contains as little as 5 to 10 per cent virgin olive oil, is cheaper to produce.

It doesn't have as strong a flavor as virgin olive oils and is best suited for frying and cooking, or even as a less expensive substitute.

Light olive oil isn't lower in fat -- it simply means the oil is made from refined olive oil. Bottles labeled "100 per cent pure olive oil" is often the lowest quality.

STORING

Depending on the quality of the oil and on how it was made, extra-virgin olive oil in a sealed bottle may last from 3 months to 2 years. After this it may begin to start to show signs of oxidation and an evident loss of quality. Bad oil will be obvious from a distinctive, unpleasant odor.

As soon as you open the bottle, the oxidation process starts and accelerates fairly rapidly. Olive oil should always be stored away from heat, light, and air.

It will solidify at 36° F (2°C), causing a white solid layer to form at the bottom of the bottle. This will not hurt the oil, which will return to normal if brought back up to room temperature.

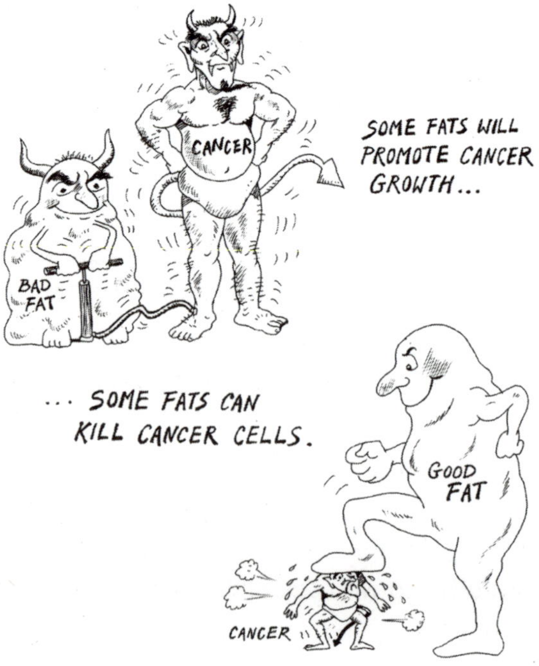

The main ways to protect the oil from light and heat are :

- Buy olive oil in dark glass bottles (or harder-to-find metal containers).
- Try to buy from a store that has a rapid turnover -- no dusty bottles sitting on the shelves for months.
- The annual olive harvest is in autumn for most varieties. Look to see if there is a date on the label, and try to get the freshest oil you can.
- Store in a dark, cool cupboard or the best is in refrigerator until ready to use, then transfer the amount you will use in a week or two to a dark glass bottle.

Olive oil in the refrigerator will solidify, but will "melt" again at room temperature. If you are purchasing olives in a can and don't want to use them immediately after opening, they can usually be safely stored in sealed container in your refrigerator for one to two weeks.

Whether brine-based, acid-based, or water-based, you can transfer the canning fluid along with the olives into your sealed refrigerator container. Glass jars of olives can be stored directly in the refrigerator for the same period of time, and in the case of some brine-cured olives, for up to one to two months.

SERVING

"Too much of a good thing is also bad", whatever oil you choose restrict the quantity to maximum of 8 teaspoons (40 gm.) per day or not more than one liter per person per month.

When cooking with olive oil, save your extra-virgin expensive oils for salads, dressings, and vinaigrettes. It can also be drizzled over slices of crusty bread or onto open-face sandwiches.

Use it on a baked potato or add it to mashed potatoes instead of butter. Extra virgin olive oil tastes great on cooked vegetables or brushed onto fish or meat before serving.

Infusing Olive Oil: It is possible to make excellent infused oil at home using dried wild herbs. The intensity of the flavor varies with the season, whether the herbs are wild or domestic, how the local growing conditions have been, etc. It takes a lot of trial and error.

It is more art than science and the people who are good at it are reluctant to share their trade secrets. The oil will pick up the flavor fairly quickly, in the first few weeks, and then slowly intensify. It is fine to leave the herbs in for a long time; eventually all the flavor leaves the herbs and the oil flavor stabilizes.

Most oil sellers keep it simple and use one herb at a time. Use dry spices and herbs; add them to the olive oil. Whole sprigs of thyme, rosemary, dried peppers, etc. can decorate the inside of the bottle this way. For other ideas, Greece is a great place to turn, as a Greek person typically consumes 26 liters of olive oil in a year!

To pit olives, press them with the flat side of a broad bladed knife. This will help break the flesh so that you can easily remove the pit with your fingers or the knife. The brine in which olives are packed can be used as a replacement for salted water in recipes.

Olive tapenade is a delicious and easy-to-make spread that you can use as a dip, sandwich spread, or topping for fish and poultry. To make it, put pitted olives in a food processor with olive oil, garlic, and your favorite seasonings.

Toss pasta with chopped olives, tomatoes, garlic, olive oil and fresh herbs of your choice.

Marinate olives in olive oil, lemon zest, coriander seeds and cumin seeds.

Add chopped olives to your favorite tuna or chicken salad recipe.

Set out a small plate of olives on the dinner table along with some vegetable crudités for your family to enjoy with the meal.

Bottom Line

1. Extra virgin cold pressed is the best for heath –olive oil.
2. For getting the full benefits use minimum heating, adding the oil in the last stage of cooking is good idea.
3. No more than one liter per person per month.

WALNUTS

Walnuts are a delicious way to add extra nutrition, flavor and crunch to a meal. They are deliciously healthy.

They are revered since ancient times as a symbol of intellectuality. They are "brain food". Physically the walnut looks a lot like the human brain. The thin, outer green cover that is taken out before the walnuts are sold is similar to the scalp.

The hard shell of a walnut is like a skull. The thin sheet inside, with its paper-like partitions between the two halves of the walnut, is like the membrane. The shape of the walnut itself represents the human brain's two hemispheres.

Walnuts help correct the human brain's serotonin levels, an important brain chemical that controls both our moods and appetite. It relieves disorders like insomnia, depression, overeating and other compulsive behavior, commonly treated with antidepressant drugs like Prozac, without the dangerous side effects.

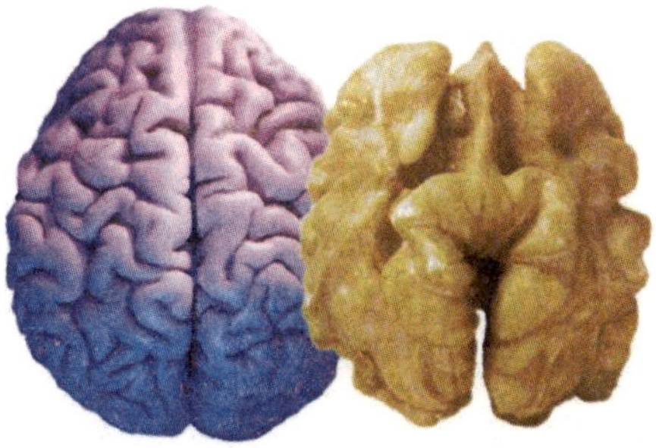

The nuts are enriched with many health-benefiting nutrients, especially omega-3 fatty acids that are essential for optimum health and body cannot make it of its own.

Walnut oil has flavorful nutty aroma and has an excellent astringent properties; helps to keep skin well protected from dryness. It has also been used in cooking, and as "carrier or base oil" in traditional medicines in massage therapy, aromatherapy, in pharmaceutical and cosmetic industry.

While walnut trees have been cultivated for thousands of years, the different types have varying origins. The English walnut originated in India and the regions surrounding the Caspian Sea, hence it is known as the Persian walnut.

Throughout its history, the walnut tree has also been highly revered; not only does it have a life span that is several times that of humans, but its uses include food, medicine, shelter, dye and lamp oil.

China is presently the largest commercial producer of walnuts in the world, with about 360,000 metric tons produced per year. The United States is second, with about 294,000 metric tons of production. After plantation, the plant takes approximately four years until it produces its first major crop.

The polyphenols found in walnuts, one of which is the most well-known Ellagic acid, can neutralize free radicals which can disrupt the body and cause cell damage, aging, atherosclerosis, cancer and loss of vision.

Incorporating walnuts into your diet will play a big part in lowering cholesterol, as well as improving the health of the whole body. All you need is 7 walnuts per day to achieve the possible health improvements.

RICH SOURCE

Walnuts are an excellent source of anti-inflammatory omega-3 essential fatty acids, in the form of alpha-linolenic acid (ALA). They are rich in anti-oxidants, including being a very good source of manganese and a good source of copper.

> *It relieves disorders like insomnia, depression, overeating and other compulsive behavior, commonly treated with antidepressant drugs like Prozac, without the dangerous side effects.*

Walnut is also a valuable source of many other minerals like calcium, chromium, iron, magnesium, phosphorus, potassium, selenium, vanadium and zinc. These nuts are packed with many important B-complex groups of vitamins such as riboflavin, niacin, thiamin, pantothenic acid, vitamin B-6, and folate.

In terms of phytonutrients, walnuts contain anti-oxidant and anti-inflammatory compounds, including more than a dozen phenolic acids, numerous tannins (especially ellagitannins, including tellimagrandins), and a wide variety of flavonoids.

These nutrients have potential health effects against cancer, aging, inflammation, and neurological diseases.

Scientists at the University of Scranton, Pennsylvania, have recently discovered that walnuts have highest levels of polyphenolic anti-oxidants than any other common edible nuts.

In addition, they are also an excellent source of vitamin E, especially rich in gamma-tocopherol; contain about 21 g per 100 g (about 140% of daily-required levels). Vitamin E is a powerful lipid soluble anti-oxidant, required for maintaining the integrity of cell membrane of mucus membranes and skin by protecting it from harmful oxygen free radicals.

The Food and Drug Administration of USA recently stated that 1 ½ ounces of walnuts each day may reduce the risk of heart disease. Dr Emilio Ros, of Hospital Clinic De Barcelona, said that this is the first whole food, and not just a component in a food, that has shown this type of effect on heart health.

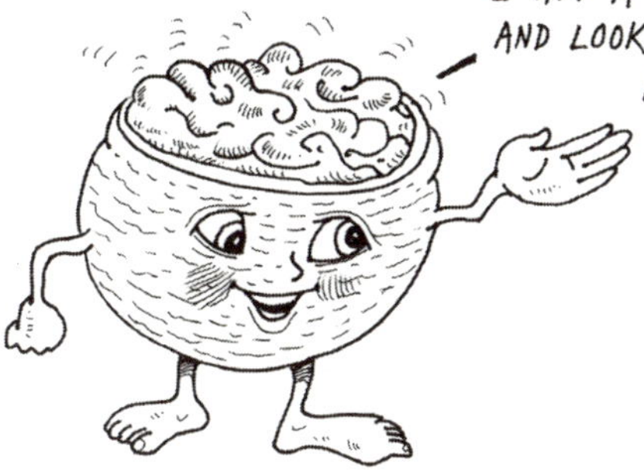

Researchers are convinced – more than ever before – about the nutritional benefits of walnuts when consumed in whole form, including the skin. We now know that approximately 90% of the phenols in walnuts are found in the skin, including key phenolic acids, tannins, and flavonoids.

Removing the walnut skin – that is whitish, sometimes waxy, sometimes flaky, outermost part of shelled walnuts is not a very good idea as this the most health–benefiting phenol-rich portion of it.

ANTI-CANCER BENEFITS

Given the wide variety of anti-oxidant and anti-inflammatory nutrients found in walnuts, it's not surprising to see research on this tree nut showing measurable anti-cancer benefits.

Some phytonutrients found in walnuts – for example, the quinone juglone – are found in virtually no other commonly-eaten foods. Other phytonutrients – like the tannin tellimagrandin or the flavonol morin - are also rare and valuable as anti-oxidants and anti-inflammatory nutrients.

The anti-oxidant properties of walnuts help lower risk of chronic oxidative stress, and the anti-inflammatory properties help lower risk of chronic inflammation, and it is precisely these two types of risk, that, when combined, pose the greatest threat for cancer development.

Prostate and Breast Cancer: Walnut consumption may provide the body with essential omega-3 fatty acids, anti-oxidants and phytosterols that reduce the risk of breast cancer, according to a study presented at the American Association for Cancer Research's 100th Annual Meeting 2009.

Prostate cancer and breast cancer are the best-studied types of cancer with respect to walnut intake, and their risk has been found to be reduced by fairly large amounts of walnut consumption.

We now know that approximately 90% of the phenols in walnuts are found in the skin, including key phenolic acids, tannins, and flavonoids.

Large in this case means approximately 3 ounces or 21 nuts per day. For prostate cancer, the evidence is somewhat stronger, and more studies have involved human subjects.

Researcher W. Elaine Hardman, Ph.D, associate professor of biochemistry at Marshall University School of Medicine in Huntington, W.Va., credits the disease-fighting omega-3 fatty acids, anti-oxidants, and in particular, phytosterols, in walnuts for the anti-cancer benefits.

Just two handfuls of walnuts a day may keep breast cancer away, a study in mice suggests. And if you have breast cancer, walnuts may help curb tumor growth, the study suggests. Hardman and colleagues studied genetically altered mice that were programmed to develop tumors within six months. Half consumed a diet that contained the human equivalent of two 1-ounce servings of walnuts per day. "One serving fits in the palm of your hand," she says.

The other half was fed a diet that did not include walnuts.

Standard testing showed that eating walnuts cut the risk of developing breast tumors in half.

"If mice did get breast tumors, the growth rate was also slowed, by 50%," Hardman says.

Looked at another way, eating walnuts delayed the development of tumors by at least three weeks in the mice. "Extrapolating to humans, this would be about a nine-year delay," she says.

The researchers are now testing the benefits of the walnut-rich diet in male mice genetically altered to develop prostate tumors. Hardman says she expected similar results, with the nuts both preventing and slowing the growth of prostate tumors.

"Phytosterols bind to estrogen receptors, so they would be expected to slow growth of breast cancers," she says. Estrogen fuels the growth of some breast tumors.

"Walnuts are better than cookies, French fries or potato chips when you need a snack," said Hardman. "We know that a healthy diet overall prevents all manner of chronic diseases."

SELECTION

When purchasing whole walnuts that have not been shelled, choose those that feel heavy for their size. Their shells should not be cracked, pierced or stained, as this is oftentimes a sign of mold development on the nutmeat, which renders it unsafe for consumption.

Shelled walnuts are generally available in prepackaged containers; avoid those that look rubbery or shriveled. If it is possible to smell the walnuts, do so in order to ensure that they are not rancid.

STORING

Due to their high oil content, walnuts are extremely perishable and care should be taken in their storage.

Shelled walnuts should be stored in an airtight container and placed in the refrigerator, where they will keep for six months, or the freezer, where they will last for one year.

Unshelled walnuts should preferably be stored in the refrigerator, although as long as you keep them in a cool, dry, dark place they will stay fresh for up to six months.

SERVING

In whatever style you decide to prepare walnuts, it's worth including the skin. Some people may not even notice that there is a walnut skin. But that whitish, sometimes waxy, sometimes flaky, outermost part of the walnut (once it has been shelled) is the skin.

Like most nuts, they can easily be added to variety of your favorite dishes. Just chop and add to your favorite salad, vegetable dish, fruit, or dessert. Some quick serving ideas include:

- Mix crushed walnuts into plain curd or yogurt.
- Add walnuts to salads or healthy sautéed vegetables.
- Purée walnuts, cooked lentils and your favorite herbs and spices in a food processor. Add enough olive or flax oil so that it achieves a dip-like consistency.
- Add walnuts to your favorite poultry stuffing recipe.
- To roast walnuts at home, do so gently—in a 160-170°F (about 75°C) oven for 15-20 minutes—to preserve the healthy oils.

Walnut allergy is a type of hypersensitivity reaction to food substances prepared using these nuts. It is due to prior sensitization of the immune system by allergens in the nuts, which may lead to severe physical symptoms like pain in abdomen, vomiting, swelling of lips and throat leading to breathing difficulty, and chest congestion. Therefore, it is advised to avoid any food preparations that contain these nut products in known case of walnut allergic individuals.

Bottom Line

1. Only seven walnuts a day can fulfill your daily need of Omega -3 fat.
2. Best is to buy fresh walnuts in shells and refrigerate them for long life and optimum nutrition.
3. Sharp brain, younger looks, healthy heart, good sleep, di-stressed body, cancer protected...list of eating walnuts is endless.

Some other Books on Cancer

BOOK	— **Anticancer, A New Way of Life**
AUTHOR	— **Dr David Seran - Shrieber,** *M.D., Ph.D.*

20 New Anticancer Rules

Dr Servan-Schreiber, M.D., Ph.D. author of the best-selling book "Anticancer, A New Way of Life" writes: "I'd like every person to know about how they can help avoid cancer - or slow it down if they have it.

FOOD RULES

1. **Go retro:** Your main course should be 80 per cent vegetables, 20 per cent animal protein, like it was in the old days. Opt for the opposite of the quarter pounder topped with a token leaf of iceberg lettuce and an anemic tomato slice. Meat should be used sparingly for taste, as when it used to be scarce, and should not be the focus of the meal.

2. **Mix and match your vegetables:** Vary the vegetables you eat from one meal to the next, or mix them together -- broccoli is an effective anti-cancer food, and is even more effective when combined with tomato sauce, onions or garlic. Get in the habit of adding onions, garlic or leeks to all your dishes as you cook.

3. **Go organic:** Choose organic foods whenever possible, but remember it's always better to eat broccoli that's been exposed to pesticide than to not eat broccoli at all (the same applies to any other anti-cancer vegetable).

4. **Spice it up:** Add turmeric (with black pepper) when cooking (delicious in salad dressings!). This yellow spice is the most powerful natural anti-inflammatory agent. Remember to add Mediterranean herbs to your food: thyme, oregano, basil, rosemary, marjoram, mint, etc. They don't just add flavor, they can also help reduce the growth of cancer cells.

5. **Skip the potato:** Potatoes raise blood sugar, which can feed inflammation and cancer growth. They also contain high levels of pesticide residue (to the point that most potato farmers I know don't eat their own grown potatoes).

6. **Go fish:** Eat fish two or three times a week – sardines, mackerel, and anchovies have less mercury and PCBs than bigger fish like tuna. Avoid swordfish and shark, which the FDA says pregnant women should not eat because they contain a high concentration of contaminants.

7. **Remember not all eggs are created equal:** Choose only omega-3 eggs, or don't eat the yolks. Hens are now fed on mostly corn and soybeans, and their eggs contain 20 times more pro-inflammatory omega-6 fatty acids than cell-growth regulating omega-3s.

8. **Change your oil:** Use only olive and canola oil in cooking and salad dressings. Go through your kitchen cabinets and throw out your soybean, corn and sunflower oils. (And no, you can't give them to your neighbors or your relatives... They're much too rich in omega-6 fatty acids!)

9. **Say "Brown is beautiful":** Eat your grains whole and mixed (wheat with oats, barley, spelt, flax, etc.) and favor organic whole grains when possible since pesticides tend to accumulate on whole grains. Avoid refined, white flour (used in bagels, muffins, sandwich bread, buns, etc.) whenever possible, and eat white pasta only al dente.

10. **Keep sweets down to fruits:** Cut down on sugar by avoiding sweetened sodas and fruit juices, and skipping dessert or replacing it with fruit (especially stone fruits and berries) after most meals. Read the labels carefully, and steer clear of products that list any type of sugar (including brown sugar, corn syrup, etc.) in the first three ingredients. If you have an incorrigible sweet tooth, try a few squares of dark chocolate containing more than 70% cocoa.

11. **Go green:** Instead of coffee or black tea, drink three cups of green tea per day. Use decaffeinated green tea if it gets you too wired. Regular consumption of green tea has been linked to a significant reduction in the risk for developing cancer.

12. **Make room for exceptions**. What matters is what you do on a daily basis, not the occasional treat.

NON-FOOD RULES

1. **Get physical:** Make time to exercise, be it walking, dancing or running. Aim for 30 minutes of physical activity at least 5 days a week. This can be as easy as just walking part of the way to the office, or the grocery store. A dog is often a better walking partner than an exercise buddy. Choose an activity you enjoy; if you're having fun, you're more likely to stick with it.

2. **Let the sun shine in:** Try to get at least 20 minutes of daily sun exposure (torso, arms and legs) without sunscreen, preferably at noon in the summer (but take care to avoid sunburns!). This will boost your body's natural production of Vitamin D. As an alternative: discuss the option of taking a Vitamin D3 supplement with your doctor.

3. **Banish bad chemicals:** Avoid exposure to common household contaminants. You should air your dry-cleaning for two hours before storing or wearing it; use organic cleaning products (or wear gloves); don't heat liquids or food in hard plastics; avoid cosmetics with parabens and phthalates; don't use chemical pesticides in your house or garden; replace your scratched Teflon pans; filter your

tap water (or used bottled water) if you live in a contaminated area; don't keep your cell phone close to you when it is turned on.

4. **Reach out (and touch someone!):** Reach out to at least two friends for support (logistical and emotional) during times of stress, even if it's through the internet. But if they're within arms reach, go ahead and hug them, often!
5. **Remember to breathe:** Learn a basic breathing relaxation technique to let out some steam whenever you start to feel stressed.
6. **Get involved:** Find out how you can best give something back to your local community, then give it.
7. **Cultivate happiness like a garden:** Make sure you do one thing you love for yourself on most days (it doesn't have to take long!).

CHAPTER 7

Master Strokes

Battle against cancer is fought at different levels. Miracles do happen. Power of the mind, and our belief systems should never be underestimated. We are what be think we are.

Modern medicine is very young, merely 200 years old, and we are surviving, living and thriving on the planet for the last 200,000 years. It is now that we have started realizing the wisdom of ancient holistic approach to cancer management.

The major difference between young modern medicine is that it targets disease, whereas holistic approach treats the cause. Modern medicine weakens the immune system, whereas holistic philosophy strengthens it.

It is difficult to imagine our winning battle against cancer without revitalizing our immune system by very harmonious body-mind relationship. They are challenging concepts, but step by step we can master them.

As the saying goes, "Body heals itself and the doctor takes the fees".

GENES

"The mind is everything; what you think, you become" - Buddha

A sour mind produces a sour stomach; this fact has been demonstrated so frequently and proved so conclusively, that it has become an accepted truth.

The age-old adage "everything looks yellow to a jaundiced eye" is also so true even today.

Every action of the brain produces a certain effect in the body. When the mental action is weak or superficial, the physical effect may be too slight to be noticed, but when this action is both deep and strong, the results will be so clearly in evidence that anyone can see it.

The power of the brain affects everything in the body, frequently producing chemical changes that we have previously believed were possible only through the use of most powerful drugs.

Modern science and medications are very young and have just about started grappling with the mysteries of mind and the immense power it has got to heal our diseases, ranging from common cold to cancer.

Science Behind: Every living organism has genes. Genes are a set of instructions that decide what the organism is like, how it survives, and how it behaves in its environment.

Your genes are responsible for your color, hair, height, how you are going to look like, chances of certain diseases including cancer.

We get our genes from our parents. Scientists say that a gene is a basic unit of heredity in a living organism. Anything that lives depends on genes. So far it was assumed that genes are fate we can do nothing to influence them barring blaming our parents.

According to Dr Bruce Lipton of the University of Virginia, USA, "Our health is not controlled by genetics, Conventional medicine does miracles," he said, "but it's limited to trauma only".

Dr Lipton elaborates "regard your physical body like a machine, in the same way that an auto mechanic regards a car. When the parts break, you replace them—a transplant, synthetic joints, and so on—and those are medical miracles."

"The problem is that while they have an understanding that the mechanism isn't working, they're blaming the vehicle for what went wrong. They believe that the vehicle, in this case our bodies, is controlled by genes.

"But guess what? They don't take into consideration that there's actually a driver in that car. The new science, epigenetics, reveals that the vehicles—or the genes—aren't responsible for the breakdown. It's the driver."

Knowing that you have a genetic risk and understanding what it means may motivate you to make preventive lifestyle and behavioral changes.

New research has revealed the science of epigenetics. According to which, it is not the genes which determine the fate of the cells, but it is the environment that is responsible for the fate of the cells. So if cells are in a healthy environment, they are healthy. If they're in an unhealthy environment, they get sick.

Dr Lipton then took this a step further, which brings us back to the cancer question. "Here's the connection"–With fifty trillion cells in your body, moving your body from one environment to another alters the composition of the 'culture medium,' the blood."

The blood's chemistry is largely impacted by the chemicals emitted from your brain. Brain chemistry adjusts the composition of the blood based upon your perceptions of life. In other words, your thoughts and perceptions have a direct and overwhelmingly significant effect on cells.

This echo, from a highly scientific point of view, what the intuitive and spiritual healers have been advocating for years: your mind can and does contribute to both the cause and healing of whatever ails you—including cancer.

Other than the mind, two other factors impact the fate of cells, according to Dr Lipton: toxins and trauma. All three factors have been associated with the onset of cancer.

ANTI-CANCER BENEFITS

According to Dr Lipton, gene activity can change on a daily basis. Research illustrates that by changing your perception, your mind can alter the activity of your genes and create over thirty thousand variations of products from each gene.

In the simplest terms, this means that we need to change the way we think if we are to heal cancer.

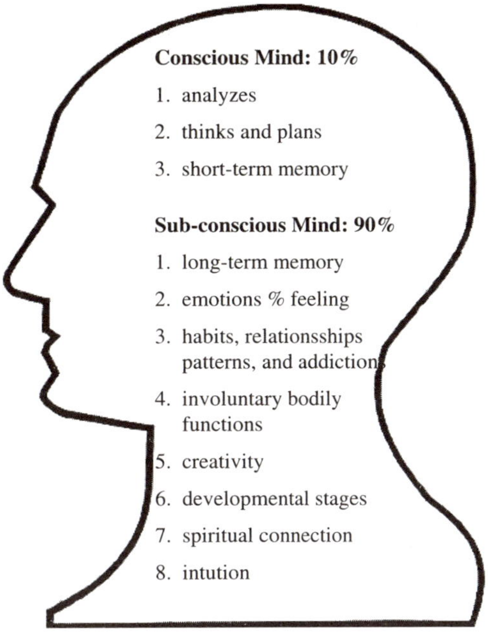

NOCEBO EFFECT

If you've been told you'll die in six months and your mind believes it, you most likely will die in six months. That's called the "nocebo" effect, the result of a negative thought, which is the opposite of the placebo effect, where healing is mediated by a positive thought.

There's the part of you that swears it doesn't want to die that is the conscious mind.

Conscious mind is overruled by the part that believes you will die as per the doctor's prognosis mediated by the subconscious mind. Which then starts the chemical reaction to make sure the body conforms to the dominant belief.

Our subconscious mind is programmed early in the childhood. The problem is that neuroscience has recognized that the subconscious mind controls 95 per cent of our lives.

This is what getting us killed. The joke, however, is that people often get better while on the way to the doctor they believe in.

Jesuits used to say, 'Give me a child until age six or seven and he'll be with the church for the rest of his life.' They knew that our subconscious minds are programmed through the experiences we have in the first six years of our lives.

Since the subconscious programs operate outside the range of consciousness, we see ourselves as victims of forces outside of our control. So we perceive ourselves as victims, and we believe that genes are in control.

Most people don't even acknowledge that their subconscious mind is at play, when the fact is that the subconscious mind is a million times more powerful than the conscious mind and that we operate 95 to 99 per cent of our lives from subconscious programs.

Dr Lipton said that to break free of the programming, you have to first recognize that your subconscious mind exists. He urges us to consider that the subconscious mind has been running programs that most likely brought the cancer on.

"You can rewire yourself," he said. "If a disease such as cancer has progressed to an advanced stage, then you might do a round or two of chemo, but at the same time you need to be reprogramming your mind and recognizing your involvement in the disease."

Think well, eat well, and exercise, and your body won't break down and need new parts. Having a genetic variant associated with cancer does NOT mean that you will definitely get cancer. A genetic variant associated with cancer is simply another risk factor.

SOLUTIONS

According to Dr Lipton, we can do this in many ways. "Through processes such as hypnosis, subliminal tapes, the religious use of affirmations, Buddhist mindfulness, or a series of reprogramming modalities collectively referred to as energy psychology.

"Other therapies such as PSYCH-K, Emotional Self-Management (ESM), Eye Movement Desensitization and Reprocessing (EMDR), and Emotional Freedom Techniques (EFT), are among many other new techniques, we can rewrite those destructive programs that occupy our subconscious field."

The core of Dr Lipton's premise is that by rewiring the subconscious thoughts that negatively impact our cells; we have a far greater chance of healing. The absence of doing this kind of work could also explain why cancer recurs, even after hard-core treatment and years of remission. You can learn more about it from Dr Lipton's book–**The Biology of Belief**.

It is a proven fact that one-third of all healings are due to the placebo effect, which is controlled by the mind. Dr Lipton talks about how powerful our minds are in changing our epigenetics to heal an illness and even correct defective organs or bones. Spontaneous Remissions happen all the time.

Our bodies can instantly reprogram our cells to be healthy or sick. Dr Lipton says a gene is like a blueprint but epigenetics can create up to 30,000 different prints of that gene. That is amazing.

POWER OF BELIEF

Studies show that between 1/3 and 2/3 of all illnesses that are corrected are because of the PLACEBO Effect and not a pill or operation. A NOCEBO effect is the opposite. It causes negative energy to cause us to be sick.

Dr Wayne Dyer, who is an internationally renowned author and speaker, talks about a man who was told he had a black spot on his lung, presumably sign of a lung cancer. Shortly thereafter he died.

Later they found old x-rays from many years before and the same black spot was there. It didn't affect him until he believed it was dangerous.

Research illustrates that by changing your perception, your mind can alter the activity of your genes and create over thirty thousand variations of products from each gene.

Another doctor was testing two different forms of knee surgery and wanted to find out which was more affective. He also did a PLACEBO effect by making an incision but doing nothing else. He showed the patient a video of someone else's surgery that they believed was happening on their knee.

It turned out all three methods had the same positive affect. Henry Ford, the founder of the Ford Motor Company said "Whether you believe you can or you can't you are correct". The power of our mind can heal us or kill us.

Gretchen Rubin, who wrote a very popular book called "The Happiness Project", writes : 'We are not predisposed to our genes because epigenetics plays our genes in different ways depending on diet, stress and thinking. It is the song that makes us who we are: sick, healthy, happy, sad, etc."

In a mice experiment that showed mice that were licked by their mothers were healthier than those that were not. Humans don't lick but we kiss, hug and touch our loved ones. Remember your epigenetics are changeable!

Dean Michael Ornish, M.D., Clinical Professor of Medicine at the University of California, San Francisco, author of Love & Survival and physician consultant to former President Bill Clinton since 1993, is a strong believer of power of mind.

Dr Ornish also directed the first randomized controlled trial demonstrating that comprehensive lifestyle changes may slow, stop, or even reverse the progression of early-stage prostate cancer. This study was done in collaboration with the Chairs of Urology and Memorial Sloan-Kettering Cancer Center, USA.

In 1998, he published research showing that comprehensive lifestyle changes affect gene expression within three months, "turning on" disease-preventing genes and "turning off" genes that promote cancer and heart disease. The research was done in collaboration with Dr Elizabeth Backburn, who was awarded the Nobel Prize in Medicine in 2009.

Bottom Line

1. Having a bad gene and expression of bad gene in your life, are two entirely different things.
2. Positive attitude, healthy lifestyle and happy thoughts can literally protect us from the ill effects of bad genes.
3. Laugh, share and prosper.

50/52

GREEN TEA

"Tea tempers the spirit, harmonizes the mind, dispels lassitude and relieves fatigue, awakens the thought and prevents drowsiness."
–Lu Yu, the Classic Art of Tea

Worldwide tea consumption is second only to that of water. All true teas whatever their color may be are made from the leaves of an evergreen tree with the botanical name of Camellia sinensis. The plant itself is very ornamental and it thrives in warm areas and the tropics, though it also grows in mountains and high altitudes.

The way the leaves are processed, are important, resulting in individual characteristics of the three predominant types of tea: green, black and oolong.

The health benefits of green tea have been extensively researched. The scientific community's awareness of its potential benefits has increased, so have the number of new studies–at the last count it were over 1000. The caffeine content of green tea is 4 times less than black tea.

Green tea drinkers appear to have lower risk for a wide range of diseases, from simple bacterial or viral infections to chronic degenerative conditions including cardiovascular disease, cancer, stroke, periodontal disease, and osteoporosis.

Green tea has always been, and remains today, the most popular type of tea from China where most historians and botanists believe the tea plant originated throughout all of Asia including India. It has the highest concentration of beneficial phytonutrients and the least caffeine of all the teas.

Tea plants grow only in warm climates but can flourish at altitudes ranging from sea level to 7,000 feet. The best teas, however, are produced by plants grown at higher altitudes where the leaves mature more slowly and yield a richer flavor.

"Better to be deprived of food for three days, than tea for one"... Ancient Chinese proverb

According to ancient Chinese legend, tea was discovered by the Chinese emperor Shen-Nung in 2737 B.C., when leaves from a wild tea bush accidentally fell into a pot of water he was boiling.

India attributes the discovery of tea to the Buddhist monk Siddhartha in the 6th century. Legend has it that the prince-turned-monk traveled north from India to China to preach Buddhism, vowing he would meditate without sleeping for nine years.

In Japan, Buddhist monks embraced tea, using it to remain alert during their own meditations and creating a simple drinking ritual that several hundred years later, tea master Sen-no Rikyu (1521-1591) developed into the high art of chanoyu, the Japanese tea ceremony.

Tea crossed the Atlantic with the American colonists, among whom its popularity led to the British imposition in 1767 of a tea tax that so infuriated the colonists that they revolted, tossing tons of tea into the harbor in 1733 in what became known as the Boston Tea Party.

Worldwide, more than 2.5 million metric tons of tea is produced each year with India, China, Sri Lanka, Kenya, Indonesia, Turkey, U.S.S.R, Japan, Iran and Bangladesh being the leading tea growing countries.

RICH SOURCE

Green tea is the least processed and thus provides the most anti-oxidant polyphenols, notably a catechin called EGCG (epigallocatechin-3-gallate). EGCG play a pivotal role in the green tea's anticancer and anti-oxidant effects.

Research shows that some of the green teas contain amazing amount of health-benefiting anti-oxidants, as high as 30% of green tea leaves, by weight.

All teas are born green. It is the amount of processing and duration of processing, that distinguishes them. The general rule, the least processed and the healthier it is, also holds good in case of tea.

Green tea is made by briefly steaming the just harvested leaves, rendering them soft and pliable and preventing them from fermenting or changing color. The resulting greenish-yellow tea has a green, slightly astringent flavor close to the taste of the fresh leaf.

Black tea production, the leaves are first spread on withering racks and air-blown, which removes about one-third of their moisture and renders them soft and pliable. Next, they are rolled to break their cell walls, releasing the juices essential to fermentation.

Fermentation turns the leaves a dark coppery color and develops black tea's authoritative flavor. Black tea immersion in hot water gives a reddish-brown brew with a stronger flavor than green or oolong teas.

The anti-oxidant activity of EGCG is about 25-100 times more potent than vitamins C and E. Just One cup of green tea may provide 20-40 mg of ECGC and has anti-oxidant effects that are greater than a serving of broccoli, spinach, carrots, or strawberries.

Oolong tea, which is made from leaves that are partially fermented, falls midway between green and black teas. Oolong is a greenish-brown tea whose flavor, color and aroma are richer than that of green tea, but more delicate than that of black.

ANTI-CANCER BENEFITS

Most of the research showing the health benefits of green tea is based on the amount of green tea typically consumed in Asian countries—about 3 cups per day.

Spanish and British scientists have discovered one of the mechanisms through which green tea helps to prevent certain types of cancer, according to a study published in the March 2005 issue of Cancer Research.

ECGC, a catechin present in green tea in amounts about 5 times higher than in black tea, inhibits the enzyme DHFR (dihydrofolate reductase), which cancer cells need to be able to grow. Green tea catechin looks a lot like the cancer drug methotrexate; it kills cancer cells in the same way as the drug.

Cancer Prevention: The evidence is so overwhelming that the Chemoprevention Branch of the National Cancer Institute of USA has initiated a plan for developing tea compounds as cancer-chemo- preventive agents in human trials.

When confronted with a cancerous cell, green tea becomes the plant kingdom's master terminator, helping to terminate cancer cells in a remarkable number of ways.

Studies also show that green tea works at the genetic level, shutting off genes in cancerous cells that are involved in cell growth, while turning on those that instruct the cancer cells to self-destruct.

One of the other mechanisms is green tea's ability to inhibit angiogenesis, the development of new blood vessels. By inhibiting angiogenesis, green tea helps starve cancer.

Cancer Drugs Efficacy: In the fight against cancer, green tea polyphenols are team players, helping cancer-killing drugs do their job more powerfully and persistently.

In a study published in the October 2004 issue of the Journal of Pharmacy and Pharmacology, green tea polyphenols caused drug-resistant cancer cells, which were able to extrude or push out one of the most commonly used cancer drugs, doxorubicin, to retain the drug, which could then destroy them.

Bladder Cancer: About 56,000 new cases of bladder cancer are diagnosed each year, making it the fifth most common cancer in the United States. About half of all bladder cancers are believed to be related to cigarette smoking.

Bladder cancer can be difficult to detect in the early, most treatable stages, yet, when not found early, the tumors can be aggressive, and more than half of patients with advanced cancers experience recurrences.

Research by a multi-departmental team from UCLA has produced valuable insights into how green tea extract might be capable of acting against the invasive growth of bladder cancer tumors.

"Cancer cells are invasive and green tea extract interrupts the invasive process of the cancer. In effect, the green tea extract may keep the cancer cells confined and localized, where they are easier to treat and the prognosis is better," explained Rao.

Brain Tumors in Children: Green tea's ability to inhibit telomerase may also translate into help for children with the most common malignant brain tumors of childhood.

In a study published in the January 2004 issue of Neuro-oncology, investigators found that telomerase activity was at least five times higher in children with these brain tumors than in normal brain cells and that EGCG strongly inhibited telomerase activity in a dose-dependent manner, again the more the merrier.

Colon Cancer: Green tea may also reduce the increased risk for colon cancer caused by a high fat diet.

An animal study published in the journal Nutrition and Cancer in 2003 found that when green tea was given along with a diet high in omega-6 type of bad fats, the amount of pro-inflammatory compounds produced in the colon was significantly lower. So were the resulting numbers of precancerous colon cells.

To evaluate the link between green tea consumption and colorectal cancer risk, researchers followed 69,710 Chinese women ranging in age from 40 to 70 for 6 years.

Women who regularly drank green tea when the study began were 37% less likely to develop colorectal cancer compared to infrequent green tea drinkers. Women who continued to drink green tea regularly throughout the study fared even better, reducing their risk of colorectal cancer by 57%.

Gallstones and Biliary Tract Cancers: Green tea lowers risk of gallstones and biliary tract cancers, suggests a large population-based, case-control study led by Ann Hsing of the National Cancer Institute, Bethesda, Maryland, USA, and published in the International Journal of Cancer, June 2006.

Milk may also block tea's effect on other things, such as cancer. Teas with high EGCG content, such as green tea, are typically consumed without milk.

Hsing's team gathered demographic, medical and dietary data from 627 individuals with biliary tract cancer, 1,037 persons with gallstones, and 959 randomly selected controls in Shanghai, China.

Among women, after taking account of age, education and body mass index, those who consumed at least one cup of tea each day for at least 6 months had a 27% reduced risk of developing gall stones, a 44% reduced risk of getting gall bladder cancer, and 35% reduced risk of bile duct cancer.

Lung Cancer: While we certainly do not recommend smoking, if you or someone you love smokes, or if you must be around smokers and are exposed to second hand smoke, drinking green tea can offer protection against lung cancer.

A human pilot study recently confirmed the protective effects of green tea against lung cancer seen in cell culture and animal studies. The study, published in the November 2004 issue of Molecular Nutrition and Food Research, evaluated the effect of green tea (5 cups per day) on 3 heavy smokers (> 10 cigarettes a day) and 3 individuals who had never smoked.

When the study subjects were drinking green tea, DNA damage caused by smoking was decreased, cell growth was inhibited, and cellular triggers for cell suicide in abnormal cells increased.

Another larger four-month study of heavy smokers involving 100 women and 33 men found that levels of urinary marker of free radical damage to DNA dropped significantly in individuals drinking decaffeinated green tea, but not with black tea.

Ovarian Cancer: Green tea consumption has been shown to enhance survival in women with ovarian cancer.

In a study published in the November 2004 issue of the International Journal of Cancer, women with ovarian cancer who drank at least 1 cup of green tea daily had a 56% lowered risk of death during the 3 years of the study compared to non-tea drinkers.

A laboratory study of human ovarian cancer cells published in the September 2004 issue of Gynecologic Oncology explains why EGCG not only suppresses the growth of ovarian cancer cells, but also induces cell suicide in these cells by affecting a number of genes and proteins.

Susanna Larsson and Alicja Wolk from the National Institute of Environmental Medicine, Stockholm, Sweden, decided to look specifically at the relationship between tea consumption and ovarian cancer.

Participants in their study were 61,057 Swedish women aged 40-76 years. Analysis of the data found that even women who averaged less than one cup of tea per day had an 18% lower risk of ovarian cancer than non-tea-drinkers.

It was also found that each additional cup of tea per day was associated with an additional 18% lower risk of ovarian cancer, the more the merrier.

Prostate Cancer: EGCG provides other benefits specific to prostate cancer prevention. A study published in the December 2004 issue of the International Journal of Cancer found that EGCG significantly inhibited, in a dose-dependent manner.

The production of prostate-specific antigen (PSA), a marker for prostate cancer risk was lowered. Not only did EGCG lower PSA levels, but it also suppressed all the activities of PSA which were examined that promote prostate cancer.

All these effects were seen in this animal study within 6 months of continuous infusion. The study suggests that daily consumption of green tea may be highly protective.

In a case-control study involving 130 prostate cancer patients and 274 hospital controls, men drinking the most green tea were found to have an 86% reduced risk of prostate cancer compared to those drinking the least.

Drinking 5 cups of green tea a day may cut the risk of advanced prostate cancer in half, shows data collected in The Japan Public Health Center-based Prospective Study. The JPHC Study followed 49,920 Japanese men aged from 40 to 69 from 1990 to 2004.

SELECTION

High altitude tea, also known as high mountain tea, is a term describing tea grown from 1000 meters (or 3000 ft) above sea level to approximately 2600 meters (8000 ft).

As a matter of fact, growing tea on high altitude mountain areas costs much more than planting on low altitudes. It is one of the reasons why prices of high mountain teas are proportional to its tea plantation altitude.

High altitude tea typically is more healthy, rich, smooth and fragrant and you can brew it more times before it loses its flavor. There are certain advantages for high altitude tea plantation such as great amount of sunlight, sufficient amount of rain, extreme temperature difference between day and night and heavily fertilized soils perfect to grow tea.

In India tea grown on hills of Darjeeling commands more premium than tea grown on the lower heights of tea gardens of Assam. Darjeeling tea is usually far more expensive than Assam because the bushes are harder to grow. It also has a shorter harvesting season than Assam.

Organic Green Teas: The most stringent standards for organic produce are found in California, Japan and Germany. Any tea that meets these standards is a high quality organic product.

The two most respected organic tea farms are in India: the Oothu Tea Estate, the first organic tea farm in the world, and Makaibari Tea Estates, which follows Rudolph Steiner's principles of harmony with nature through organic, sustainable methods of agriculture.

Indian Green Teas: Although green teas are a very small part of overall tea production in India, the following are notable.

Bherjan Estate: an organic green tea grown in Assam, India's most plentiful tea district. Assam teas are renowned for their hearty taste and "strength" in aroma and body.

Ambootia Tea Estate: a Darjeeling district organic green tea that produces a light, fragrant cup.

Makaibari Tea Estates: a multiple award winning Darjeeling green tea, flavorful but light.

Craigmore Estate: grown at high altitudes in the spectacular range of the Nilgiris, India's Blue Mountains, these green teas are exceptionally fragrant and sweet.

Whenever possible, ask for a sample of prepared tea before buying. Most high-quality teas will produce a pale-green to yellow-green cup.

Loose Tea: To test for freshness, tightly squeeze a small amount and smell the aroma. The freshest, most flavorful tea will smell sweet and grassy. Since a single ounce of tea should produce 15 to 30 cups, the best way to ensure your tea is fresh is to purchase it in small amounts—two to four ounces at most at one time.

Japanese Green Teas : A good night time choice as it is very light and low in caffeine is Sencha. About 75% of the green tea harvested in Japan is Sencha, making it the most commonly consumed green tea in Japan.

Sencha is especially rich in vitamin C and provides a clear rich yellow-green liquor that is grassy sweet and cleanly astringent. Made from a higher quality leaf than bancha or houjica, Sencha is often called "guest tea."

Shin-cha: In Japanese, "shin" means new and "cha" means tea. Shincha is literally "new tea" as it consists of leaves very lightly steamed immediately after harvesting.

Gyokuro (in Japanese means "jewel dew") is a fine and expensive type of shaded green tea from Japan. It differs from the standard sencha, a classic unshaded green tea, in being grown under the shade rather than the full sun. Its EGCG content is considered the highest.

STORING

To retain freshness and flavor in both loose and bagged tea, store it in a tightly constructed opaque container to protect it from light, moisture and food odors.

Dark glass or ceramic containers are best; tins often leak as their seams are soldered. Use a small container just large enough to accommodate the amount of tea; tea exposed to the air in a half-empty large container will continue to oxidize.

It's best to store tea in a dark, cool, dry cupboard. Tea stored in the refrigerator is vulnerable to moisture and odors from other foods and the water condensation that occurs when frozen tea is defrosted can ruin it.

SERVING

Green tea should be handled tenderly, just as you would do it to fresh green leafy vegetables.

Water : Spring water is the ideal choice for brewing tea, followed by filtered water. Distilled water should never be used; the brew it produces will be flat since the minerals removed from it are essential to bringing out tea's flavor.

Piping Hot Drinking Temperature : Piping hot tea consumption has been linked to a higher risk for esophageal cancer: "In the case-control study, risk for esophageal cancer was increased for drinking hot tea vs lukewarm or warm tea.

Effect of Milk on Tea : A study at the Charité Hospital of the Berlin Universities showed that adding milk to tea will block the normal, healthful effects that tea has in protecting against cardiovascular disease. This occurs because casein from the milk binds to the molecules in tea that cause the arteries to relax, especially EGCG.

Milk may also block tea's effect on other things, such as cancer. Teas with high EGCG content, such as green tea, are typically consumed without milk.

Plant-based "milks", such as soy milk, do not contain casein and are not known to have similar effects on tea. In fact in one study it was found that combination of soya products enhances the anti-cancer benefits of green tea.

Effect of Citrus on Tea : Drinking tea, particularly green tea, with citrus such as lemon juice is common. Studies, including a study from Purdue University in 2007, found that most of the anti-oxidant catechins are not absorbed into the bloodstream when tea is drunk by itself.

The study also found that adding citrus to the tea lowers the pH in the small intestine and causes more of the catechins to be absorbed. Fresh lime green tea at lukewarm temperature is the ideal way to drink tea.

Although heartily boiling water is used to brew black and oolong teas, green tea needs much lower temperatures (160-170°F; 79-85°C) and also should be brewed for a longer time.

Let the water barely reach the boiling point to liberate its oxygen, then allow it to cool slightly before pouring over your tea. Brewing for 30 seconds to one minute is usually ideal for normal black tea; however, green tea should be brewed for 6-7 minutes, as this will enhance the ECGC content many folds.

Some other great ideas to increase your consumption of green tea are, brew green tea with thinly sliced ginger and lemon, or sprigs of spearmint. Add one teaspoon of honey per cup, stir and serve hot or use half the amount of hot water, allow the tea to brew and cool, then pour over ice cubes.

Make a green tea chai by brewing green tea in hot vanilla soy milk and topping with a dash each of cinnamon, black pepper, ginger and allspice.

Brew 1-2 teaspoons loose leaf green tea in 8 ounces cool water for 20-30 minutes to develop flavor without bitterness and add to stir-fries, marinades, dressings, soups and sauces.

Cook noodles in green tea for about 5 minutes, then remove from heat and leave noodles in tea until cool. Drain and toss lightly with soy sauce and sesame oil. Add thinly sliced tofu, scallions, mushrooms, and chopped cilantro, and serve.

Combine cooled green tea half and half with a fruit juice, such as peach, pineapple or papaya. Sweeten with a teaspoon of honey per cup. Blend and pour over ice.

Get in the habit of drinking green tea by taking one liter of iced green tea to work and sip throughout the day or take it to the gym to provide exceptional preventive health benefits just after hard workout and simultaneously replenishing fluid needs.

Bottom Line

1. Green tea has got the maximum cancer killing properties.
2. Mixing milk with tea will greatly reduce its ability to fight cancer.
3. The ideal combination is high altitude green tea, with fresh lime or soya milk at lukewarm temperatures, three times a day and freshly prepared.

51/52

STEP BY STEP

"Resting is rusting"

"Humans learnt walking about 6 million years back. It comes naturally to us. It's free, safe, simple, doesn't require any practice, and can be done anywhere. It is the world's most underrated exercise. You may be surprised that it has got HUGE health benefits.

Can walking make you happy? Can it help you deal with life stress? Can it help you work through relationship problems? Can it lead to a deeper spiritual and religious life? For many, the answer to all is yes, yes.

Walkers have less incidence of cancer, heart disease, stroke, diabetes and other killer diseases. They live longer and get mental health and spiritual benefits. Walking is a gentle, low-impact, practically injury-free exercise, accessible to just about everybody.

A study in 2011 showed that older adults walking 40 minutes a day, three times a week, reduced the normal age-related shrinkage of the brain's hippocampus, which is where the brain processes memory and emotions. After a year, they improved their performance on spatial memory tasks.

SCIENCE BEHIND

Exercise, such as walking, increases the blood flow to the brain. A 1999 study of people over age 60 found that walking 45 minutes a day at a 16-minute mile pace improved thinking skills.

The participants started at 15 minutes of walking and built up their time and speed. The result was that the same people were mentally sharper after taking up this walking program.

I have two doctors, my left leg and my right leg"

– G.M. Trevelyan

Walking and other exercise leads to the release of the body's natural happy drugs -- endorphins. Walkers who walk at a higher heart rate pace will notice this effect more than those who walk at a slower heart rate pace. But even at a slower pace, most people notice an improvement in mood.

By getting your brain to release more of the happy chemicals – the endorphins -- you achieve naturally what many prescription drugs and herbs try to do artificially. There many changes happen inside your body as you start walking and continue to walk.

Minutes 1 to 5: Your first few steps trigger the release of energy-producing chemicals in your cells to fuel your walking. Your heart rate increases from about 70 to 100 beats per minute (bpm), boosting blood flow and warming muscles.

Any stiffness subsides as joints release lubricating fluid to help you move more easily. As you get moving, your body burns 5 calories per minute, compared with only 1 calorie per minute at rest. Your body needs more fuel and starts pulling from its carbohydrate and fat stores.

Minutes 6 to 10: Heartbeat increases from 100 to about 140 bpm, and you're burning up to 6 calories a minute as you pick up the pace. A slight rise in blood pressure is countered by the release of chemicals that expand blood vessels, bringing more blood and oxygen to working muscles.

Minutes 11 to 20: Your body temperature keeps rising, and you start to perspire as blood vessels near the skin expand to release heat. As your walk becomes brisker, you'll be burning up to 7 calories a minute and breathing harder. Hormones such as epinephrine and glucagon rise to release fuel to the muscles.

One-third of the more than 500,000 cancer deaths in the U.S. each year are attributable to diet and physical activity habits, such as being overweight or obese. That's about the same number of cancer deaths caused by tobacco.

Minutes 21 to 45: Feeling invigorated, you start to relax as your body releases tension, thanks in part to a dose of feel-good chemicals such as endorphins in your brain. As more fat is burned, insulin (which helps store fat) drops--excellent news for anyone battling excess weight or diabetes.

Minutes 46 to 60: Your muscles may feel fatigued as carbohydrate stores are reduced. As you cool down, your heart rate decreases and your breathing slows. You'll be burning fewer calories but more than you were before you started. Your calorie burn will remain elevated for up to 1 hour.

ANTI-CANCER BENEFITS

Taking the occasional flight of stairs or short walk from the parking garage to the office simply isn't enough to put a dent in your cancer risk. Needless to say they are very good habits and should be continued with more vigor, with no opportunity lost philosophy.

New cancer prevention guidelines from the American Cancer Society say at least 30 minutes a day of dedicated exercise above and beyond the usual activities of daily life on five or more days a week is needed to really reduce your cancer risk.

"For years, we've told people what habits to adopt to lower their cancer risk, but it has become increasingly clear we need to create environments that make it easier to make healthy choices," says researcher Colleen Doyle, MS, RD, director of nutrition and physical activity for the American Cancer Society, in a news release.

"Just as excise taxes and smoke-free laws have been critical to reducing tobacco's cancer toll," says Doyle, "community action is essential to create a social environment that promotes healthy food choices and physical activity."

Researchers say that for non-smokers, weight control, physical activity, and dietary factors are the most important modifiable cancer risk factors. The guidelines, which are updated every five years, are based on the most current scientific evidence related to diet, activity and cancer risk.

American Institute of Cancer Research (AICR) experts estimate that overall, about 1/3 of cancers in the 1.5 million cancers that occur every year in the US could be prevented by following these guidelines. For several specific types of cancer, following them could prevent even more cases.

Burn-Baby-Burn : Excess fat in the body is an open invitation to cancer. The World Cancer Research Fund (WCRF) report is the most comprehensive ever published on the link between cancer and diet, physical activity and weight.

And its key finding is that maintaining a healthy weight is one of the most important things you can do to prevent cancer.

The number of types of cancer where there is "convincing" evidence that body fat is a cause has risen from one to six since the last WCRF report was published in 1997, including colorectal cancer and post-menopausal breast cancer.

The good news is that your body gets better at using oxygen and burning fat when you do regular aerobic exercise; your heart pumps more blood, your muscles consume more oxygen, and you produce more usable energy.

Aerobic: Aerobic simply means "with oxygen". It's any activity that stimulates your heart rate and breathing to increase but not so much that you can't sustain the activity for more than a few minutes.

Walking, dancing, swimming, water aerobics, biking, hiking, climbing steps, low-impact dance classes, kick-boxing, all the cardio machines at the gym -treadmill, elliptical, bike, rower, x-c skiing, stair-climber, are all examples of aerobic or cardio activities.

But they can be anaerobic too if they are performed at a high enough intensity. The bottom line is that the intensity at which you perform an activity determines if it's aerobic or anaerobic.

Anaerobic: It simply means without air exercise. It is the type where you get out of breath in just a few moments, typically like when you lift weights for improving strength, when you sprint, or when you climb a long flight of stairs.

Perhaps no area of exercise science has been more studied than the benefits of aerobic exercise. There is a mountain of evidence to prove that regular aerobic exercise will improve your health, your fitness, and dramatically reduce your chances of getting cancer.

Colon Cancer: Research is clear that physically active men and women have about a 30%-40% reduction in the risk of developing colon cancer compared with inactive individuals.

It appears that 30-60 minutes per day of moderate-to-vigorous-intensity physical activity is needed to decrease the risk, and there is a dose-response relationship, which means that the risk declines the more active you are.

Breast Cancer: There is reasonably clear evidence that physically active women have about a 20%-30% reduction in risk compared with inactive women. Like colon cancer, it appears that 30-60 minutes per day of moderate-to-vigorous-intensity physical activity is needed to decrease the risk.

Prostate Cancer: Research shows that physical activity plays role in the prevention of this prostate cancer.

Lung Cancer: There are relatively few studies on physical activity and lung cancer prevention. The available data suggest that physically active individuals have a lower risk of lung cancer.

Cancer Treatment : There's some good news for people undergoing cancer treatment. In one study, aerobic exercise performed five days per week for 30-35 minutes for six weeks at 80% of maximal heart rate reduced fatigue in women being treated for cancer.

In another study, 10 weeks of aerobic exercise at 60% of maximum heart rate for 30-40 minutes, four days per week, reduced depression and anxiety in female cancer patients.

Walking Meditation: In fact, the medical benefits of walking are similar to those seen from meditation and more specifically, walking meditation.

Herbert Benson, MD, founder of the Benson-Henry Institute for Mind Body Medicine at Massachusetts General Hospital, has found that like sitting meditation, focused walking is highly efficient at reducing anxiety and triggering a "relaxation response."

Walk with 'soft vision' allowing the eyes to relax and focus upon nothing, while aware of everything. Smile softly with your eyes. Gradually allow the smile to spread from your eyes to your face and throughout your body.

This is called an "organic smile" or a "thalamus smile". Imagine every cell of your body smiling softly. Let all worry and sadness fall away from you as you walk. Walk in silence, both internal and external.

Be mindful of your walking, make each step a gesture, so that you move in a state of grace, and each footprint is an impression of the peace and love you feel for the universe. Walk with slow, small, deliberate, balanced, graceful footsteps.

Be mindful of your breathing also, without trying to control it. Allow the breath to become diaphragmatic if possible, but always make sure your breathing feels natural, not artificial. Allow the breath to become circular, and fluid. Notice the beauty of your surroundings, both externally and internally.

This effect of walking meditation has significant long-term health benefits, including lowering blood pressure, slowing breathing rates, reducing incidents of chronic pain, and reducing insomnia.

Bottom Line

1. The Gold standard for walking is 10,000 steps a day that is approximately a distance of 8 KM or 5 Miles. Built up slowly to this number.
2. Use pedometer to track your daily numbers and never be out of breath during walking or any other aerobic exercise.
3. Brisk walking for more than 30 minutes a day is called fat stripping exercise, and thus reducing the chances of number of cancers.

YOGA

"Yoga heals, nourishes, and challenges us. The practice infiltrates every corner of our lives." – Valerie Jeremijenko

Stars do it. Sports do it. Judges in the highest courts do it. Let's do it. Yoga is the in thing. A path to enlightenment that winds back 5,000 years in its native India, yoga has suddenly become so hot, so cool, so very this minute.

It's the exercise cum meditation for the new millennium.75% of all U.S. health clubs offer yoga classes. Oprah Winfrey, arbiter of moral and literary betterment for millions of American women, devoted a whole show to the benefits of yoga.

Yoga typically means 'union' between the mind, body and spirit. It involves the practice of physical postures and poses, which is sometimes referred to as 'asana' in Sanskrit.

The oldest physical discipline in existence known to humankind, Yoga brings stability to the body and the wavering mind. It increases the lubrication of joints, ligaments and tendons of the body.

Studies in the field of medicine suggest that Yoga is the only form of physical activity that provides complete exercise to the body, because it massages all the internal organs and glands. Yoga makes use of different movements, breathing exercises, relaxation technique and meditation.

Yoga can create a positive permanent difference to the lifestyle of anybody practicing it on a regular basis. It is called yogic way of living - when anger does not hurt you and you do not become mad in joy. This is what reduces the risk of many diseases including cancer.

The East treats the person; the West treats the disease. "Our system of medicine is very fragmented," says Dr. Carrie Demers of the Himalayan International Institute of Yoga Science and Philosophy of the USA.

"The East treats the person; the West treats the disease. "Our system of medicine is very fragmented," says Dr. Carrie Demers"

"We send you to different specialists to look at different parts of you. Yoga is more holistic; it's interested in the integration of body, breath and mind."

SCIENCE BEHIND

Yoga relaxes you. When you do yoga — the deep breathing, the stretching, the movements that release muscle tension, the relaxed focus on being present in your body — you initiate a process that turns the fight-or-flight system off and the Relaxation Response is switched on.

That has a dramatic effect on the body. The heartbeat slows, respiration decreases, blood pressure decreases. The body seizes this chance to turn on the healing mechanisms.

But the process isn't automatic. Especially in their first sessions, yoga students may have trouble suppressing those competitive beta waves. We want to better ourselves, but also to do better than others; we force ourselves into the gym-rat race.

It may take a while for the enlightenment bulb to switch on — for you to get the truth of the yoga maxim that what you can do is what you should do.

But when it happens, it's an epiphany, like suddenly knowing, in your bones and your dreams, the foreign language you've been studying for months. In yoga, this is your mind-body language.

BENEFITS OF PRANAYAMA

One of the many wonderful Pranayamas that Yoga offers us, Kapalbhati is one of the most favorite breathing exercise.

It is so simple and safe that even children can do it. When done even for a short time consistently, its benefits are undeniable.

If there was only one Pranayama that you elected to do, Kapalbhati might well be the one to pick - it's that good! Kapalbhati primarily affects stomach, pancreas, liver, spleen, intestine, prostate and kidney to function more efficiently.

These are very significant parts of human body. Kapalbhati is beneficial even in the case of those diseases which are impossible to be cured by medicines like cancer, diabetes, asthma.

According to Swami Ramdev, Kapalbhati is sanjeevani (one that infuses life) on earth. Numerous patients have gained healthy and happy life by adopting it, in their daily life.

'Kapalbhati' is a Sanskrit word. 'Kapal' means forehead and 'Bhati' means light. It refers that

> *You don't win by punishing your body. You convince it, seduce it, and talk it down from the ledge of ambition and anxiety. Yoga is not a struggle but surrender.*

by this breathing exercise forehead becomes luminous and lustrous, which means all diseases disappear and body becomes pure, healthy and happy.

Place : The best place for pranayama is peaceful, holy river bank or some open area like garden with lush greenery, where atmosphere is full of natural oxygen in early mornings otherwise you can choose a peaceful, neat, clean room with the access to fresh and healthy oxygen.

Best Time : The best time for pranayama is early morning along with empty stomach. Though it can also be practiced after 4 hours of having a major meal.

Some patients of chronic diseases are advised to practice pranayama twice a day, in the morning and evening. After pranayama, food should NOT be taken for at least 20 minutes.

Preparations : At the time of practicing pranayama yoga, cloths should be loose and comfortable with the body. Kapalbhati is practiced in any one of comfortable poses of asana like Padmasana, Siddhasana, Vajrasana or Sukhasana sitting on the floor on yoga mat. Spinal cord must be straight.

Practitioners unable to sit on the floor due to any disease can sit on the chair with straight spinal cord. Pranayama should never be practiced on the bare floor or in standing position.

How to do : It is very easy to practice for everyone. The primary thing is to breathe in normally and breathe out forcefully so as to influence the organs of the abdominal area.

Technique : Sit in a comfortable asana with normal breathing. Inhale normally and exhale forcefully. Also keep the body easy and relax, don't feel like stressed. As a beginner, the force should be very low as per the body strength. Continue this practice till you can perform comfortably.

Whenever feel tired take a break with normal breathing and then resume. Optimize your practice to make "one stroke per second". In the beginning the practitioner may feel little pain in the abdomen and back because of new strain on the body, which disappears in few days.

At the time of forcefully 'exhaling', the practitioner should assume like throwing all impurities, toxins, diseases out of the body.

Those who want to get rid of anger, greed, self-ego, attachment etc. should develop a feeling of throwing out all the negative and injurious elements along with the air exhaled. This procedure will give you additional advantages and quick results.

Duration : A new practitioner should try for 3–5 minutes per day. The body gains more stamina as days pass. After 1-2 months, practitioner can perform five minutes in single stretch. Practice should be increased up to 10–15 minutes daily after 2-3 months.

Patients suffering from acute and chronic diseases must practice for 15 minutes at least along with precautions.

Cures: It includes obesity, diabetes, flatulence, constipation, acidity and diseases pertaining to kidneys and prostate glands etc. Women diseases like uterus cysts, breast cysts, cancer cysts or any type of cysts in the body are permanently dissolved without any surgery.

Parkinson's disease, Liver Cirrhosis and Hepatitis-B is permanently cured with devoted practice. It removes snoring problems and cures sinusitis completely.

Swami Ramdev maharaj claims to control 'Cancer' with kapalbhati and anulom-vilom. Even he has proved that with some patients in his ashram in India. According to him, any disease can be cured by the combination of Pranayama practice.

Precautions: Women should avoid kapalbhati pranayama during periods and pregnancy. Patients with severe heart problems should not do with force and they must practice under an experienced yoga teacher.

Blood pressure patients should also avoid doing with force in the beginning. In the beginning, any pranayama practice must be done under experienced yoga teacher's training.

ANTI-CANCER BENEFITS

Author and one of the world's best US doctors, in preventive health care, Dr Dean Ornish is in the midst of a study involving men with prostate cancer. Can diet, yoga and meditation affect the progress of this disease? So far, Ornish will say only that the data are encouraging.

Dr Ornish hoped for more than the respect of his peers: he wanted action. "I used to think good science was enough to change medical practice," he says, "but I was naive. Most doctors still aren't prescribing yoga and meditation. We've shown that heart disease can be reversed."

Sue Cohen, 54, an accountant, breast-cancer survivor and five-year yoga student at the Unity Woods studio in Bethesda, USA, says : "After my cancer surgery," I thought I might never lift my arm again. Then here I am one day, standing on my head, leaning most of my 125-lb. body weight on that arm I thought I'd never be able to use again."

Chemotherapy, surgery and some medications can rob you of mental acuity, but yoga helps compensate for the loss. It impels you to do things you never thought you were capable of doing.

"The sensible practice of yoga does more than slap a Happy Face on your cerebrum. It can also massage the lymph system" says Dr Mehmet Oz, a cardiac surgeon at New York Presbyterian Hospital in Manhattan.

Lymph is the body's dirty dishwater; a network of lymphatic vessels and storage sacs crisscross over the entire body, in parallel with the blood supply, carrying a fluid composed of infection-fighting white blood cells and the waste products of cellular activity.

Exercise in general activates the flow of lymph through the body, speeding up the filtering process; but yoga in particular promotes the draining of the lymph. Certain yoga poses stretch muscles that from animal studies are known to stimulate the lymph system.

Researchers have documented the increased lymph flow when dogs' paws are stretched in a position similar to the yoga "downward-facing dog."

"All the drugs we give people have side effects," McCall says. "Well, yoga has side effects too: better strength, better balance, peace of mind, stronger bones, cardiovascular conditioning, and lots of stuff.

"Here is a natural health system that, once you learn the basics, you can do at home for free with very little equipment and that could help you avoid expensive, invasive surgical and pharmacological interventions. I think this is going to be a big thing."

At Cedars Sinai Medical Center in Los Angeles, cardiac doctors suggest that their patients enroll in the hospital's Preventive and Rehabilitative Cardiac Center, which offers yoga, among other therapies.

Why have so few studies tested the efficacy of yoga? For lots of reasons. Those sympathetic to yoga think the benefits are proved by millenniums of empirical evidence in India; those who are suspicious think it can't be proved.

"In modern medicine, we're actually doing a lot more guesswork than we let on," says Dr. Demers. "We want to say we understand everything. We don't understand half of it. It's scary how clueless we are."

"Thousands of research studies have shown that in the practice of yoga a person can learn to control such physiologic parameters as blood pressure, heart rate, respiratory function, metabolic rate, skin resistance, brain waves and body temperature, among other body functions."

Made for Each Other: Yoga and Sattvic food are made for each other. It is an eating philosophy based on a wholesome vegetarian diet in combination with spices and herbs that have therapeutic value and delicious flavors.

"You are what you Eat" – a commonly used phrase in yoga, has a powerful meaning. Yoga believes that food not only influences your body in the physical sense but is also known to directly influence emotions and feelings.

It can induce bliss or anger, contentment or restlessness, thoughts of the sacred or the profane. The quality of the food you eat literally creates your state of mind and emotions.

The teachings of yoga advocate a vegetarian diet with special emphasis on foods that bring peace to body, mind, and spirit.

The yogic belief is that several health disorders can be traced to faulty nutrition, poor diet and difficulty in digestion. A vegetarian yoga diet ensures that all faculties of digestion work smoothly—absorption, assimilation, and elimination. The diet also contains high amounts of fiber and anti-oxidants.

Sattvic foods include foods rich in vitamins and minerals such as fresh vegetables, fruits, herbs; essential dietary fiber and carbohydrates required by the body include whole and unrefined grains.

Protein-rich foods such as legumes, nuts, seeds. Natural sweeteners such as honey and raw sugar, therapeutic spices in small quantities, oil and ghee (Indian clarified butter) in small quantities from the grass fed domestic cow, for the required fat in the body.

Bottom Line

1. Yoga is a way of living life, it is not merely a combination a few stretches and asanas.
2. The major difference between normal exercise and yoga is that yoga focuses on massaging the internal organs, whereas exercise targets our outer muscles.
3. Oxygenation of blood, purification of mind and spiritual bliss all can be achieved by simply practicing Yoga.

Miscellaneous

Feeding the Baby

Cancer is a chronic disease. The seed of cancer takes very long time to become full blown cancer, which then becomes visible in X-rays or CT scan etc. It passes through three stages -initiation, promotion and progression. It may be residing in your body for over 40 years.

Promotion is the stage where we have maximum window of opportunity. Latest research conclusively proves that some foods, habits and lifestyles are responsible for feeding the cancer.

If you are able to control these modifiable factors then the chances are that cancer may never bother you. Seed will never become a tree.

Top 13 Modifiable Factors for Cancer Control

1. Smoking

When people think of cancers caused by smoking, the first one that comes to mind is always Lung. Most cases of lung cancer death, close to 90% in men, and 80% in women, are caused by cigarette smoking.

There are several other forms of cancer attributed to smoking as well, and they include cancer of the oral cavity, pharynx, larynx, esophagus, bladder, stomach, cervix, kidney and pancreas, and acute myeloid leukemia.

Inhaling secondhand smoke causes lung cancer in non-smoking adults. Approximately 3,000 lung cancer deaths occur each year among adult non-smokers in the United States as a result of exposure to secondhand smoke.

The U.S. Surgeon General estimates that living with a smoker increases a non-smoker's chances of developing lung cancer by 20 to 30 per cent.

2. Milk

Research finds animal proteins found in cow's milk can cause a wide range of cancers. Casein, an animal protein found in cow's milk and used in products from

Paneer (cottage cheese), curd, yogurt, cheese and protein supplements, has been found to cause cancer.

Casein makes up about 87 per cent of cow's milk and has also been linked to autism in some studies. T. Colin Campbell, Ph.D, world-renowned Cornell University Nutritionist and co-author of the groundbreaking book The China Study, states, "Casein is the most relevant carcinogen that humans ingest. It is more potent than DDT or dioxin."

Epidemiologists reported that cancer of the lung, breast, and colon increased two to three times among Japanese women between 1950 and 1975. During that period, milk consumption increased fifteen times; meat, eggs, and poultry climbed seven and a half times.

3. Sugary Drinks

Mark Pereira of the University of Minnesota, USA, who led the study on sugary drinks found that "The high levels of sugar in soft drinks may be increasing the level of insulin in the body, which we think contributes to pancreatic cancer cell growth."

Writing in the journal Cancer Epidemiology, Biomarkers & Prevention, Pereira and colleagues said they followed 60,524 men and women in the Singapore Chinese Health Study for 14 years.

Over that time, 140 of the volunteers developed pancreatic cancer. Those who drank two or more soft drinks a week had an 87 percent higher risk of being among those who got pancreatic cancer. Incidentally the insulin, which helps the body metabolize sugar, is made in the pancreas.

4. Refined Wheat

A new study published in the journal Cancer Epidemiology, Mile Markers, and Prevention is presenting evidence of the link between the consumption of refined carbohydrates and cancer.

This case-controlled study looked at the dietary habits of over 1,800 women in Mexico, and found that those who got 57% or more of their total energy intake from carbohydrates showed a 220% higher risk of breast cancer than women with more balanced diets.

This study shows that foods with high glycemic index values -- that is, foods that more quickly raise blood sugar levels in the human body-- actually accelerate the growth of cancer cells and tumors in the human body.

Researchers involved with the study propose that the correlation between the consumption of refined carbohydrates and breast cancer could be related to elevated levels of insulin and the fact that many breast cancer tumors are encouraged and supported by high levels of insulin in the body.

The story is no different in the case of rice. More than 70% of the rice consumed in developed countries such as the US and UK is white.

Like other wholegrain foods, brown rice is high in fiber and releases its energy slowly and In contrast, white rice has had all the bran and some of the germs removed during milling. This gives white rice a higher glycemic index (GI) - a measure of how much a food raises blood sugar levels compared with the same amount of glucose.

An Indian cancer researcher concluded that thorough chewing lowered the risk of cancer. "The proper chewing of meals ensuring that mucous-rich saliva mixed with the food seemed to be protective factors." Cancer also appeared to be more prevalent in South India where white rice is used in cooking, which hardly requires any chewing.

Whiter the bread or the rice the sooner you are dead.

5. Obesity

Results from the 2007-2008 National Health and Nutrition Examination Survey (NHANES) shows that whopping 68 per cent of U.S. adults are overweight or obese.

Obesity is associated with increased risks of the following cancer types, and possibly others as well: Esophagus, Pancreas, Colon and Rectum, Breast, Endometrium (lining of the uterus),Kidney, Thyroid and Gall bladder.

One study, using NCI Surveillance, Epidemiology, and End Results (SEER) data, estimated that in 2007 in the United States, about 34,000 new cases of cancer in men and 50,500 in women were due to obesity.

This analysis also found that if every adult reduces its weight roughly just by 1 kg (or 2.2 lbs), this would prevent about 100,000 new cases of cancer by 2030 in USA alone.

Several possible mechanisms have been suggested to explain the association of obesity with increased risk of certain cancers:

Fat tissue produces excess amounts of estrogen, high levels of which have been associated with the risk of breast, endometrial, and some other cancers.

Obese people often have increased levels of insulin and insulin-like growth factor-1 (IGF-1) in their blood which may promote the development of certain tumors.

Obese people often have chronic low-level, or "sub-acute," inflammation, which has been associated with increased cancer risk.

6. Excessive Drinking

Alcohol is associated with an increased risk of a number of cancers. 3.5% of cancer deaths worldwide are attributable to the consumption of alcohol. Breast cancer in women is linked with alcohol intake. Alcohol also increases the risk of cancers of the mouth, esophagus, pharynx and larynx, colorectal cancer, liver cancer, stomach and ovaries.

Together, these cancers kill more than 125,000 people annually in the United States alone. Preliminary studies show that alcohol may affect cancer development at the genetic level by affecting oncogenes at the initiation and promotion stages of cancer.

It has been suggested that acetaldehyde, a product of alcohol metabolism, impairs a cell's natural ability to repair its DNA, resulting in a greater likelihood of mutations causing cancer initiation.

In general, these risks increase after about one daily drink for women and two daily drinks for men. A drink is defined as 12 ounces of regular beer, 5 ounces of wine, or 1.5 ounces of 80-proof liquor. Large amount of alcohol drinking in one sitting also called binge drinking is extremely harmful.

Also, using alcohol with tobacco is riskier than using either one alone, because it further increases the chances of getting cancers of the mouth, throat, and esophagus.

Studies indicate that alcohol enhances tobacco's ability to stimulate tumor formation in rats. In humans, the risk for mouth, tracheal, and esophageal cancer is 35 times greater for people who both smoke and drink than for people who neither smoke nor drink.

7. Ugly Fat

Hydrogenated oils and trans fatty acids are silent killers. Research studies show conclusively these deadly oils cause non-insulin dependent type II diabetes. This is a disease which can eventually burn out the pancreas.

These changed molecular oils dramatically increase the risk of coronary heart disease, breast cancer, lung cancer, other many types of cancer and auto immune diseases. Over 100 research studies show how harmful these oils are to the human body.

However, these findings have been largely ignored by the mass media and the FDA and other governments world over. In addition, the Commercial Edible Food Industry has suppressed these research findings many times.

Why? Money and lots of it! Food processing companies and the companies that own the patents on this process would lose billions of dollars if they had to change their method of food production of hydrogenating oils.

The main reason oils are hydrogenated is that the hydrogenation of the oils act as a preservative. This leads to increased shelf life of products and less returns or spoilage of products. But at what cost is it to the human body?

Hydrogenated oils are molecularly changed oils that are toxic to the body. Over the last fifty years since the introduction of hydrogenated oils, the diseases has increased over 1000%. Over 90% of the foods produced today contain hydrogenated oils. All bakery items from biscuits, breads to cakes and pastries, contain these fats.

There is NO difference between hydrogenated oil vs partially hydrogenated oils.

They are equally as bad. Packaged foods contain as high as 35% hydrogenated trans-fats.

Researchers found that calories from dietary fat were highly significantly associated with lung cancer mortality. For example, male lung cancer deaths are highest in West European countries where a high-fat diet is consumed, and lowest in Thailand, Philippines, Honduras, Guatemala, and Japan where a low-fat diet is eaten.

While noting that smoking is still the major causative factor of lung cancer, the scientists theorized that a high-fat diet might also trigger the process by which cigarette smoke is harmful to the lungs. It is conceivable that "tobacco smoke is readily oxidized to the ultimate carcinogen as a consequence of a high-fat diet."

8. Excessive Antibiotics

How ironic that the very thing we were taught would save us may actually be increasing our chances of death from a fatal disease. Recent research has established the link between antibiotic use and cancer.

International Journal of Cancer issue reported a nationwide cohort study to determine whether antibiotic use predicts the development of various cancers. The research included 3,112,624 individuals, aged 30-79 years, with no history of cancer.

Antibiotic use was associated with increased risk of cancer. For the person taking more than 6 prescriptions group, the risk of cancer was increased to 37% as compared to person in the one prescription group. Relative risks for the most common primary sites of the cancer were 1.39 for prostate, 1.14 for breast, 1.79 for lung, 1.15 for colon, and 2.60 for endocrine gland.

Then in 2004, scientists from the University of Washington, the National Cancer Institute, the Group Health Cooperative and Fred Hutchinson Cancer Research Center in Seattle sought to examine the association between the use of antibiotics and risk of breast cancer.

They found that increasing cumulative days of antibiotic use were associated with increased risk of incidence of breast cancer. These findings show that the risk of breast cancer doubled in those who had used antibiotics for more than 500 cumulative days.

Antibiotics were shown to be an even greater risk factor than synthetic hormone replacement therapy (HRT), according to the lead researcher. Synthetic HRT has been shown to pose a 30-40 per cent increased risk to women for getting breast cancer.

As an adult human, you have three to four pounds of beneficial bacteria and yeast living within your intestines. These microbes compete for nutrients from the food you eat. Usually, the strength in numbers beneficial bacteria enjoy both keeps the ever-present yeasts in check and causes them to produce nutrients such as the B vitamins.

However, every time you swallow antibiotics, you kill the beneficial bacteria within your intestines. When you do so, you upset the delicate balance of your intestinal terrain. Yeasts grow unchecked into large colonies and take over and is the cause of many diseases.

Undoubtedly it is best to handle suspected infections without the use of antibiotics. You can keep your intestinal tract well populated with friendly bacteria by using a good probiotic, or by consuming fermented foods and cultured foods containing live bacteria such as yogurt or kefir.

You can also include pre-biotic foods like raw Jerusalem, raw artichoke, raw dandelion greens, raw garlic, raw Leek, raw onions and raw asparagus in your daily diets. As per one research, 70% of antibiotics are coming through your food chain it makes sense to eat organic products.

9. Over Stress

Jim Kiefert of Olympia, Wash., is absolutely convinced that stress led to his prostate cancer. It was diagnosed in 1989, when he was 50. Mr. Kiefert was a school superintendent, and he was in the midst of difficult negotiations with teachers over their contracts. "I was stressed out," he says. "I know stress caused my cancer."

The question of whether there is a link between stress and cancer has puzzled and intrigued researchers as well as patients. Study after study has asked whether people who developed cancer had more stress in the years before the diagnosis, and conversely, whether people who experienced extreme stress were more likely to develop cancer.

Investigators have also explored possible mechanisms, asking, for example, whether stress might suppress the immune system cells that might be needed to squelch rogue cancer cells. What has emerged is a tenuous connection between stress, the immune system and cancer.

Polly Newcomb, the head of the cancer prevention program at the Fred Hutchinson Cancer Research Center in Seattle, decided to ask whether stress caused breast cancer, because women seemed convinced that it did.

"There are small increases in certain types of cancers," Dr. Applebaum said, but those tend to be cancers that are associated with infections - like stomach cancer, associated with ulcer -causing *Helicobacter pylori*.

Liver cancer, associated with hepatitis B and hepatitis C infections; Kaposi's sarcoma, associated with herpes virus and infections; lymphoma, associated with Epstein-Barr virus ; and cervical cancer, associated with human papillomavirus.

10. Resting is Rusting

Following a sedentary lifestyle is more dangerous for your health than smoking, says a new study reported in the South China Morning Post, and carried out by the University of Hong Kong and the Department of Health.

In the study, researchers looked at the level of physical activity in people who died and were able to correlate their level of physical activity with their risk of dying.

The results are fascinating: 20% of all deaths of people 35 and older were attributed to a lack of physical activity. That's more deaths than can be attributed to smoking. Looking at specific diseases, the risk of dying from cancer increased 45% for men and 28% for women due to lack of physical activity.

The risk of dying from respiratory ailments was 92% higher for men and 75% higher for women. The risk of dying from heart disease was 52% higher for men and 28% higher for women, all due to a lack of physical activity. It turns out that being a couch potato can kill you, literally.

This is really no surprise to naturopathic physicians, holistic healers, holistic nutritionists, and other people in the natural healing fields: physical activity is absolutely critical for the health of the human body. In fact, it's fair to say that the human body was designed to be used.

In fact, the more you use your body, the healthier it gets -- up to a point of course; you don't want to overexert yourself and cause injury, but very few people run the risk of actually doing too much exercise in modern society.

Sadly, in today's world, a lot of people just sit around. They spend endless hours watching TV, and they hold jobs that require them to sit behind a desk for 8 or 9 or 10 hours a day engaging in virtually no physical movement at all.

As a result, they are being diagnosed with chronic diseases like cancer, heart disease, diabetes, and respiratory ailments -- all related to a lack of regular physical exercise.

Physical exercise, if done outside, also exposes you to the healing effects of natural sunlight, an essential nutrient for the human body that is deficient in most people. Getting enough sunlight on your skin can prevent and even reverse an astounding number of chronic diseases such as breast cancer, prostate cancer, osteoporosis and more.

A mere 30 minutes a day of walking, swimming, jogging, cycling or other cardiovascular exercise can have astounding positive health effects.

No one can do it for you, no prescription drugs can give you the same effects, no surgical procedure can create the health that your body would create on its own when you engage in regular physical exercise. This is something you must pursue on your own if you desire to experience the positive health results it offers.

11. Salt

A diet overloaded with salt is putting millions of us at twice the risk of contracting stomach cancer, research has revealed. Processed foods and ready meals are among the worst culprits.

The expert panel found that salt and salt-preserved foods increase the chance of developing stomach cancer. Studies have shown that high salt intake can damage the lining of the stomach.

But even everyday items such as bacon, bread and baked beans can boost salt to dangerous levels in the body. Eating just 12g of salt a day doubles the likelihood of stomach cancer, which kills more than 6,400 Britons a year, Cancer Research UK says.

The recommended daily allowance is 6g or one small teaspoon. We actually need much less than this. Some ready meals - particularly curries, Chinese dishes and pizzas - contain virtually all the daily salt allowance in a single serving.

Most of the salt we eat comes from processed and packaged foods such as sauces, processed meats, stock cubes and soups as well as breads and cereals.

Both salt and salt preserved foods are probably associated with an increased risk of stomach cancer. Salt is also a leading cause of high blood pressure and cardiovascular disease.

National Health and Medical Research Council's (NHMRC) Dietary Guidelines, recommends that people choose foods low in salt, and avoid adding salt at the table or in cooking.

Ways to limit salt intake include purchasing "no added salt" or "low salt" foods in the supermarket, flavouring foods with herbs and spices instead of salt, eating more fresh fruit and vegetables and limiting processed and take-away foods.

Our daily intake of salt should be less than 2,400 milligrams. Most people in the United States currently consume more than 2,400 mg, but there are simple ways to cut down on our intake.

Most of the salt in our diets comes from processed foods. We are not always aware that these foods are high in salt because they may not taste "salty," so make sure to read the sodium content on the Nutrition Facts label. Watch out for breakfast cereals, bread, frozen meals, pizza and chips.

Also, check the amount of sodium in canned products, such as soups and sauces, and avoid processed meats. Even sweet foods like cookies can contain high levels of salt. Lesser the better.

12. Burnt Foods

Even though some people love to eat the crispy, dark pieces that result from cooking burgers, steaks or chicken on the barbecue, did you know that these bits and pieces can increase your risk of cancer?

Cancer Causing Chemicals When foods such as beef, pork, chicken, and fish are cooked at very high temperatures, they produce compounds called heterocyclic amines (HCA). Different cooking methods yield different levels of HCA's.

Frying, deep-frying, broiling and barbequing are cooking techniques that produce the highest amount of HCA's. Grilling also poses an additional problem because the smoke that rises from the coals is absorbed by the meat, which we ultimately ingest.

These compounds have the potential to increase your risk of cancer--especially colon and stomach cancer. These are highly concentrated in well-done, charred food. It's the combination of amino acids (building blocks of protein) and creatinine (a compound found in muscle) reacting together at high temperatures that produce HCAs.

Other protein foods, such as eggs, tofu, milk and liver have little to no HCA's when cooked.

Higher HCAs, Higher Colon Cancer In a study evaluating the relationship between colon cancer and meat intake, it was found that there is a strong association between increased consumption of HCAs and diagnosis of colon cancer.

The study categorized meat intake by how well it was cooked and what cooking method was used. Another study showed that HCAs tripled when cooking temperatures were increased from 392 to 482 degrees F.

The Harvard Medical School (Health Letter, June 2007) suggests the following tips for safer and healthier grilling: cook smaller pieces (this helps to cook your food more quickly using lower temperatures); choose leaner meat (less fat will reduce flames and therefore your food will be exposed to less smoke); flip frequently (both sides have time to absorb or lose too much heat).

13. Meat Eating

According to the World Health Organization, up to 40 per cent of all cancers are preventable, and the American Cancer Society reports that one-third of all cancer deaths in the United States can be attributed to nutritional factors.

According to the Physicians Committee for Responsible Medicine, this means that vegetarians "are about 40 per cent less likely to get cancer than non-vegetarians, regardless of other risks such as smoking, body size, and socio-economic status."

A vast array of studies from top universities and independent researchers has found that eating the flesh of chickens, cows, and other animals promotes cancer. Here are a few:

- One study compared cancer rates of vegetarians and meat-eaters in 34,000 Americans. The results showed that those who avoided meat, fish, and poultry had dramatically lower rates of prostate, ovarian, and colon cancer compared to meat-eaters.
- An 11-year-long German study involving more than 800 vegetarian men found that their cancer rates were less than half those of the general public. The lowest cancer rates were found in those who had avoided meat for 20 years or more.

- A 2007 study of more than 35,000 women published in the British Journal of Cancer found that women who ate the most meat had the highest risk of breast cancer.
- A study comparing the dietary habits of men in 32 countries found that the highest risk factors for prostate cancer mortality were meat and dairy products. By contrast, another study of men diagnosed with prostate cancer showed that a diet rich in fruits, vegetables, and grains can slow or even halt the progression of the disease.
- Scientists from the Bremen Institute for Prevention, Research, and Social Medicine and the German Cancer Research Center observed in the American Journal of Clinical Nutrition that "the relationship between a vegetarian and fiber-rich diet and a decreased risk for colon cancer has been reported in many studies."

Dr. T. Colin Campbell, arguably the foremost epidemiological researcher alive today, believes that animal proteins are the prime carcinogen in meat and dairy products.

He points out that "human studies also support this carcinogenic effect of animal protein, even at usual levels of consumption. ... No chemical carcinogen is nearly so important in causing human cancer as animal protein."

Fat is a culprit, too: Higher-fat diets raise estrogen levels, whereas plant-based diets tend to keep them at a safe level, which doesn't promote the growth of cancer cells. But fiber—a nutrient plentiful in vegetarian diets—can help our bodies eliminate excess estrogen, cutting the risk of cancer.

It seems that with every bite of meat, we increase our risk of cancer. Luckily, we can eliminate animal products from our diets and replace them with vegetable proteins that protect our health instead of harming it.

Anti-oxidants

When a cut apple changes its color to brown-black, it is called oxidation.

Oxidation occurs when oxygen is exposed to cells and causes them to change. Our bodies typically use oxygen in an efficient way, but sometimes cells get harmed in the process and free radicals are created.

Free radicals are unstable oxygen molecules that often collide with other cells and cause interference with normal cell functioning. This sometimes causes a chain reaction and can result in the disruption of a living cell and ultimately cause DNA damage.

Free radicals are also created from environmental pollution, smoke from cigarettes, radiation and other chemicals. The resulting oxidation is linked to a variety of health problems such as cancer, diabetes, macular degeneration and heart disease.

Anti-oxidants prevent and stop free radicals to have free go at our cells. Food is the best source of anti-oxidants. Plant-based foods such as vegetables, fruits, legumes, whole grains and nuts contain complex combinations of anti-oxidants.

Well-known anti-oxidants are vitamin C, vitamin E and selenium. Phytochemicals are plant compounds that are rich in anti-oxidants. There are more than thousand known phytochemicals. Some of the well-known phytochemicals are lycopene in tomatoes, isoflavones in soy and flavanoids in fruits.

It is best to obtain these anti-oxidants from foods instead of supplements. In addition, minimize the exposure of oxidative stress such as smoking and sunburn.

Top 10 Resources

Books:

1. Anticancer: A New Way of Life - by Dr David Servan-Schreiber, M.D., Ph.D
2. The Cancer-Fighting Kitchen - by Rebecca Katz MS
3. The China Study - by Dr T. Colin Campbell
4. Foods to Fight Cancer - by Dr Richard Béliveau
5. Jungle Effect - by Dr Daphne Miller MD
6. The Biology of Belief - by Dr Bruce H. Lipton, Ph.D.
7. Healing with Spices - by Dr Bharat B. Aggarwal, Ph.D

Websites:

8. www.livestrong.com
9. www.whfoods.com
10. www.pcrm.org - Physicians Committee for Responsible Medicine

Index